God, Race, and History

God, Race, and History
Liberating Providence

Matt R. Jantzen

LEXINGTON BOOKS
Lanham • Boulder • New York • London

Published by Lexington Books
An imprint of The Rowman & Littlefield Publishing Group, Inc.
4501 Forbes Boulevard, Suite 200, Lanham, Maryland 20706
www.rowman.com

6 Tinworth Street, London SE11 5AL, United Kingdom

Copyright © 2021 by The Rowman & Littlefield Publishing Group, Inc.

All rights reserved. No part of this book may be reproduced in any form or by any electronic or mechanical means, including information storage and retrieval systems, without written permission from the publisher, except by a reviewer who may quote passages in a review.

British Library Cataloguing in Publication Information Available

Library of Congress Control Number: 2020947614

ISBN 978-1-7936-1955-6 (cloth)
ISBN 978-1-7936-1957-0 (pbk)
ISBN 978-1-7936-1956-3 (electronic)

For Amy

Contents

Acknowledgments	ix
Abbreviations	xi
Introduction	1
1 The Problem of Providence in Contemporary Theology: From Recovery to Liberation	11
2 G. W. F. Hegel: Providence in Time, Space, and Race	37
3 Karl Barth: Providence between East and West	67
4 James H. Cone: Providence as the Cities Burned	107
5 Liberating Providence: The Spirit, Christ's Presence, and Creaturely Participation	137
Conclusion	167
Bibliography	179
Index	191
About the Author	197

Acknowledgments

Writing this book has been a journey, and along the way there have been many guides and traveling companions without whose company I could not have completed it—or even taken the first steps. At the very beginning, there was Allen Verhey, who believed in me more than I believed in myself and who first encouraged me to pursue this project in a conversation at the Federal in Durham, NC. I miss him dearly. My doctoral mentor Luke Bretherton was perpetually generous with his time, energy, and support over the years, devoting countless hours to reading and discussing my work. He has contributed to my development as a teacher and a scholar in innumerable ways. Willie Jennings, Stanley Hauerwas, and J. Kameron Carter were my teachers and conversation partners for the better part of a decade at Duke Divinity School and served on my dissertation committee, along with James Chappel. I am deeply grateful to them all.

A number of other individuals and groups helped to support and advance my work on this book at key moments. I received valuable feedback from workshops and presentations on different portions of the manuscript at the Society of Christian Ethics, the Political Theology Network, the Center for Barth Studies at Princeton, the Theology and Ethics Graduate Colloquium at Duke, the Fellowship for Protestant Ethics, and the Theology Seminar at Hope College and Western Theological Seminary. Todd Billings was a gracious guide as I navigated the world of academic book publishing for the first time. I was continually energized by my wonderful students at Duke University, Duke Divinity School, Meredith College, and Hope College, especially the students in the Emmaus Scholars Program, who display the love and courage that is necessary to move falteringly toward Christ's presence through the Spirit in the world today. The editorial staff at Lexington

Books has persevered through a pandemic to bring this book to press, and I owe Michael Gibson, Mikayla Mislak, and Becca Beurer a debt of gratitude.

The book was shaped along the way by the witness and work of a number of organizations and communities in which I was involved while I wrote. I drew inspiration from the organizers and leaders of Durham C.A.N. (Congregations, Associations and Neighborhoods) and from Rev. William J. Barber II and the North Carolina NAACP's Forward Together movement. I also learned much about discerning the Spirit in a world governed by whiteness from the people of Durham Church and Iglesia Emanuel.

I am so very thankful for the friends who supported me as I worked on this project. I was fortunate to be a part of a wonderful group of graduate students in the Divinity School and the Graduate Program in Religion at Duke University, including Justin Ashworth, Carole Baker, Sarah Barton, Tanner Capps, Matt Elia, Emily Dubie, Sam Fong, Aaron Griffith, Mike Grigoni, Joelle Hathaway, Ryan Juskus, SueJeanne Koh, Alberto La Rosa, Tomi Oredein, Amanda Pittman, Mandy Rodgers-Gates, Kara Slade, Derek Taylor, Marvin Wickware, Michelle Wolff, and Colin Yuckman. Brett McCarty was a faithful friend after the death of our mentor Allen Verhey. I was sustained by the laughter and tears of Thursday night dinners with Evan, Ashley, Dustin, Jen, James, Eliza, Aaron, Ben, Lauren, Derek, and especially the Very Reverend Michael Richard Boone, who left us too soon. Robin Barefoot encouraged me from start to finish, and Gordon Cooper's friendship has been unfailing.

I am especially grateful to my family. My grandparents, Bob and June Vetter, shared with me their faith, as well as their passion for learning, writing, and laughing. My parents, Deb and Dan, have offered steady, unconditional support, while my siblings and their partners—Elissa, Hugh, Colby, and Brenna—have been ready sources of laughter and solidarity. My children, Luke and Will, are slowly teaching me to receive the gift of creatureliness. Finally, I dedicate this book to Amy, my wife and partner, whose life is a beacon of God's lavish, life-giving, death-defying love for the world.

Abbreviations

BTBP   Cone, James H. *Black Theology and Black Power.* Maryknoll, NY: Orbis Books, 1997.
BTL   Cone, James H. *A Black Theology of Liberation.* Maryknoll, NY: Orbis Books, 1986.
CD III/3   Barth, Karl. *Church Dogmatics.* Edited and translated by G. W. Bromiley and T. F. Torrance. Vol. III/3. Edinburgh: T&T Clark, 1960.
LPWH   Hegel, G. W. F. *Lectures on the Philosophy of World History: Volume 1: Manuscripts of the Introduction and the Lectures of 1822-3.* Edited and translated by Robert F. Brown and Peter C. Hodgson with the assistance of William G. Geuss. Oxford: Oxford University Press, 2011.
GO   Cone, James H. *God of the Oppressed.* Maryknoll, NY: Orbis Books, 1975.

Introduction

God's providence is back in the headlines. As the 2016 U.S. presidential election unfolded, influential Christian leaders in the United States began discerning a higher power at work in the candidacy of Donald Trump. In June 2016, Paula White, a televangelist, megachurch pastor, and future member of the Trump administration, offered a theological interpretation of Trump's candidacy in an interview with the Christian Broadcasting Network. When asked how to make sense of what God was doing in making Trump the Republican nominee for president (a question that many of Trump's opponents were no doubt asking as well), White began with a brief appeal to the inscrutability of God's providence: "First off, do we ever make sense of God, you know? I think that His plans are not our plans." Then, without skipping a beat, White proceeded to try to make sense of God's plans: "There's no way in 'the natural'—if we were to use that terminology—that you could take a man against seventeen other candidates . . . very qualified candidates, and then here he is, the nominee. That has to be providence." Trump's surprising success, despite his lack of qualifications, was evidence that something more than politics as usual was at work. This was the "hand of God."[1]

White's verdict has since been repeated by other high profile political and spiritual figures in the United States, especially after Trump went on to defeat Hillary Clinton in the general election. In response to Trump's victory, Franklin Graham proclaimed that "God showed up."[2] Former U.S. Congresswoman Michele Bachmann similarly weighed in: "The glory goes to the God Almighty, the God of the Universe, the Sovereign Lord. He is the one who did this for us."[3] For more than a few outspoken Christians in the world today, it seems that God's providence has aligned itself—once again—with the impulses of toxic nationalism.

However, nationalism is not the only idolatrous providential discourse that shapes the social life of humanity in the twenty-first century. The invisible hand of the capitalist market economy is at least an equal claimant to that title. Contemporary capitalism has perfected the art of mimicking God's providence. It is irresistible in its sovereign power, omnipresent in its scope, unquestionable in its omniscient reconfigurations of global society and the planet itself, and seemingly eternal in duration: "It is easier to imagine the end of the world than to imagine the end of capitalism."[4]

One of the many manifestations of capitalism's pseudo-providential rule over the common life of humanity in recent years has been the calm, systematic, and merciless onslaught of gentrification and displacement in cities across the United States. Cities like Durham, NC, where African American communities that had existed since the Civil War have been pillaged for profit. Having endured and persisted through the collapse of Reconstruction, the violence of Jim Crow, and successive waves of redlining, urban "renewal," and economic disinvestment, these communities are now facing the possibility that it is not economic deprivation, but rather the "revitalization" of their city that will lead to the dissolution of their communities at the hands of trendy coffee shops, real estate developers, and liberal white professionals and graduate students.[5] The mysterious—and racialized—judgments of market providentialism elect some for flourishing and others for displacement.

What might Christian theology have to say in the face of nationalism and capitalism—these racialized counterfeits of the doctrine of providence? Ironically, while these idolatrous deformations of the doctrine of providence are increasingly in the ascendancy, the same cannot be said with respect to the treatment of the doctrine within the field of Christian theology.

Long deemed one of the most notable and resilient aspects of Christian doctrine due to its central place in the theologies of the Reformation and Protestant liberalism, the doctrine of providence now bears the opposite reputation in most theological circles. In the last half a century, the doctrine of providence has been notable only by its absence, and the resilience of the doctrine is now widely identified with a stubborn resistance to efforts to revive it.[6] Thus, even as the providential hand of the market tears apart communities of color, and as popular Christian figures like Paula White easily associate God's providence with a political campaign that trafficked in racism and authoritarianism, academic Christian theologians seem to have difficulty saying anything at all about the doctrine. The experiment in Christian doctrine that occupies the following pages suggests that these realities might be related to one another. It does so by delving to the theological roots of the relationship between providence and race in the modern world. The book exposes the entanglement of the Christian doctrine of providence in modern racial visions of history and geography and articulates an alternative political theology of providence, following in the wake of those who have sought to discern the liberative character of God's action in history.

My interest in the topic of God's providence began as a casual observation years ago that the doctrine seemed underrepresented in contemporary theological discourse. It quickly developed, however, into a conviction that the doctrine of providence provided an important case study of key transformations that Christian theology underwent in modernity through symbiotic and mutually constituting relationships with political and racial discourse. Furthermore, I came to believe that grappling with these transformations might shed light on the disappearance of providence from recent academic theology and perhaps even point to a path forward for the doctrine. Working from this central conviction, the present study develops a theology of providence that engages interdisciplinary conversations about religion and race in the modern world and that grows out of an inquiry in intellectual history into three key figures in modern Protestant theology.

As a work of constructive theology, my argument also addresses itself to conversations in my discipline about the noticeable lack of attention that the topic of providence has received in recent times. Beginning in the 1950s, a broad consensus emerged within the field of systematic theology that the doctrine of providence was in a state of crisis and that efforts to repair and retrieve it were necessary.[7] Over the past half century, there have been repeated efforts to diagnose the reasons leading to this "collapse" of the doctrine of providence and to offer new formulations of the doctrine in response.[8] The present study engages this mid-century diagnosis of a crisis for the doctrine of providence. However, in order to do so, the book first raises some critical questions about the way that this crisis has been narrated by white European and U.S. American theologians in the last seventy years. I offer an alternative construal of the problem that the doctrine poses for contemporary Christian theology and formulate a constructive theological account of providence in response. This alternative construal of the problem has everything to do with the twisted trail that Christian theology and racial discourse have blazed together through the modern world.

Recent years have witnessed a surge of interest in the relationship between religion and race in modernity. This interdisciplinary conversation reflects a mutual convergence of scholars of race, religion, and theology around a common verdict. That verdict is summarized in Willie Jennings's suggestion that "race has a Christian architecture, and Christianity in the West has a racial architecture."[9] This study examines the specific aspect of this symbiotic architecture that has been constituted around the theological concept of providence.

The doctrine of providence provided a powerful ordering vision of God and creation, time and space, self and other, which European thinkers appropriated as an intellectual framework for imagining a racialized world. These racial visions then went on to distort Christian attempts to discern the providence of God in history. The book examines a specific case of this vicious circle in one of the most influential theological and philosophical thinkers of the modern world, Georg Wilhelm Friedrich Hegel, as well as two attempts to wrestle theologically with the problem that Hegel embodied, which were undertaken in the twentieth century by Karl Barth and James Hal Cone. The book exposes the contested racial imaginations within modern Protestant theological reflection on the doctrine of providence, exploring how Christian theologies of providence have served as an intellectual site at which race and whiteness have been both constructed and resisted.[10]

At this point, a clarification on the use of a few key terms is in order. In the present study, I will identify the doctrine of providence's relationship to whiteness as one of the central problems that Christian theology must confront in its efforts to engage the doctrine today. From the outset, it is important to define what I mean by whiteness and to explain the relationship between this term and its close relative: white supremacy. Most basically, I define whiteness as what Pierre Bourdieu calls a habitus or a "socialized subjectivity."[11] Whiteness is a set of flexible and shifting perceptions, dispositions, practices, structures, and processes that are historically, socially, politically, and culturally produced through relationships to land and people defined by dislocation and domination.[12] Importantly, as has been recently demonstrated, these historical, social, political, and cultural practices and processes, which originally produced whiteness, had their roots in Christianity in general and Christian theology specifically.[13]

What this means is that whiteness and the concomitant racial system that it generates are neither natural or neutral. It is not the case that race is merely a descriptive category—a way to classify biological or physiological differences within humanity—that only later is corrupted into racism, when used as the basis for hierarchical and comparative evaluation. Rather, as Nell Irvin Painter has suggested, race and racism are "inevitable partners" that together follow "a crooked road, constructed by dominant peoples to justify their domination of others."[14]

It is for this reason that I choose to identify whiteness—as opposed to white supremacy—as the primary problem to be confronted in this study. To use the term white supremacy would leave open the possibility for misinterpretation, as if the problem is not racial thinking as such, but merely racial thinking used for domination through comparative evaluation. Racial thinking, however, was born out of the quest for domination through comparative evaluation. Whiteness, as it has existed thus far in human history, is inherently white supremacist.[15] Therefore, this study sets out to interrogate the way in which the doctrine of providence has provided a powerful theological vision that has contributed to the construction of the racial subjectivity of whiteness, comfortably resided within it, but also been used to wrestle against it. The book pursues this line of inquiry using the tools of intellectual history to trace these theological issues across the writings of three central figures in the history of modern Protestant theology.

As a work of intellectual history, the central chapters of the book examine how G. W. F. Hegel, Karl Barth, and James Cone engaged in theological reflection about the doctrine of providence as a way to either promote or contest the political and racial realities of their day. These three figures have been selected both for their relevance to the particular topic at hand, as well as their significance in shaping the contemporary field of Christian theology.

Each of these figures engaged in theological reflection about providence in historical moments of heightened significance for the relationship between race and Christianity, and careful attention to the productive interplay between their historical contexts and their theological writings reveals otherwise overlooked dimensions of their theological projects. Hegel engaged the doctrine in the midst of rising—if mostly frustrated—German colonial ambitions in the 1820s. Barth wrestled with the doctrine in the aftermath of National Socialism and the early stages of the Cold War at the end of the 1940s, while Cone's reflections on providence took place in the context of uprisings in cities across the United States and the Black Power movement at the end of the 1960s and beginning of the 1970s. In Hegel, Barth, and Cone's theological accounts of providence, the often-repressed racial architecture of modern doctrines of providence rises closer to the surface and becomes more visible, making these three figures ideal conversation partners to engage on the central theological questions of this study.

The selection of these figures is further merited by the narrative arc that emerges from placing them in conversation. Hegel's *Lectures on the Philosophy of World History* presents the doctrine of providence at the peak of its powers in shaping a vision of European modernity. While other figures engaged the doctrine of providence in their political philosophies—Immanuel Kant being the most obvious example—none can rival Hegel in terms of the scope and confidence of his use of the doctrine.[16] In the hands of Hegel, the doctrine of providence becomes the basis for a philosophical theory that orders all of time and space around the incarnation of the divine in modern European humanity and its civilization.[17] In composing his doctrine of providence in *Church Dogmatics* III/3, Karl Barth explicitly engages Hegel as a key interlocutor over and against whom Barth articulates his theology. Similarly, in his early writings, James Cone is engaged in a running dialogue with Barth's theology. Methodologically, therefore, the study represents, what H. Richard Niebuhr calls a "pilgrim's venture": an attempt at historical inquiry made by one who is "interested more in prospect than in retrospect but who, seeing the continuity of present with past, know[s] that without retrospect no real prospect is possible."[18] In order to develop a contemporary account of the doctrine of providence that is responsive to the problematic symbiosis between racial and Christian providential discourse in the modern world, I examine historical case studies in which significant Christian intellectuals wrestled with the same task in their own contexts.

In terms of structure, the book begins with an assessment of the problem that the doctrine of providence poses for the field of contemporary Christian theology, which it then addresses through interpretive engagements with the work of Hegel, Barth, and Cone, before circling back to articulate a constructive theological account of providence in response to contemporary racial politics. The first chapter frames the problem that the doctrine of providence poses for Christian theology today. It opens with a critique of the dominant way that the infamous twentieth-century "crisis" of the doctrine of providence has been narrated within the field of Christian theology by figures like Langdon Gilkey and G. C. Berkouwer. The chapter challenges this dominant narrative of the doctrine's collapse, which states that providence fell into a crisis in the twentieth century because it could not render intelligible the suffering of European humanity in the two world wars.

Over and against this narrative, I argue in chapter 1 that there is a more historically and conceptually basic problem for a Christian account of providence in modernity: the use of the doctrine to justify the massive suffering inflicted upon global humanity by Christian Europe throughout the modern period. The chapter makes the argument that this suffering—like Abel's blood crying out from the ground in Genesis 4—is a wound to which theological reflection on providence must respond. The book then takes up the work of crafting such a response by engaging with three key figures in modern Protestant theology who wrestled with this issue in very different ways.

Chapter 2 offers a critical case study of G. W. F. Hegel's *Lectures on the Philosophy of World History*, which exemplify the problematic distortion of the Christian doctrine of providence with which this study is concerned. It argues that in these lectures Hegel deploys the Christian doctrine of providence as a conceptual framework through which he theorizes world history as a teleological process of divine incarnation, articulated in terms of historical, geographical, and anthropological progress. These temporal, spatial, and anthropological lines of analysis converge in Hegel's thought around one figure, who emerges from the lectures as the divine subject of world history: European man. Indeed, in these lectures, the figure of European man replaces Jesus Christ as the center of the doctrine of providence, displacing the latter and identifying the former as the human subject around which divine providence would be calibrated in world history. As a result, the doctrine of providence, which had been a way to articulate God's rule over the cosmos, became a way to articulate European humanity's rule over the globe. The chapter closes with an assessment of Hegel's problematic vision that outlines the basic challenge to which the rest of the book responds. That challenge is to articulate an account of God's providence that will resist attempts to transform it into an account of European humanity's providential rule over the globe. The following two chapters explore Karl Barth and James Cone's different attempts to respond to that challenge.

The third chapter examines the relationship between Karl Barth's doctrine of providence in *Church Dogmatics* III/3 and the historical context within which Barth composed it, namely, the end of the Third Reich in Germany and the emergence of the Cold War. I argue that Barth cast his own account of providence in radical antithesis to Hegel's vision, offering an alternative theological exposition of the relationship between providence, history, and humanity centered upon the God revealed in the covenant with Israel and the incarnation of the Jewish human being Jesus of Nazareth. While Hegel wielded the doctrine of providence as a conceptual resource through which to forge a vision of European man as the quasi-divine subject of history, Barth bases his own doctrine of providence on an alternative vision of Jesus Christ as the center and telos of world history. The chapter recovers a radical Barth, whose writings on providence unmask a distorted understanding of Christian identity that Barth held responsible for the rise of National Socialism in Germany and the emergence of anti-Communist hysteria in the Western world. On this reading, Barth's Christological reformulation of the doctrine of providence in *Church Dogmatics* III/3 is an attempt to articulate an account of providence that challenges Hegel's providential discourse of European world-governance.

In chapter 4, I turn to James H. Cone's account of providence and divine action, which he articulated in the midst of the Black Power movement in the late 1960s and early 1970s. The chapter argues that Cone's theology contains an understanding of divine action in human history that fosters particular and contingent judgments about how Jesus Christ continues to be active in world history through the Holy Spirit in relationship to human struggles for liberation and justice. While Cone is obviously critical of attempts to reinterpret God's activity in line with the subjective interests of white people, he also wants to avoid a simple inversion of that ideological formulation which would reverse the equation and align God's activity with the subjective interests of Black people. Rather, Cone develops a nuanced and contextual approach for discerning God's liberating presence in history that resists the attempt to deploy it ideologically as a mask for subjective human values and interests.

The fifth and final chapter draws together the strands of analysis from the three preceding chapters in order to identify a developing trajectory of thought in Hegel, Barth, and Cone. Building on this trajectory, I formulate a constructive account of providence as the work of the Holy Spirit in making Jesus Christ present to creation between ascension and eschaton and enabling human creaturely participation in Christ's presence in this time between the times. More succinctly, I argue for a pneumatological conception of providence in terms of Christological presence and anthropological participation. I then fill out this framework in conversation with the work of Delores S. Williams and M. Shawn Copeland, examining the Spirit's specific relationship to bodies, community, and time, yielding an account of providence that identifies Jesus Christ at work through the Spirit in ordinary, overlooked, and oppressed human beings who are daily engaged in the work of carving out a flourishing life for themselves, their families, their communities, and their world.

Finally, by way of conclusion, the study offers some reflections on how this constructive theology of providence might help to shape practical judgments about where, how, and in whom God is active today. I demonstrate how the account of divine providence developed over the course of this study might guide discernment of God's relationship to particular times and places through a case study of practices of community organizing and fusion politics in the city of Durham, NC in the second decade of the twenty-first century.

For more than fifty years, Christian theologians have worried about the doctrine of providence. This book suggests that these worries must be understood in light of the doctrine's entanglement with whiteness in the modern world and that it is only by doing so that contemporary theology might begin to imagine theologies of providence that enable liberating and just interpretations of the relationship between God's providential action in history and contemporary racial politics. In this regard, the book's subtitle operates in two senses: the book seeks both *to liberate* the doctrine of providence from its symbiotic entanglement with racial vision and to articulate an account of the *liberating* character of God's providence. Ultimately, the present study reflects my attempt to craft a theology of providence that might help to guide myself and others in discerning God's relationship to a world governed by the distorted racial logics of whiteness. My hope is that such discernment might lead to actions that are responsive to—and perhaps even participate in—what God is doing in the world today. As James Cone has suggested, "We must speak of God and his work, if we intend to join him."[19]

NOTES

1. David Brody, "Donald Trump, Paula White and the Gospel," *Christian Broadcasting Network*, June 21, 2016, https://www1.cbn.com/thebrodyfile/archive/2016/06/21/donald-trump-paula-white-and-the-gospel. While Paula White's prosperity gospel televangelism has been viewed by many as an unorthodox departure from the theological brand of previous presidential faith advisors, her providential

interpretation of political events sits firmly within a quintessential tradition of U.S. Christianity that climaxed during the Civil War, as Mark Noll has documented in *The Civil War as a Theological Crisis* (Chapel Hill, NC: University of North Carolina Press, 2006), 83: "If natural causes (that is, God's mediated control over events) seemed to point in one direction and yet something different happened, commentators leapt to the conclusion that God's unmediated actions must be the explanation."

2. Lauren Markoe, "Did God Choose Trump? What it Means to Believe in Divine Intervention," *Religion News Service*, January 17, 2017, http://religionnews.com/2017/01/17/did-god-choose-trump-what-belief-in-divine-intervention- really-means/.

3. Brooke Seipel, "Michele Bachmann on Trump Victory: 'God Did This,'" *The Hill*, November 9, 2016, https://thehill.com/blogs/ballot-box/presidential-races/305227-michele-bachmann-on-trump-victory-god-did-this.

4. Frederic Jameson, "Future City," *New Left Review* 21 (May/June 2003): 76.

5. Gillian B. White, "The Downside of Durham's Rebirth," *The Atlantic*, March 31, 2016, https://www.theatlantic.com/business/archive/2016/03/the-downside-of-durhams-rebirth/476277/.

6. Langdon Gilkey offered the paradigmatic account of this sea change in the doctrine of providence in his landmark essay "The Concept of Providence in Contemporary Theology," *Journal of Religion* 43, no. 3 (1963): 171–192. I discuss Gilkey's essay at length in the next chapter.

7. Gilkey, "The Concept of Providence," 171–192; G. C. Berkouwer, *The Providence of God*, trans. Lewis B. Smedes (Grand Rapids, MI: Wm. B. Eerdmans Publishing Company, 1952).

8. Langdon Gilkey, *Reaping the Whirlwind: A Christian Interpretation of History* (New York: The Seabury Press, 1976); Albert C. Outler, *Who Trusts in God: Musings on the Meaning of Providence* (New York: Oxford University Press, 1968); Peter R. Baelz, *Prayer and Providence: A Background Study* (New York: The Seabury Press, 1968); Michael J. Langford, *Providence* (London: SCM Press Ltd., 1981); Benjamin Wirt Farley, *The Providence of God* (Grand Rapids, MI: Baker Book House, 1988); T. J. Gorringe, *God's Theatre: A Theology of Providence* (London: SCM Press Ltd., 1991); Paul Helm, *The Providence of God* (Downers Grove, IL: InterVarsity Press, 1994); E. Frank Tupper, *A Scandalous Providence: The Jesus Story of the Compassion of God* (Macon, GA: Mercer University Press, 1995); John Sanders, *The God Who Risks: A Theology of Providence* (Downers Grove, IL: InterVarsity Press, 1998); Reinhold Bernhardt, *Was heißt "Handeln Gottes"?: Eine Rekonstruktion der Lehre von der Vorsehung* (Gütersloh: Chr. Kaiser/Gütersloher Verlagshaus, 1999); Charles M. Wood, *The Question of Providence* (Louisville, KY: Westminster John Knox Press, 2008); Francesca Aran Murphy and Philip G. Ziegler (ed.'s), *The Providence of God:* Deus Habet Consilium (London: T&T Clark, 2009); Terry J. Wright, *Providence Made Flesh: Divine Presence as a Framework for a Theology of Providence* (Milton Keynes: Paternoster Press, 2009); Hans S. Reinders, *Disability, Providence, and Ethics: Bridging Gaps, Transforming Lives* (Waco, TX: Baylor University Press, 2014); David Fergusson, *The Providence of God: A Polyphonic Approach* (Cambridge: Cambridge University Press, 2018).

9. Willie James Jennings, "Overcoming Racial Faith," *Divinity*, Spring 2015, 5.

10. In invoking the racial unconscious, I draw upon Willie James Jennings's development of Frederic Jameson's concept of the political unconscious in *The Christian Imagination: Theology and the Origins of Race* (New Haven: Yale University Press, 2010), 252, 342 n. 14. According to Jameson, the political unconscious is "the repressed and buried reality" which must be restored "to the surface of the text." See Frederic Jameson, *The Political Unconscious: Narrative as a Socially Symbolic Act* (Ithaca: Cornell University Press, 1981), 20.

11. Pierre Bourdieu and Loïc J. D. Wacquant, *An Invitation to Reflexive Sociology* (The University of Chicago Press, 1992), 126. See also Pierre Bourdieu, *The Logic of Practice*, translated by Richard Nice (Stanford: Stanford University Press, 1990), 53: "The conditionings associated with a particular class of conditions of existence produce *habitus*, systems of durable, transposable dispositions, structured structures predisposed to function as structuring structures, that is, as principles which generate and organize practices and representations."

12. For a similar account, see Robin DiAngelo, "White Fragility," *International Journal of Critical Pedagogy* 3, no. 3 (2011): 56–58.

13. J. Kameron Carter, *Race: A Theological Account* (Cambridge: Cambridge University Press, 2008); Jennings, *The Christian Imagination.*

14. Nell Irvin Painter, *The History of White People* (New York: W.W. Norton, 2010).

15. Whether there is the possibility of a future transformation of whiteness beyond white supremacy—the creation of a positive white identity—is a heavily debated question. Elsewhere, I have engaged this debate and argued that the path forward for those racialized as white in the struggle against whiteness lies through conversion from whiteness. See Matt R. Jantzen, "Neither Ally, Nor Accomplice: James Cone and the Theological Ethics of White Conversion," *Journal of the Society of Christian Ethics* 40, no. 2 (2020).

16. See, in particular, Immanuel Kant, "Idea for a Universal History with a Cosmopolitan Intent," in *Perpetual Peace and Other Essays: On Politics, History, and Morals*, trans. Humphrey (Cambridge: Hackett Publishing Co., 1983); Immanuel Kant, "To Perpetual Peace: A Philosophical Sketch," in *Perpetual Peace and Other Essays: On Politics, History, and Morals*, trans. Humphrey (Cambridge: Hackett Publishing Co., 1983).

17. The decision to focus on Hegel is also warranted by Hegel's tremendous influence on those who came after him. In the words of Maurice Merleau-Ponty, "All the great philosophical ideas of the past century—the philosophies of Marx and Nietzsche, phenomenology, German existentialism, and psychoanalysis—had their beginnings in Hegel." See Maurice Merleau-Ponty, *Sense and Non-Sense*, trans. Dreyfus and Dreyfus (Chicago: Northwestern University Press, 1964), 63. Cited in Charles Taylor, *Hegel* (Cambridge: Cambridge University Press, 1975), 538.

18. H. Richard Niebuhr, *The Kingdom of God in America* (Middletown, CT: Wesleyan University Press, 1988), 1.

19. James Cone, *Black Theology and Black Power* (Maryknoll, NY: Orbis Books, 1997), 49 (hereafter cited as *BTBP*).

Chapter 1

The Problem of Providence in Contemporary Theology

From Recovery to Liberation

In the July 1963 issue of *The Journal of Religion*, the U.S. American theologian Langdon Gilkey sounded the alarm: the doctrine of providence was in crisis. In his essay entitled "The Concept of Providence in Contemporary Theology," Gilkey exposed a serious deficit in contemporary theological reflection on the doctrine of providence, arguing that providence "had nearly disappeared from present theology" and was the only one of the major classical loci of Christian doctrine that had not enjoyed a considerable renaissance in the twentieth century.[1] Indeed, according to Gilkey, the only significant feature of theological reflection on providence in the twentieth century was its rapid disappearance:

> Today this concept of Providence is notable mainly in its absence from theological discussion. This absence is in turn the more striking because, first, the two past traditions that have greatly influenced contemporary theology—the Reformation and Liberalism—both had carefully elaborated and very significant conceptions of Providence; and, second, because the question most frequently asked in contemporary theological discussion—What is the meaning, if any, of history?—might seem to call for an equally strong view of God's providential rule over historical events.[2]

The rapid erosion of one of the central doctrines of Christian theology led Gilkey to an important question about "the forgotten stepchild of contemporary theology": "Why has Providence in our generation been left a rootless, disembodied ghost, flitting from footnote to footnote, but rarely finding secure lodgment in sustained theological discourse?"[3]

More than half a century later, Gilkey's question remains relevant. Despite repeated efforts to account for the neglect of providence and to engage in a recovery of the doctrine, there remains a broad consensus among contemporary theologians: "The situation has not changed markedly since Gilkey wrote."[4] Indeed, David Fergusson has recently published a major work on providence—one of the few to appear in the last several decades—which he frames as a project of doctrinal "recovery" and "reconstruction," ascribing "magisterial" significance to Gilkey's mid-century analysis.[5] Thus, even when the doctrine does occasionally receive attention in contemporary theology, it often does so precisely because of its beleaguered condition, and the dominant framework for continuing theological engagements with providence remains that of collapse and recovery.[6]

Gilkey's alarm is still ringing after more than fifty years. Like pain pulsing from the site of a wound that refuses to heal, the continued relevance of Gilkey's analysis indicates that something is wrong with the doctrine of providence and calls for a response. This protracted doctrinal impasse is both a cause for concern and an invitation for further reflection. As Mary McClintock Fulkerson has argued, "Theologies that matter arise out of dilemmas. . . . Creative thinking originates at the scene of a wound. Wounds generate new thinking. Disjunctions birth invention."[7] The dramatic collapse of the doctrine of providence in twentieth-century theology is an intellectual wound, a painful disruption of established belief that holds within itself the possibility of restoration and new growth. However, the path to those latent, hope-filled possibilities runs directly through some difficult questions: what caused the doctrine of providence to fall into its present state of crisis, and why have repeated attempts to resolve that crisis made so little progress? This chapter explores these diagnostic questions in dialogue with Gilkey and others, arguing that the intellectual wound that providence represents has not been healed after all these years because it has not been properly diagnosed.

In terms of diagnosis, there is widespread agreement among scholars that one of the principal reasons for the collapse of the doctrine of providence was the sheer amount of human suffering and violence that marked the modern era. But whose suffering? And which violence? It is at this point that a critical revision of the scholarly consensus is necessary, for the wound runs far deeper than most Christian theologians have been able to acknowledge.

Within the field of Christian theology, the mid-twentieth-century perspectives of Langdon Gilkey and the Dutch Reformed theologian G.C. Berkouwer have provided the guiding framework for conversations about the collapse and recovery of the doctrine of providence. Both Gilkey and Berkouwer identified the root cause of providence's collapse specifically in the profound suffering of European humanity in the first half of the twentieth century in the trenches of World War I, the bombed-out cities of World War II, and the gas chambers of the Shoah. According to Gilkey and Berkouwer, the contemporary crisis of the doctrine of providence resulted from Christian theology's inability to reconcile belief in God's providence with the suffering and dislocation experienced by European humanity in the first half of the twentieth century. While there is some truth to their assessment, it only scratches the surface of the challenge that human suffering in modernity poses to the doctrine of providence.

There is a depth to this problem of human suffering that Gilkey and Berkouwer were unable to acknowledge, and that inability has everything to do with the way that race has shaped the Christian theological imagination in modernity. When European civilization came under duress in the first half of the twentieth century, it registered within the dominant streams of Christian theology—through the writings of leading theologians like Gilkey and Berkouwer—as a fundamental threat to the basic viability of a Christian doctrine of providence. Yet, even as they lamented the violence, suffering, and radical alienation that European humanity experienced in the world wars and the Holocaust, Gilkey and Berkouwer completely failed to address—or even recognize—the violence, suffering, and radical alienation that has marked *non-European* humanity's experience of the modern world dating back to its very foundations. Even more problematically, where European suffering seemed to be radically incompatible with God's providence, the suffering of non-European others through slavery, conquest, and colonialism was articulated within large swaths of Christian Europe for hundreds of years as deeply compatible with God's providential ordering of the world.

While much ink has been spilled addressing the perceived incompatibility between belief in God's providence and the suffering of European humanity in the twentieth century, the field of Christian theology still struggles to come to grips with the problem posed by the long and enduring perception of compatibility between European Christian visions of providence and the enslavement, suffering, and death of non-European peoples in modernity. More than fifty years ago, Gilkey asked why providence had ceased to function as a meaningful theological category in the face of the suffering of European humanity in the first half of the twentieth century. This question has dominated the imaginations of many Christian theologians interested in providence ever since, inspiring a number of attempts to "recover" the doctrine from its state of crisis. However, there is another question that Christian theology needs to ask, one which is potentially far more troubling, but which has been largely neglected in contemporary discussions: how could the Christian doctrine of providence have functioned so well as a theological category through which European Christians rendered intelligible and theologically justified the suffering and violence that they inflicted upon non-European peoples for hundreds of years before the twentieth century? Reframing the problem that the doctrine of providence represents for contemporary Christian theology in light of this latter question leads to the conclusion that providence does not so much need to be *recovered* from its collapse into obscurity, as it needs to be *liberated* from its captivity to race.

THE PROBLEM OF PROVIDENCE: COLLAPSE OR CAPTIVITY?

Alongside Langdon Gilkey's landmark article in *The Journal of Religion*, Gerrit Cornelius Berkouwer's *The Providence of God* implanted the story of the collapse of the doctrine of providence in mid-century European and North American theology. Berkouwer was one of the leading figures in twentieth-century Dutch Reformed theology, as well as an important Protestant contributor to ecumenical dialogue with the Roman Catholic Church after the Second World War. He held the chair in dogmatics at the Free University of Amsterdam from 1945 to 1974, a chair whose previous occupants included Abraham Kuyper and Herman Bavinck. His ecumenical work earned him a personal invitation to attend the Second Vatican Council as an observer. He wrote five books on Roman Catholicism and the eighteen volume series *Studies in Dogmatics*.[8] Published in 1952 as the second volume of that series, *The Providence of God* contained Berkouwer's frank description of what he identified as the "crisis of the providence doctrine in our century."[9]

According to Berkouwer, the nature of the crisis was not simply that a particular configuration of theological ideas no longer made sense, but that an entire way of seeing and being in the world which that configuration of ideas had supported had become untenable. It was not only the doctrine of providence that was in crisis but also the fundamental ordering of Christian European society that had been animated and held together by that doctrine. Writing from his postwar vantage point in 1950, Berkouwer surveyed the landscape of a European humanity whose experience in the first half of the twentieth century radically called into question the church's confession of the providence of God. In a century which will forever be marked as a time "of the concentration camps and the pogroms, of war and hatred, of attack on the worth of humanity itself," Berkouwer suggests that the providence of God "has today become a profound problem—*the* problem for persons who have never even considered it before." Yet while this problem has manifested as a problem with God and God's providence, its roots lie first and foremost in "the problem of man."[10]

A half-century of self-inflicted mass slaughter produced a European humanity whose fundamental outlook on existence is defined by a sense of "radical displacement and estrangement." Berkouwer labels this pervasive attitude "dread," the result of being "more or less ruthlessly snatched out of an old and trusted order and forced into a strange, hostile world." Importantly, according to Berkouwer, "The trusted order out of which man is plucked is the order of Providence."¹¹ As he sees it, modern European humanity stands at a crossroads where it is forced to choose between "the comfort of the old confession of God's providence," which now seems to ring hollow, and "the *dread* that rises from the events of our century," which presents itself in nihilism and atheism as the "one realistic world and life view" and the "only logical and permissible conclusion."¹²

The swift collapse of providence in the face of this radical alienation of "man" from "his trusted order" is all the more surprising to Berkouwer in light of providence's previous reign as "one of the most self-evident articles of the Church's confession." Long after other Christian doctrines like the virgin birth, the resurrection, and the ascension were subjected to strident criticism, providence continued to elicit almost "universal assent" from nineteenth-century humanity.¹³ Berkouwer explains providence's rapid fall from grace as the result of a gradual watering down of the doctrine within eighteenth- and nineteenth-century Christian theology which corroded the doctrine from the inside out, leading to its catastrophic demise at the hands of the twentieth-century horrors.

Appearing just over a decade after the publication of *The Providence of God*, Langdon Gilkey's "The Concept of Providence in Contemporary Theology" offered an account of the status of the doctrine in contemporary theology that echoed Berkouwer's sentiments. In his essay, Gilkey argues that the disappearance of the doctrine of providence from twentieth-century theology is indicative of more than just an intellectual problem within the academic guild of Christian theology. Paralleling Berkouwer's assertion that the problem with providence is more fundamentally a "problem of man," Gilkey suggests that the root cause of providence's demise lies "in the general character of our cultural situation."¹⁴ While past centuries have seen obstacles to belief in the doctrine of providence—such as the Lisbon earthquake in 1755—the twentieth century proved unique in posing seemingly insurmountable challenges to the doctrine which appeared to leave no possibility of a reconfiguration or adaptation of providence to the new cultural circumstance. Gilkey shares Berkouwer's assessment that the deathblow to providence was struck by the catastrophic devastation that European humanity had inflicted upon itself in the first half of the twentieth century. He links the doctrine's demise primarily to the "violent irruption of evil" in the twentieth century, which left the "field of life . . . filled with the very real screams of mangled bodies and littered with very dead corpses."¹⁵

Berkouwer and Gilkey agree that the collapse of the doctrine of providence means more than just a loss of a particular set of intellectual truth claims about God's relationship to the world. For Gilkey, the collapse of the doctrine means that "our" cultural situation was now defined by the fact that "*no* purpose, direction, or meaning of any sort could be seen in the general passage of historical events."[16] Similarly, according to Berkouwer, "man" has been alienated "from his trusted order."[17] For both thinkers, the collapse of the doctrine of providence leads ineluctably to the death of a certain way of being in the world for European Christian humanity: "God is estranged from man; and man becomes a stranger in His world."[18] Western civilization as a whole was reeling from an encounter with dread, suffering, estrangement, and alienation which was—in their eyes—unprecedented in the modern world. Neither Berkouwer nor Gilkey recognized that there is, in fact, one very obvious precedent for suffering and alienation of this magnitude in modernity: the experiences of non-European peoples who endured hundreds of years in the crucible of European colonial and imperial ventures—ventures which were theologically narrated through the lens of divine providence.

On January 10, 1838, John C. Calhoun, a former vice president, current U.S. senator from South Carolina, and perpetually vociferous defender of slavery, took to the floor of the U.S. Senate to offer an apology for the South's peculiar institution. In his remarks, Calhoun concocted a defense of slavery that mixed paternalism and white supremacist racial theory with an appeal to God's mysterious providential ordering of human political and economic relations:

> A mysterious Providence had brought together two races, from different portions of the globe, and placed them together in nearly equal numbers in the Southern portion of this Union. They were inseparably united beyond the possibility of separation. Experience had shown that the existing relation between them secured the peace and happiness of both. Each had improved; the inferior greatly; so much so, that it had attained a degree of civilization never before attained by the black race in any age or country. Under no other relation could they co-exist together. To destroy it was to involve a whole region in slaughter, carnage, and desolation; and, come what will, we must defend and preserve it. . . . Many in the South once believed that it was a moral and political evil; that folly and delusion are gone; we see it now in its true light, and regard it as the most safe and stable basis for free institutions in the world.[19]

Not content with simply defending the continued existence of the Southern slavocracy on the grounds of political pragmatism—as a regrettable but necessary evil—Calhoun met the moral critiques of his abolitionist opponents head-on. Attempting to outflank his enemies and seize the moral high ground, Calhoun argued that when viewed from the perspective of God's beneficent, providential organization of human society, slavery was revealed to be an unqualified good for all involved, promoting the improvement and development of masters, slaves, and society at large.

In taking this position, Calhoun echoed the view that his fellow South Carolinian James Henry Hammond had expressed in the U.S. House of Representatives just two years earlier. According to Hammond, "The camel loves the desert; the reindeer seeks the everlasting snows; the wild fowl gather to the waters; and the eagle wings his flight above the mountains. It is equally the order of Providence that slavery should exist among a planting people beneath a southern sun." Far from being evil or unjust, Hammond concluded, slavery was "the greatest of all the great blessings which a kind Providence has bestowed upon our glorious region."[20]

Calhoun and Hammond's grotesque appeals to providence to defend the Southern system of chattel slavery point to a critical problem that is missed by Berkouwer and Gilkey in their descriptions of the twentieth-century collapse of the doctrine of providence: the way that race has persistently infiltrated and distorted Christian discernment of the work of divine providence in the modern world. As Willie James Jennings argues in *The Christian Imagination: Theology and the Origins of Race*, when European Christians discovered and conquered the lands and peoples of Africa and the Americas, they used a "hermeneutic of providence" to narrate what they were doing theologically. The doctrine of providence served as "a powerful tool," an "epistemic imaginary" that helped Europeans to interpret and situate themselves in relationship to the new places and peoples with whom they came into contact.[21] The problem, of course, is that this hermeneutic of providence was idolatrously calibrated to a racialized vision of humanity.

In terms of the breadth and the depth of this problem, it is no exaggeration to say that this problem has been one of the perennially recurring features of European Christianity over the last 500 years, cutting across historical, geographical, and confessional boundaries with alarming ease. Whether one considers Spanish and Portuguese Catholics in the fifteenth and sixteenth centuries, British Anglicans in the seventeenth and eighteenth centuries, Presbyterians and Methodists in the United States in the nineteenth century, or German Lutherans and South African Dutch Reformed Christians in the twentieth, the empirical results are ominously consistent given the vast distances in time, space, and theological tradition that separate these different situations: the mass suffering, enslavement, and death of people of color at the hands of white Christians who explicitly and self-consciously invoked divine providence as the lens through which to render their actions theologically intelligible and claim them as righteous. Like Abel's blood crying out from the ground in Genesis 4, this suffering is a wound to which theological reflection on providence must respond.

The modern era was not the first, of course, to witness the misuse of the doctrine of providence to justify immoral human action, and in response Christian theologians have come up with a number of different solutions to serve as checks against problematic appeals to God's activity in history. In reaction against the use of providence to justify an unjust status quo by appealing to God's providential ordering of human affairs, theologians have tried to offer an alternative account of providence that might animate social change. Conversely, where providence has been invoked in order to baptize unjust human political projects as part of God's salvific work in the world, theologians have sought to confine providential politics to modest, quotidian goals. Yet neither of these two dominant strategies for combating the misuse of Christian providential visions is adequate for grappling with the racialized subversion of the doctrine of providence in modernity. Indeed, both of these supposed theological "correctives" were easily co-opted by Christian defenders of chattel slavery in the United States.

One historic misuse of the doctrine of providence invokes God's providential ordering of the world as little more than a divine stamp of approval for an unjust status quo. It is an inherently conservative reading of the political consequences of providence whose maxim is "that which is, is good"—or perhaps better yet, "God willed it, I accept it, that settles it." On this conservative model, appeals to God's providence function to maintain the order of things even when that order is unjust. According to the logic of this model, if God's all-encompassing providence establishes, maintains, and governs everything that happens in world history, including the affairs of humanity, then everything that happens is a result of the direct decision and action of God—including unjust and oppressive realities like slavery. To try to fight back against injustice or liberate oneself—the argument goes—would be to engage in rebellion against the God who willed for you to be taken or born into slavery.

Over and against this conservative use of the doctrine of providence to underwrite an unjust status quo, efforts have been made to articulate a more progressive doctrine of providence that, as Philip Ziegler suggests, "can underwrite and animate a critical politics of social and political change."[22] With an alternative construal of divine providence, the doctrine might serve as the theological basis for efforts to critique and transform unjust social structures. Where a conservative reading of providence emphasizes the importance of maintaining the God-ordained order of things as they already exist in the present, this alternative construal views God's providential engagement in history as dynamically related to the unfolding of God's will for the future. Given this progressive view of divine providence, Ziegler argues, Christians should not equate fidelity to God's providence with maintaining the established order of things. Rather, they should be open to the idea that God's dynamic providential action may express itself through human efforts to change the existing order of things.[23] This theological strategy admirably attempts to free Christian political judgment from complicity in uncritically maintaining the present order of things and seeks to mobilize the doctrine of providence as a resource for political resistance and change.

However, it is important to see that this critique of conservative visions of God's providence does not in itself answer the question of how the doctrine of providence could be pressed inside of racialized visions of the world in modernity. While defenders of slavery certainly invoked ideas of providential order to justify slavery, conserve an unjust status quo, and discourage slaves from seeking freedom, it is equally true that they invoked progressive providential visions as a theological rationale for creating, maintaining, and expanding a new global economy based upon human slavery. In this case, the proposed theological solution to problematic visions of God's providence was itself part of the problem.

William Henry Holcombe's pamphlet *The Alternative*, published in 1860, exemplifies a theological interpretation of slavery in the United States that envisioned it in relationship to the transformative and dynamic movement of God's providence in the world. Holcombe was the son of Virginia slave owners who emancipated their slaves and moved him to Indiana when he was still young. However, his parents' emancipatory actions did not shape Holcombe's mature views on the topic of slavery and, after becoming a doctor and gaining national repute for his cholera treatments, he moved south to Mississippi in 1852 and took up the pro-slavery cause with a vengeance.[24]

In *The Alternative*, Holcombe conceives of the relationship between divine providence and the institution of slavery not in terms of the static preservation of a divinely established order, but in terms of the mission of white Christian humanity to respond to the *dynamic* and *active* movement of God in the world:

> The South is now fully convinced of the benefits and blessings it is conferring upon the Negro race. It is beginning to catch a glimpse of the true nature and extent of its mission in relation to this vast and growing institution. The government of the South is to protect it; the Church of the South is to Christianize it; the people of the South are to love it, and improve it and perfect it. God has lightened our task and secured its extension by making our interests happily coincide with our duty. We anticipate no terminus to the institution of slavery. It is the means whereby the white man is to subdue the tropics all around the globe.... African slavery is no retrograde movement, no discord in the harmony of nature, no violation of elemental justice, no infraction of immutable laws, human or divine—but *an integral link in the grand progressive evolution of human society as an indissoluble whole.*[25]

Surprisingly, Holcombe's understanding of the relationship between divine providence and human political judgment on display in *The Alternative* matches quite closely the supposedly radical view that humanity's obligation in relationship to divine providence "is to keep abreast of the present *ruling* of the God who is ever free according to his good purposes 'to will a world in which human efforts alter human social orders.'"[26] The politics of slavocracy in the United States could, in fact, quite comfortably take the form of a critical politics of social change—this was not the problem. The problem was that they were a critical politics of social change produced inside the logics of whiteness.

While conservative invocations of providence to legitimize an unjust status quo represent one of the classic political misuses of the doctrine of providence, a second archetypal misuse of the doctrine of providence aligns human political activity with the unfolding of the messianic age. According to this second vision, faith in providence enables Christians to decipher the manifestations of God's salvific action in history, in such a way that political history merges with salvation history as human political projects are caught up in the divine work of redeeming the cosmos. This misuse of the doctrine of providence dramatically and inappropriately raises the expectations associated with human political endeavors, inviting triumphalism and extremism.

In response to this error, theologians taking their cues from the writings of St. Augustine have formulated alternative accounts of divine providence that encourage a more modest use of the doctrine. Rather than folding providence into the salvific logic of eschatology, these theologians insist on the distance between the two. Providence, they argue, must be clearly demarcated from salvation history. God's providence is about the preservation of creation, not the salvation of creation, and, therefore, any political vision that builds upon the doctrine of providence must have similarly modest ambitions: "What befits human endeavor in the field of divine providence is pursuit of modicums of peace and justice such as can be humanly achieved—not less, but not more."[27] Appeals to divine providence cannot license messianic attempts to inaugurate the eschatological kingdom of God through human political activity, because providence is concerned with the preservation of creation history, not the unveiling of salvation history. When confronted by historical examples of Christians whose understanding of providence too quickly licensed their belief in the special divine authorization of a political movement or leader, one quickly appreciates the benefits of this formulation of the doctrine of providence for Christian political activity. However, a closer examination of the theological debates about slavery in the United States in the 1850s ironically reveals that those voicing the position closest to this modest conception of the political ramifications of the doctrine of providence were the defenders of slavery.

In *Providence and the Invention of the United States, 1607-1876*, Nicholas Guyatt offers a careful analysis of the various ways in which Christians in the United States construed the doctrine of providence and its relationship to national politics. While Guyatt insightfully explores the complexity and malleability of the doctrine of providence in a variety of episodes in the history of the United States, his exposition of the theological debates of the 1840s and 1850s about the meaning and place of slavery in relationship to divine providence are particularly relevant to the present discussion. Guyatt argues that while there were Christians who steadfastly warned against the imperialism that results from divinizing human political agendas through joining them to an interpretation of God's providential action in history, they were the defenders of slavery.

As the debates about slavery rose to a fever pitch in the years prior to the Civil War, the defenders of slavery increasingly embraced a moderate realism in regards to the doctrine of providence, while simultaneously accusing Northern abolitionists of messianic triumphalism in aligning emancipation with the redemptive movement of God in the world. A particularly clear example of the thinking that increasingly came to dominate the pro-slavery position on providence comes from the writings of Benjamin Palmer, who became famous as a champion of Southern secessionism.[28] Palmer's deepest engagement with the relationship of the doctrine of providence to human slavery appeared in his *Vindication of Secession* published in 1861. In the *Vindication*, Palmer fiercely criticized the pro-slavery, but anti-secession position of the Presbyterian minister Robert J. Breckinridge—whose belief in a providential destiny for the United States prevented him from endorsing an action that could lead to its dissolution.

Palmer condemned Breckinridge's resistance to secessionism precisely on the grounds that Breckinridge had imparted too much significance to the role that the United States played within God's providential activity in history. Palmer lumped Breckinridge together with the Northern "imperialists," who embraced a "providential presumptuousness" that "led the United States towards empire."[29] Southerners, Palmer argued, had the good sense to maintain a modest and restrained understanding of God's providence, in sharp contrast to the feverish messianism of the abolitionist cause. Palmer played the part of Augustine to the United States' Roman Empire, vociferously criticizing those who would take up the role of a latter-day Eusebius and lend the progressivism of Northern visions of emancipation divine sanction. Drunk on eschatological messianism, Northerners had forsaken the pursuit of "modicums of peace and justice" for the prospect of a progressive reforging of an entire world order in an attempt to inaugurate their interpretation of the eschatological destiny of the human race in the present through their own efforts.[30]

The foregoing analysis reveals that two of the standard theological critiques that Christian theology has historically leveled against unjust and immoral providential visions do not provide adequate theological solutions to the doctrine of providence's entanglement with racialized visions of humanity in modernity. Theologians have worried that the doctrine of providence lends itself to conservative appeals to maintaining an unjust status quo, and they have sought to articulate progressive accounts of providence in which God's activity is compatible with social change. Conversely, theologians have worried that appeals to providence have the effect of baptizing human political projects as part of God's eschatological work of salvation, and they have worked to elaborate modest and restrained accounts of the relationship between human and divine action.

However, neither of these theological correctives successfully resolves the problem at hand regarding providence and race in modernity. The problem is not that providence was conceived by the defenders of slavery so as to foreclose on the possibility of a critical politics of social change, but that the critical politics of social change to which interpretations of providence gave birth were calibrated around an idolatrous vision of white Christian humanity. Similarly, the problem is not simply that the doctrine of providence gave birth to a triumphalist, messianic politics of European global domination, but that even calls for a modest providentialism could be deployed in the service of unthinkable violence against fellow creatures. There is a deeper problem, which these standard theological critiques of distorted visions of providence do not sufficiently diagnose: the doctrine of providence provided an intellectual and religious framework for the construction of an idolatrous, racialized vision of global humanity, which could flexibly inhabit and subvert appeals to providence that were conservative or progressive, messianic or moderate. The challenge for contemporary theology, then, is to properly diagnose how providence has functioned so effortlessly and flexibly as a theological justification for racialized colonialism, genocide, and slavery, and to offer a constructive alternative that might liberate providence from its captivity to whiteness.

A PATH FORWARD: FROM RECOVERY TO LIBERATION

It should now be apparent that Langdon Gilkey and G. C. Berkouwer's articulation of the problem that the doctrine of providence represents for contemporary theology is only the tip of the iceberg. Above the surface, Gilkey and Berkouwer struggled to reconcile belief in God's providence with the suffering of European humanity in the first half of the twentieth century. But below the surface, obscured from Gilkey and Berkouwer's view of the modern world, providence provided an intellectual framework that seamlessly reconciled belief in the Christian God with a global, racialized system predicated upon the suffering, enslavement, and death of non-European humanity. Why, then, did prominent Christian theologians in Europe and the United States only declare that the doctrine of providence was in crisis when the suffering, violence, and dislocation that had marked the experiences of non-European peoples for hundreds of years finally manifested in Europe itself in the twentieth century?

In their lamentations over the collapse of the doctrine of providence, Gilkey and Berkouwer are theologically performing a role common among first-world intellectuals in the latter half of the twentieth century, which Chela Sandoval has theorized as "the disoriented first world citizen-subject." Stumbling out from the ruins of European civilization in the middle of the twentieth century, this subject "longs for the solidity of identity possible only—if at all—under previous eras," and—unable to recover that solidity—finds itself threatened with "an irrevocable and tragic fall into despair." To this formerly centered and secure modern subject of the first world, a sense of history that once reliably linked past to present to future seems to dissolve into a view of history as "sheer heterogeneity, random difference" that leaves the subject disoriented, unable to map his or her location in social and cultural time and space.[31]

Sandoval is of course not specifically thinking of Gilkey and Berkouwer in her account of the disoriented first world citizen-subject. Yet that only makes the accuracy of her description all the more striking, for she could hardly have written a more concise and accurate summary of the perspective expressed by Gilkey and Berkouwer. Berkouwer's lament for the collapse of "an old and trusted order"—"the order of providence"—that has left European humanity with a sense of "radical displacement and estrangement" exemplifies the perspective of Sandoval's disoriented first world subject, as does Gilkey's account of a widespread cultural sentiment that "no purpose, direction, or meaning of any sort could be seen in the general passage of historical events."[32] In their landmark accounts of the collapse of providence, Gilkey and Berkouwer are doing more than simply making an observation that theologians are not paying as much attention to a particular doctrine as they once did. They are offering, in Sandoval's terms, a "eulogy, a funeral dirge for a lost time and place where it was once possible to know exactly who you were and where you stood; a time when it was possible to map your position in social space and to consider from what Archimedean point you could court the possibility of action."[33] Gilkey and Berkouwer offer a theologically inflected version of this lamentation, identifying this lost time and space as one that was underwritten by the Christian doctrine of providence.

Yet, as Sandoval points out, the conditions that precipitated the centered, first world citizen-subject's fall into abject despair are not without precedent in the modern world. To the contrary, "subordinated, marginalized, or colonized Western citizen-subjects" have been forced to navigate almost these exact conditions "as a pre-condition of survival" for hundreds of years before the first world citizen-subject finally encountered them in the twentieth century.[34] The disorientation experienced by the first world citizen-subject is not due to his or her emergence into a new state of human existence, but rather his or her relatively late encounter with "the emotional states of peoples whose native territories were replaced, their bodies subordinated to other dominants, their futures unclear."[35] In short, the conditions which cause the first world subject to fall into total despair are none other than the conditions that the first world subject imposed on enslaved and colonized subjects, precisely as the means by which the first world subject created itself as such in the first place.

There is, therefore, an internal connection between the violence that erupted in Europe in the first half of the twentieth century and the violence that Europe inflicted upon the rest of the world in the centuries prior. It is a connection that Aimé Césaire explores in his *Discourse on Colonialism*, published in 1955, in between the appearance of Berkouwer and Gilkey's respective accounts of the crisis of the doctrine of providence. Césaire claims that the violence that European humanity inflicted upon itself in the twentieth century should be understood as a "boomerang effect" of the prior violence that European humanity inflicted upon the rest of the world through colonialism. "Colonization," Césaire writes, "works to *decivilize* the colonizer, to *brutalize* him in the true sense of the word, to degrade him, to awaken him to buried instincts, to covetousness, violence, race hatred, and moral relativism." It is a "poison" that "has been distilled into the veins of Europe and, slowly but surely, proceeds toward *savagery*."[36]

The savagery instilled by colonialism built up within European humanity until it finally erupted within Europe itself in the twentieth century in the guise of Nazism. This leads Césaire to conclude that, while it is true that Nazism "is barbarism, the supreme barbarism, the crowning barbarism that sums up all daily barbarisms," it is also true that before European peoples were the victims of Nazi barbarity, "they were its accomplices; that they tolerated that Nazism before it was inflicted on them, that they absolved it, shut their eyes to it, legitimized it, because, until then, it had been applied only to non-European peoples."[37] The critical point underlying Césaire's poetic analysis is that modernity is not strictly a European phenomenon, and, therefore, the questions and crises generated by modernity cannot be sufficiently analyzed without attention to this fact. As Enrique Dussel has argued, "Modernity is, in fact, a European phenomenon, but one constituted in a dialectical relation with a non-European alterity that is its ultimate content."[38] Modernity is two-sided. In addition to its more prominent European "topside," it has an "underside" or a "darker side," which is constituted by the global colonial relations between Europe and the non-European world.³⁹ The crises generated by modernity—including the crisis of the doctrine of providence in the twentieth century—cannot be understood without considering both sides of modernity or the full context of modernity/coloniality as a global whole. Long before modernity fell into crisis for first world subjects in the twentieth century, it was experienced as a crisis by Europe's colonial subjects.

Yet it is precisely this crucial insight that eludes Gilkey and Berkouwer. Their accounts of the crisis of providence remain firmly entrenched within the narrow perspective of the first world citizen-subject whose vision is confined within the limits of the topside of modernity. They lament the loss of the old and trusted providential order, in which it was possible for the Christian subject to locate itself in time and space in relationship to God, and they long for its recovery. Yet they fail to see that this modern providential order looked very different from the perspective of the enslaved and colonized peoples dwelling on the darker side of modernity. Indeed, Gilkey and Berkouwer's accounts of the collapse of providence are predicated on the forgetting of these peoples and their perspectives, which would otherwise disrupt the story that Gilkey and Berkouwer seek to tell. To take these people and their perspectives seriously requires reframing the problem that the doctrine of providence poses for contemporary theology. The problem is not only that providence *could not* render intelligible the suffering experienced by European humanity in the first half of the twentieth century but also that it *could* render intelligible the suffering inflicted upon the colonized and the enslaved by European humanity for hundreds of years. Furthermore, if Césaire's analysis is accurate, it will only be possible to understand the former issue if one first understands the latter.

The problem of providence in contemporary theology, therefore, is not simply its *collapse* in the face of European suffering, but rather its ideological *captivity* to a racialized vision of humanity within which it offered the Christian theological rationale for colonization and slavery. While Gilkey and Berkouwer adeptly diagnose *the collapse* of providence as a problem for Christian theology, they are unable to grasp *the captivity* of providence as a problem, precisely because their theological vision remains partially constrained by it. They write from the perspective of first world citizen-subjects, lamenting the loss of a world ordered by divine providence and failing to recognize that—for many of the inhabitants of the darker side of modernity—this providentially ordered world was precisely the problem.

The doctrine of providence has gone missing in contemporary theology. In response, there has been a running conversation within the field for more than fifty years about whether and how it might once again be found. Various attempts have been made to "recover" the doctrine, but they have had limited success—a clear indication of which is the fact that theologians are still using the language of recovery to frame their engagements with the doctrine half a century later. In this chapter, I have tried to show the limitations of continuing to frame contemporary engagements with providence in terms of a recovery or reconstruction of the doctrine following its collapse or crisis in the twentieth century. I have argued that there is a more basic problem with which Christian theologies of providence must wrestle today: the fact that—long before the doctrine of providence fell into crisis in mid-twentieth-century theology—it provided a key theological framework for modern Christianity's diseased social imagination.[40] In other words, though the doctrine of providence may have "died" in the middle of the twentieth century, it had been terminally ill for centuries prior. To understand the cause of death, it is necessary to understand the illness which preceded it. This book takes up that task, attempting to understand the theological role that the doctrine of providence played in constructing powerful narratives about European progress, the superiority of Western civilization, and white racial supremacy in the modern world.

In order to execute this task, the following chapters engage with three key figures in the history of modern Christian theology who engaged the doctrine of providence precisely on these grounds: G. W. F. Hegel, Karl Barth, and James Cone. Each of these theologians explicitly understood that doctrinal expositions of the nature and shape of divine providence served as interpretive lenses through which Christians located themselves in time and space in relationship to God and fellow humanity. Furthermore, all three figures saw the way in which these providential lenses were deeply interwoven with racialized visions of modern global humanity.

Perhaps most importantly, Hegel, Barth, and Cone did not simply address these issues as distant, theoretical problems. All of them were themselves historical subjects, seeking to locate themselves in time and space in relationship to the social and political events of their respective historical moments. Therefore, as they wrestled with these theoretical issues, they did so with one eye fixed firmly on the practical implications of their reflections. Hegel articulated his own account of providence in *The Lectures on the Philosophy of World History* in the context of Germany's growing colonial anxieties and ambitions in the opening decades of the nineteenth century. Barth, for his part, composed his doctrine of providence in *Church Dogmatics* III/3 in response to the end of the crisis of Nazism in Germany and the emerging new world order of Western capitalism following the Second World War. Finally, James Cone developed his own theological account of God's providential action in order to interpret the rise of Black Power and urban rebellions in Newark, Detroit, and beyond in the 1960s and 1970s. It is by situating their theologies of providence in these respective historical and social contexts that they are able to truly shed light on questions about providence, politics, and race for modern Christian existence.

Therefore, the following chapters place historical inquiry in the service of constructive theological reflection. By investigating and reflecting upon the history of diverse attempts to engage the doctrine of providence in the context of racialized modernity in chapters 2–4, I hope to discover the tools, concepts, and insights that will make possible my own constructive analysis of the doctrine in chapter 5. In this way, historical inquiry serves as an important resource for constructive theological reflection because it provides a repository of suggestive examples, potential models, and otherwise forgotten possibilities—all of which can contribute to the imaginative formulation of a contemporary treatment of the topic.[41]

In addition to the role that history plays in uncovering resources for contemporary theological reflection, there is another reason why a turn to history is particularly appropriate for a study on the doctrine of providence. From the start, the doctrine of providence contains an innate connection to history. The doctrine of providence is concerned with what happens to creation and creatures *in time*. Therefore, the basic subject matter of the doctrine of providence naturally suggests the necessity of some attention to the category of history and the importance of connecting reflection on providence to the people, places, and things which shaped that reflection in the first place.

At their best, Christian theologies of providence have recognized this fact. Augustine's reflections on providence in *The City of God* emerged as a response to the sack of Rome by Alaric the Visigoth in 410.[42] Dante analyzed divine providence in *De Monarchia* in light of the advent of Henry VII's armies to Italy in 1312.[43] John Calvin's doctrine of providence attempted to make sense of sixteenth-century historical existence: natural disasters, varying yields from agricultural production, and material poverty in Geneva all lie just beneath the surface of his doctrine in *The Institutes* I.16.[44] Nor has this simply been a premodern phenomenon. One need look no further than the seismic unsettling of the doctrine of providence that followed from the Lisbon earthquake of 1755, the intellectual aftershocks of which—most famously visible in Voltaire's critique of the doctrine in *Candide*—have reverberated through more than two centuries of European thought.[45] As these examples demonstrate, history provides an anchor that ties individual instances of theological reflection on the doctrine of providence to the particular people, places, and things that shaped them and made them intelligible in the first place.

Without this historical anchoring, it can seem like the doctrine of providence is most fundamentally a collection of timeless theological ideals which different theologians have variously assembled and configured. Yet the difference between Augustine, Calvin, and Barth's accounts of the doctrine of providence cannot simply be reduced to differing configurations of eternally unchanging truths. The most obvious difference—and one that ought to matter for theological reflection—is that Barth wrote his doctrine of providence in the late 1940s in Basel, while Augustine wrote *The City of God* in North Africa at the beginning of the fifth century and Calvin wrote Book 16 and 17 of *The Institutes* in Geneva in the sixteenth century. By paying attention to this, one can put one's doctrine on the ground, reading it against the background of particular historical persons and places, while locating it in the midst of the messy machinations of real human lives. As Langdon Gilkey says, "It cannot be questioned that as an authentic human is *historical*, deeply related intentionally and unintentionally to social changes in which he or she is immersed, so an authentic religion and a valid theology must be historical."[46] As a doctrine addressing the history of creation, providence provides the site at which theological reflection ought to most obviously connect to the actual lived histories of the human beings who do the reflecting.

In recent times, when theologians have turned to history as a resource for theological thinking, they have more often than not turned to a particular mode of historical investigation. This type of historical work has largely taken the form of grand meta-narratives and has come to be associated with names like Alasdair MacIntyre, Charles Taylor, John Milbank, and Brad Gregory.[47] The canonical works of this genre of historical inquiry roughly share a certain profile. First, they cover massive historical periods and geographical areas, stitching them together into linear accounts of historical development. Second, they seek to discover causal explanations of how contemporary human life and thought came to be the way it is today as a result of past developments. Furthermore, while not locating this historical causality solely within the history of ideas, they tend to subordinate social or cultural developments to intellectual ones in their descriptions of these causal relationships.[48] The present study deploys a very different mode of historical investigation than the one embodied in the meta-narrative genre.

Where meta-narratives attempt to integrate diverse geographical locations and expansive historical periods into a single historical plotline, the present study attempts to judiciously paint three distinct historical portraits. Furthermore, where meta-narratives seek causal historical explanations in which a straight line can be drawn from the past to the present, the present study contents itself with outlining a series of historical possibilities, which do not necessarily share a common trajectory to the present. In other words, I seek to paint a series of portraits, drawing out the connections between particular constructions of the doctrine of providence and attempts to discern God's relationship to particular historical episodes.

In summary, whereas historical meta-narratives too often present themselves as universal causal narratives which leverage explanations of why things went the way they did in order to explain the way things are today, the historical thrust of the present study pushes toward a mode of thick description, making a series of sketches of past figures who have engaged Christian theology to negotiate the complicated relationship of providence, politics, and race. This work of thick description seeks to discover continuities, discontinuities, surprises, and ironies that might be sources of wisdom aiding contemporary efforts to engage the same issues. The reasons for preferring this latter mode of historical inquiry as an ally for theological reflection are of two types: empirical and theological.

The empirical reasons relate to the accuracy of the meta-narratival mode of history. A chief problem with the meta-narrative genre is that the very features that give it its appeal also threaten to undermine it in a number of ways. The author of such a narrative is constantly tempted to oversimplify complex historical phenomena, falsely equate concepts and ideas that may bear the same name but actually emerge from very different historical conditions and intellectual traditions, and draw simplistic conclusions about the overall trajectory of this history (usually in terms of either decline or progress).[49] Thus, while these narratives wield great explanatory power in their memorability and simplicity, they usually do so at the cost of attention to nuance and detail—to the warp and woof of the individual threads of which they are composed. Once someone tugs on one of these loose ends, the story that held such great power over the imagination of the reader all too often unravels.

A particularly egregious example of this is Mark Lilla's *The Stillborn God*, which articulates a simple and persuasive story about the birth of modern political theory out of the violent death throes of medieval Christendom's religious fanaticism. Lilla's basic claim is that modern political philosophy emerged as an attempt to articulate a modest, peaceful politics that offered humanity a way to free itself from the hold of medieval political theology. The problem with all political theology, according to Lilla, is that it dangerously amplifies the conflict that is already an inherent property of politics through appeals to divine revelation.[50] Lilla holds up Thomas Hobbes as the great revolutionary who led modern humanity's escape from this deplorable tradition of theologico-political thought.

As Lilla tells it, in the aftermath of the destruction wrought by political theology "something happened—or rather, many things happened, and their combined force would eventually bring the reign of political theology to an end in Europe. Not just Christian political theology, but the basic assumptions upon which all political theology had rested. . . . A Great Separation took place, severing Western political philosophy decisively from cosmology and theology."[51] The first—and most important—thing that happened in the construction of the Great Separation, according to Lilla, was the publication in 1651 of Hobbes's *Leviathan*, which contained "the most devastating attack on Christian political theology ever undertaken and was the means by which later modern thinkers were able to escape from it."[52] Indeed, Lilla boldly asserts that "the aim of Leviathan is to attack and destroy the entire tradition of Christian political theology."[53]

While this is certainly a powerful explanatory story, it rings hollow when held up to a critical light. Indeed, Hobbes's Great Separation was neither great—in the sense of an unprecedented revolutionary creation *ex nihilo*—nor a separation. While Hobbes certainly made some unique, perhaps even revolutionary, contributions to Western political thought, advocating for a separation between ecclesiastical and secular authorities was not one of them. One can think of a number of examples that demonstrate that the idea of separating ecclesiastical and secular authorities did not originate in 1651, from Dante's *De Monarchia* (c. 1312), to Marsilius of Padua's *Defensor Pacis* (1324), to Luther's *On Secular Authority* (1523).[54] Furthermore, if anything, Hobbes did not advocate the separation of theology and politics, but rather their joining—prompting Rousseau's comment that Hobbes brought about a reunion of "the two heads of the eagle."[55] Most problematically, Lilla's work totally fails to address the fact that fully half of *Leviathan* is taken up with biblical exegesis and theological reflection—nor, for that matter, does his reading of Hobbes make any sense of the full title of the work: *Leviathan, or the Matter, Forme, and Power of a Commonwealth, Ecclesiastical and Civil*. Therefore, while *The Stillborn God* tells a very persuasive tale that serves as a kind of creation myth for a particular vision of liberal politics, it proves totally unconvincing when one examines its component parts in any great detail.

In addition to this practical concern about the accuracy of the meta-narratival approach to history, there are also good theological reasons for eschewing this form of intellectual inquiry, which are integrally connected to a Christian doctrine of providence. The meta-narrative genre too easily produces works that succumb to the temptation to produce an all-encompassing history of an idea, a field, or a civilization articulated from a quasi-divine perspective, which claims to uncover a "key" or "guiding thread" to history. Given that the doctrine of providence has functioned at least since Augustine to check human pretensions to be able to read history from a quasi-divine perspective, the meta-narrative approach to a historical exploration of the doctrine of providence would be a performative contradiction. Instead, the doctrine of providence calls for a chastened mode of historical inquiry that takes seriously the particularities, complexities, and contradictions of a history interpreted by finite human creatures. In this study, I attempt to deploy the tools of intellectual history in precisely this mode.

For all these reasons, thick historical description serves as an ideal means to generate a set of diverse theological perspectives on the relationship between the doctrine of providence and race in modernity that can inform a constructive account of the doctrine of providence today. Locating important historical treatments of the doctrine of providence in their sociopolitical contexts brings the inherent connection between providence and the modern racial imagination into focus, illuminating the practical nexus where interpretations of divine providential action meet judgments about appropriate human political action in the context of racialized modernity.

CONCLUSION

The next three chapters examine how three prominent figures in the history of modern Protestant theology theologically negotiated the relationship between providence, politics, and race in the modern world. In doing so, they offer resources for resisting the distortion of Christian belief and practice that occurs when the doctrine of providence becomes entangled within the logics of whiteness. If there is a path forward for the doctrine of providence in contemporary theology, it is one which must seek to do more than simply gather up the pieces of a doctrine which fell apart in the middle of the twentieth century in order to somehow stitch them back together again. The path forward for the doctrine of providence lies in liberating the doctrine from its deep entanglement within European Christianity's racialized visions of humanity and its idolatrous projects of global discovery, conquest, and rule. In the next chapter, I examine a paradigmatic example of this entanglement, analyzing the doctrine of providence's foundational role in the racial and colonial vision of one of the modern era's most philosophically and theologically influential intellectuals, Georg Wilhelm Friedrich Hegel.

NOTES

1. Gilkey, "The Concept of Providence," 171–192. Of all of the classical theological doctrines, Gilkey suggested, providence "is the single one which has not been reinterpreted and revitalized by contemporary theology."
2. Ibid., 171.
3. Ibid., 174, 171.
4. Charles M. Wood, "Providence," in *The Oxford Handbook of Systematic Theology*, ed. Kathryn Tanner, John Webster, and Iain Torrance (Oxford: Oxford University Press, 2007), 93.
5. Fergusson, *The Providence of God*, 11, 243.
6. For other representative expressions of the consensus view in addition to Wood and Fergusson, see Julian N. Hart, "Creation and Providence," in *Christian Theology: An Introduction to Its Traditions and Tasks*, ed. Peter C. Hodgson and Robert H. King (Minneapolis, MN: Fortress Press, 1994), 141; Peter C. Hodgson,

"Providence," in *A New Handbook of Christian Theology*, ed. Donald W. Musser and Joseph L. Price (Nashville, TN: Abingdon Press, 1992), 394–6; Sung-Sup Kim, *Deus providebit: Calvin, Schleiermacher, and Barth on the Providence of God* (Minneapolis, MN: Fortress Press, 2014), 210–224; Wolf Krötke, review of *Was heisst 'Handeln Gottes'?*, by Reinhold Bernhardt, *Theologische Literaturzeitung* 125: 1190–1993; E. Frank Tupper, "The Providence of God in Christological Perspective," *Review & Expositor* 82 (1985): 579–595.

7. Mary McClintock Fulkerson, *Places of Redemption: Theology for a Worldly Church* (Oxford: Oxford University Press, 2007), 13–14.

8. Eduardo Echeverria, *Berkouwer and Catholicism: Disputed Questions* (Leiden: Brill, 2013), 1.

9. Berkouwer, *The Providence of God*, 7.

10. Ibid., 8, 11, 12. Emphasis in the original.

11. Ibid., 12, 12, 12.

12. Ibid., 12. Emphasis in original.

13. Ibid., 17, 10, 11.

14. Gilkey, "The Concept of Providence," 173.

15. Ibid., 175.

16. Ibid., 173.

17. Berkouwer, *The Providence of God*, 17.

18. Ibid., 17.

19. John C. Calhoun, "Further Remarks in Debate on His Fifth Resolution," in *The Papers of John C. Calhoun*, ed. Clyde N. Wilson (Columbia, SC: University of South Carolina Press, 1981), XIV: 84.

20. James Henry Hammond, *Remarks of Mr. Hammond of South Carolina on the Question of Receiving Petitions for the Abolition of Slavery in the District of Columbia* (Washington: Duff Green, 1836), 11, 11.

21. Jennings, *The Christian Imagination*, 93, 90.

22. Philip Ziegler, "The Uses of Providence in Public Theology," in *The Providence of God: Deus Habet Consilium*, ed. Murphy and Ziegler (London, T&T Clark, 2009), 308.

23. Ibid., 308.

24. David Brion Davis, *Antebellum American Culture: An Interpretive Anthology* (Lexington, MA: D. C. Heath and Co., 1979), 463.

25. William Henry Holcombe, "The Alternative," in *Antebellum American Culture*, ed. Davis (Lexington, MA: D. C. Heath and Co., 1979), 465–466. Emphasis added. Holcombe was not alone in holding this view. As David Brion Davis argues throughout *Slavery and Human Progress* (Oxford: Oxford University Press, 1984), despite the eventual consolidation of discourses of progress by the antislavery movement, progressive visions can be found at the heart of movements of imperial expansion and mass enslavement throughout history.

26. Ziegler, "The Uses of Providence," 308.

27. Ibid., 320. Emphasis in original.

28. Nicholas Guyatt, *Providence and the Invention of the United States, 1607-1876* (Cambridge: Cambridge University Press, 2007), 249–250.

29. Ibid., 251–252.
30. Ziegler, "The Uses of Providence," 320.
31. Chela Sandoval, *Methodology of the Oppressed* (Minneapolis: University of Minnesota Press, 2000), 9, 9, 17.
32. Berkouwer, *The Providence of God*, 12; Gilkey, "The Concept of Providence," 173.
33. Sandoval, *Methodology of the Oppressed*, 23.
34. Ibid., 9.
35. Ibid., 34.
36. Aimé Césaire, *Discourse on Colonialism*, trans. Joan Pinkham (New York: Monthly Review Press, 2000), 35, 36. Emphasis in original.
37. Ibid., 36.
38. Enrique Dussel, "Eurocentrism and Modernity (Introduction to the Frankfurt Lectures)," *boundary 2* 20, no.3 (1993): 65.
39. Enrique Dussel, *The Underside of Modernity: Apel, Ricouer, Rorty, Taylor, and the Philosophy of Liberation*, trans. Mendieta (Atlantic Highlands: Humanities Press, 1996); Walter D. Mignolo, *The Darker Side of Western Modernity: Global Futures, Decolonial Options* (Durham, NC: Duke University Press, 2011).
40. Jennings, *The Christian Imagination*, 6.
41. As Ted Smith and David Daniels suggest, turning to history enables the work of "unforgetting" otherwise suppressed alternatives in order to think critically and constructively about the present. The retrieval of historical resources fuels the task of contemporary revision and reconstruction. See David D. Daniels III and Ted A. Smith, "History, Practice, and Theological Education," in *For Life Abundant: Practical Theology, Theological Education, and Christian Ministry*, ed. Dorothy C. Bass and Craig Dykstra (Grand Rapids, MI: William B. Eerdmans Publishing Co., 2008), 236.
42. Augustine, *The Retractions*, trans. Sister M. Inez Bogan (Baltimore, MD: The Catholic University of America Press, 1968), 209: "Meanwhile, Rome was destroyed as a result of an invasion of the Goths under the leadership of King Alaric, and of the violence of this great disaster. The worshipers of many false gods, whom we call by the customary name pagans, attempting to attribute its destruction to the Christian religion, began to blaspheme the true God more sharply and bitterly than usual. And so, 'burning with zeal for the house of God,' I decided to write the books, *On the City of God*, in opposition to their blasphemies and errors. This work kept me busy for some years because many other things, which should not be deferred, interfered and their solution had first claim on me. But finally, this extensive work, *On the City of God*, was completed in twenty-two books."
43. See Shaw's discussion in the introduction to Dante, *Monarchy*, ed. Prue Shaw (Cambridge: Cambridge University Press, 1996), x, xxiv, xxxiii.
44. John Calvin, *Institutes of the Christian Religion*, 197–210. During his explication of the doctrine of providence, Calvin addresses the relationship between God's providence and the varying amounts of breast milk produced by nursing mothers (200), individuals killed by shipwreck and falling trees (199), crops destroyed by drought and hail (203), and the existence of economic disparity in human societies (205).

45. For extensive expositions of the significance of the Lisbon earthquake for modern European thought and culture, see Susan Neiman, *Evil in Modern Thought: An Alternative History* (Princeton: Princeton University Press, 2002) and the essays compiled in Theodore E. D. Braun and John B Radner (ed.'s), *The Lisbon Earthquake of 1755: Representations and Reactions*, volume 2005:02 of *Studies on Voltaire and the Eighteenth Century* (Oxford: Voltaire Foundation, 2005).

46. Gilkey, *Reaping the Whirlwind*, 34. Emphasis in original.

47. See Alasdair MacIntyre, *Whose Justice? Which Rationality?* (Notre Dame, IN: University of Notre Dame Press, 1989); Charles Taylor, *Sources of the Self: The Making of the Modern Identity* (Cambridge, MA: Harvard University Press, 1989); Charles Taylor, *A Secular Age* (Cambridge, MA: Harvard University Press, 2007); John Milbank, *Theology and Social Theory: Beyond Secular Reason* (Oxford: Blackwell Publishing, 1990); Brad Gregory, *The Unintended Reformation* (Cambridge: The Belknap Press, 2012).

48. The causal priority given to ideas is perhaps most visible in MacIntyre's *Whose Justice, Which Rationality?* which traces the development of conceptions of justice and practical rationality through a series of talking heads (Plato, Aristotle, Augustine, Aquinas, Hutcheson, and Hume) in order to offer an explanation of and solution to what he sees as the crisis of liberal individualism. Charles Taylor's work offers a far more complex example. In *Sources of the Self*, he strongly asserts that a full historical explanation of any concrete development in history must attend to both ideas and practices as driving forces of historical development: "Change can come about in both directions, as it were: through mutations and developments in ideas ... and also through drift, change, constrictions, or flourishings of practices, bringing about the alteration, flourishing, or decline of ideas" (205). Taylor justifies his preoccupation with the development of ideas with the clarification that he does not take his work to be offering historical explanations at all. Rather he sees himself as attempting to answer an interpretive question about the power and attraction of certain ideas regardless of how they came to be. However, he admits that he is walking a fine line: "This discussion ... has to serve as a warning to me not to lose from sight the context of practices in which this identity developed, and the powerful forces shaping them. Pressures so massive on the history of civilization as those I have been describing have to be kept in mind even when they are not—rightly not—the focus of attention" (207). The fact that Taylor has produced such a massive output of work dedicated to understanding modern identity without any substantial reflection about the importance of colonial and imperial practices for the creation of that identity suggests that perhaps he has not taken his own warning seriously enough.

49. On the contemporary prevalence of narratives of progress and decline in recent theological histories, see Ted A. Smith, *The New Measures: A Theological History of Democratic Practice* (Cambridge: Cambridge University Press, 2007), 11. Smith is critical of such narratives for their failure both to "account for complexities and discontinuities" within historical phenomena and to "recognize the indirect, ironic relationships between human projects and the saving work of God."

50. Mark Lilla, *The Stillborn God: Religion, Politics, and the Modern West* (New York: Vintage Books, 2008), 52: "All politics involves conflict, but what set Christian

politics apart was the theological self-consciousness and intensity of the conflicts it generated—conflicts rooted in the deepest ambiguities of Christian revelation."

51. Ibid., 58.
52. Ibid., 75.
53. Ibid., 75.
54. See Dante, *Monarchy*, 63–94; Marsilius of Padua, *The Defender of Peace*, ed. and trans. Annabel Brett (Cambridge: Cambridge University Press, 2005); Martin Luther, "On Secular Authority," in *Luther and Calvin on Secular Authority*, ed. Harro Höpfl (Cambridge: Cambridge University Press, 1991).
55. Jean-Jacques Rousseau, "The Social Contract," in *The Social Contract and Other Later Political Writings*, ed. Victor Gourevitch (Cambridge: Cambridge University Press, 1997), 146.

Chapter 2

G. W. F. Hegel
Providence in Time, Space, and Race

Standing before the irate Ashanti ruler, Thomas Edward Bowdich watched silently as his party's mission teetered on the brink of disaster.[1] Commissioned in April 1817 by Governor John Hope Smith at the behest of the Company of Merchants Trading to Africa, Bowdich and his companions had spent nearly a month traveling from British colonial headquarters to the Ashanti capital of Kumasi with instructions to establish diplomatic relations and open a path for commerce and exploration into the African interior. It was with this purpose that the embassy to the Ashanti had set out from Cape Coast Castle under the leadership of Frederick James on April 22. Bowdich was assigned the supporting role of scientific observer, charged with keeping track of latitude and longitude and recording notes about the land and people along the route. Twenty-eight days later, after unwanted encounters with severe weather and a panther, the party arrived at Kumasi on Monday, May 19. They were received in a ceremony which Bowdich found "indescribably imposing," lasting for more than six hours and including a processional of Ashanti warriors that Bowdich estimated at 30,000.[2]

Treaty negotiations began the next day and proceeded favorably until Thursday, May 22, when the success of the mission was suddenly thrown into serious jeopardy. The Ashanti king summoned the visitors to his house, where he showed them written records of financial commitments made by the colonial governor that suggested the British had not made their approach to the Ashanti in good faith. Faced with these allegations and an angry Ashanti ruler, Frederick James, who had been leading the negotiations for the British, faltered. Rather than attempting to conciliate the king, Mr. James became desperate to extricate himself from the deteriorating situation. He absolved himself of personal responsibility—laying the blame directly at the feet of the governor—and announced his intention to return to Cape Coast Castle imminently. The king interpreted this response as an admission of guilt and threatened to retaliate by invading the coastal region. Bowdich looked on as Mr. James's mismanagement of the situation imperiled not only the immediate objectives of the mission but also the security of the British colonial settlements. As a defeated Mr. James fell silent before the king, Thomas Edward Bowdich spoke.

Breaking ranks with his superior, Bowdich asked to be heard by the king directly. The room fell silent as Bowdich addressed the king, reassuring him that the intentions with which they had undertaken their mission to Kumasi were entirely friendly. The Governor, Bowdich explained, had sent them to reach a comprehensive agreement with the king and to resolve any conflicts or misunderstandings. Mr. James was ill and thus understandably wished to return to the coast. However, Bowdich pledged to remain in Kumasi until correspondence with the governor could resolve the conflict, offering his own life as collateral until a satisfactory resolution was reached. To Bowdich's great relief, the king received the speech favorably, extending his hand to Bowdich as applause rang out around them. When word of Bowdich's desperate intervention reached Cape Coast Castle, the governor relieved Mr. James of command and put Bowdich in charge of the mission. Following several months of further negotiation, Bowdich achieved his objective on September 9, 1817, when the Ashanti ruler signed a general treaty with the British Government.

After completing his mission, Bowdich published his official account of the experience, which included an extensive compilation of notes and observations about the region's land and people. *Mission from Cape Coast Castle to Ashantee, with a statistical account of that kingdom, and geographical notices of others parts of the interior of Africa* appeared in 1819, joining the deluge of travel literature flooding Europe at the end of the eighteenth and beginning of the nineteenth century. Demand for travelogues such as Bowdich's was particularly high in Germany, whose population had become the foremost consumers of the genre in Europe.[3] Among the German armchair explorers who read Bowdich's *Mission from Cape Coast Castle* was a certain influential professor of philosophy at the University of Berlin: Georg Wilhelm Friedrich Hegel.[4]

While travel literature like Bowdich's narrative generated popular interest across German society, Hegel engaged the genre with a particular academic interest in mind: his developing work on the philosophy of world history. This work reached its most mature form in his lecture cycles on the subject, which he delivered in Berlin five times over the last decade of his life between 1822 and 1831. One of the challenges facing Hegel in his attempt to develop a philosophical interpretation of the history of the entire world was, of course, the fact that he never ventured outside of Europe a single time during his whole life.⁵ In travel literature, therefore, Hegel found a source of valuable information about the world that might otherwise have remained inaccessible to him. Travelogues like *Mission from Cape Coast Castle* provided Hegel with much needed "raw material" that he could draw upon when constructing his philosophical account of world history.⁶

In approaching travel literature with this systematizing intent, Hegel planted himself firmly within a quintessentially German tradition of the European colonial enterprise. Lacking colonies of their own until the late nineteenth century, Germans made up for this absence by imagining themselves as the "intellectual arbiters" of Europe's colonial endeavors.⁷ As Susanne Zantop has argued, German intellectuals allocated a "special role" for themselves in European colonialism, precisely "derived from their position as outsider looking in."⁸ Making a virtue out of necessity, Germans engaged in what Zantop calls "intellectual colonialism": they "compiled, edited, evaluated, and processed any information available on colonial activities," engaging in the "exploration and appropriation of hitherto undiscovered worlds into Eurocentric categories."⁹ In the *Lectures on the Philosophy of World History*, Hegel contributed to this uniquely German colonial enterprise on the grandest of scales.

Through the *Lectures on the Philosophy of World History*, Hegel attempts to work out a comprehensive theory, not only of the world and its peoples in the early nineteenth century, but of the relationship between divinity, history, and humanity as such and in total. As Hegel boldly declared to his students in the opening lines of his very first introduction to the lecture cycles in 1822, "The subject of these lectures is the *philosophical history of the world*. Our concern is to work our way through universal world history as such."¹⁰ In the lectures, Hegel sets out to analyze the shape, direction, and purpose of the history of the world in its entirety. Importantly, Hegel does so from the perspective of divine providence: attempting to map the relationship between God and the world that constitutes the world-historical process. Hegel develops an account of world history as the movement of divine spirit toward self-consciousness in the world through the providential progression of historical epochs, the rise and fall of states, the heroic exploits of world-historical individuals and the atoning deaths of those who lose their lives upon the slaughter bench of history. As one commentator suggests, Hegel views history as "the autobiography of God."¹¹

Hegel explicitly acknowledges the central conceptual role played by the doctrine of providence in his lectures, expounding at length the foundational connection between the Christian doctrine of providence and the philosophical first principle guiding his lectures: "The conception that reason governs the world."¹² Yet, Hegel does not simply repristinate traditional Christian thinking about providence to serve as the framework of his philosophical approach to world history. Rather, he attempts a revolutionary transformation of the doctrine of providence in light of what he sees as the unprecedented epistemological powers made available to humanity within the advanced conditions of European modernity. Theologically speaking, then, the *Lectures on the Philosophy of World History* represent Hegel's attempt to construct a comprehensive reading of world history in light of his particular construal of the doctrine of providence.

In the hands of Hegel, the doctrine of providence becomes a powerful conceptual lens that—he believes—enables him to read the movement of the divine in history with unprecedented clarity. Indeed, his chief criticism of the doctrine of God's providence as it has traditionally been articulated within Christianity is its insistence on epistemological humility. He firmly rejects the idea that God's providential activity in history is mysterious and hidden from human eyes, decisively parting ways with figures like Augustine of Hippo and John Calvin, who identify the hiddenness of divine providence as a key aspect of the doctrine.[13] Hegel articulates his understanding of providence in direct opposition to this stream of Christian reflection on the doctrine. However, Hegel does not consequently reject the Christian theological tradition as a whole in order to formulate his theory about the relationship of the divine to world history. To the contrary, he casts his alternative conception of divine providence as an internal critique of the doctrine *from within* the Christian tradition itself, suggesting that the emphasis on humility and mystery in prior Christian accounts of providence fails to account properly for the truth that God has revealed Godself in history.

As Hegel construes it, the activity of divine self-revelation is a teleological process, occurring progressively in and through history. Hegel argues that with the advent of a fully mature European modernity, the time has come when the trajectory of revelation has reached its zenith, allowing Hegel himself to map the movement of the divine in history.[14] Importantly, Hegel draws the chief warrant for his critique of traditional Christian understandings of divine providence from his understanding of the central truth of Christianity itself: the incarnation.

For Hegel, the fundamental truth of the incarnation—that God reveals Godself to humanity—establishes both the possibility and the necessity of a more confident and robust approach to interpreting divine providence, requiring modern Europeans like Hegel to set aside traditional admonitions about the hidden and mysterious nature of providence and embrace their ability to read perspicaciously the movement of God in history. Hegel frames the guiding philosophical first principle of the lectures—that world history is governed by reason—not as a rejection or subversion of the content of the Christian doctrine of providence, but rather as an understanding of the content of the doctrine that more faithfully reflects the central truths of Christianity.

Armed with this modified doctrine of providence, Hegel endeavors in his lectures to map the movement of the divine in world history. He maps this movement along three related axes: the temporal, the spatial, and the anthropological. While this providential process unfolds temporally or historically—from past to present—it also occurs spatially or geographically: from east to west.[15] Furthermore, on Hegel's account it is not simply certain geographical *spaces* that stand in closer relationship to the divine than others, but, more precisely, the *peoples* that inhabit those spaces.[16] Hegel interprets the movement of divine providence in relationship to history, geography, and anthropology in order to produce a providential account of the incarnation of the divine in the world.

Hegel deploys the doctrine of providence in the *Lectures on the Philosophy of World History* as a conceptual apparatus through which he theorizes world history as a teleological process of divine incarnation, articulated in terms of historical, geographical, and anthropological progress. These temporal, spatial, and anthropological lines of analysis converge in Hegel's thought around one figure, who emerges from the lectures as the divine subject of world history: European man.[17] Indeed, in his lectures Hegel sacralizes European Christian civilization, envisioning it as the *telos* of world history, the intrahistorical eschaton in which the divine life of spirit reaches final consummation. The inhabitants of this civilization become, for Hegel, the final bearers of divine presence in history—those in whose humanity the divine is most fully incarnate.

In what follows, I will first explore the theological grammar that undergirds Hegel's lectures in order to make clear the foundational role that the doctrine of providence plays in Hegel's approach to world history. After establishing the nature of the relationship between the doctrine of providence and the conceptual apparatus of Hegel's lectures, I will examine the specific interpretation of history and global humanity that emerges from Hegel's attempt to relate divine providence to the particulars of history, geography, and anthropology. I will display how Hegel uses the doctrine of providence to imagine the location of various peoples within the divine economy of incarnation—from Africans and the indigenous inhabitants of the Americas, who are entirely cut off from participation in the divine, to Western Europeans, in whom spirit finds its final resting place.

THE CONCEPT OF PROVIDENCE IN THE *LECTURES ON THE PHILOSOPHY OF WORLD HISTORY*

Hegel understands the core philosophical grammar that undergirds the *Lectures on the Philosophy of World History* as an amplification, expansion, and perfecting culmination of the Christian theological doctrine of providence. In his lectures, he utilizes the doctrine of providence as the basic conceptual lens through which to envision a rational theory of history as the progressive incarnation of the divine. While it is tempting here to use the language of "secularization" to describe Hegel's transformation of Christian doctrine, if anything, Hegel's approach is the opposite.[18] As I will make clear, Hegel wants to intensify and expand upon the concept of providence found in Christian theological discourse. He does not resolve the tension between the religious and the secular, the divine and the human, or the transcendent and the immanent by removing one and preserving the other, but by seeking their final reconciliation. As Robert Bernasconi suggests, "On Hegel's account of history, the secular and the spiritual are reconciled . . . without either being diminished."[19] Like Jesus in Matthew 5:17, Hegel asserts that his philosophical account of world history has not come to abolish the Christian doctrine of providence, but to fulfill it.

In mapping the contours of Hegel's reception and transformation of the doctrine of providence in the lectures, I follow the formal outline of the philosophy of world history utilized by Hegel in the introduction to the 1830/1 lecture cycle, first examining the general relationship between the doctrine of providence and Hegel's concept of world history before turning to the specific contours of Hegel's appropriation of the doctrine in his account of the actualization of spirit in history.[20]

Providence and the General Concept of World History

Hegel opens the lectures of 1830/1831 by addressing a potentially devastating critique of his impending endeavor to approach history philosophically.[21] This opening defense of the basic principles behind his approach bears decisive witness to the central place occupied by the doctrine of providence in Hegel's own understanding of his enterprise. In these first paragraphs of his introduction to the lectures, Hegel suggests that the time has come for the philosophy of world history to take up the mantle of the Christian doctrine of providence and make good on that doctrine's long unrealized promise to articulate fully the relationship between God and the world. He does this through an extensive comparison of his philosophical view of history, which is predicated upon the conviction that the world is governed by reason, with the traditional Christian theological view of history, which is predicated upon the conviction that the world is governed by divine providence. Hegel believes that the former conviction, while not opposed to the latter, definitively surpasses it by giving determinant content to the otherwise abstract theological conviction of providential rule. As Hegel understands it, while his philosophy of world history is *more than* a theological doctrine of providence, it is certainly not less than one.

Hegel singles out one critique of his philosophical approach to world history in particular as requiring immediate refutation at the outset of his lectures on the topic. This is the critique of the historical positivists—which has since come to be associated, perhaps too closely, with Leopold von Ranke—that a philosophical approach to history necessarily brings with it preconceptions and assumptions which distort its reading of the historical data.[22] Hegel emphatically denies the relevance of this critique for his approach, not because he believes that it is acceptable for philosophical preconceptions to play fast and loose with history, but because he does not believe that his approach is founded upon such preconceptions.

Hegel argues that his philosophical approach to history brings with it only one presupposition: "The sole conception that [philosophy] brings with it is the simple conception of *reason*."[23] As Hegel sees it, all historians—even the most rigorous positivists—approach their task with categories not derived from the historical data. Where the positivists delude themselves with feigned objectivity, Hegel sees himself as owning up to his one fundamental preconception and defending it as the right one to have. In the course of his exposition of this most crucial of methodological first principles for the philosophical approach to world history, Hegel narrates this fundamental conviction that reason governs world history as a development of the content of the Christian doctrine of providence.

Hegel locates his own position on these matters by rehearsing a brief genealogy of the conviction that reason governs the world. The conviction has appeared in three paradigmatic forms, each of which has been an improvement on the previous iteration: the Greek conception, the Christian conception, and Hegel's own conception.[24] However, the dialectical progression is not linear. For, according to Hegel, while the relationship between his own conception and the Greek conception of reason's cosmic rule is marked by a difference in *kind*, his conception of reason and the Christian conception of providence differ only in *degree*.

Anaxagoras was the first person to suggest that reason rules the world. However, there were two problems with his account. First, he restricted reason's dominion to the realm of nature. Second, even with respect to nature, Anaxagoras' formulation of nature's rule remained abstract; he failed to apply it to concrete nature. This is the criticism of Anaxagoras' principle voiced by Socrates in the *Phaedo*.[25] The Christian conception of the conviction that reason governs the world avoids the first problem of Anaxagoras' account, while succumbing to the second. While Anaxagoras' account remains severely inadequate to the extent that it confines the rule of reason solely to the natural, Hegel suggests that the Christian doctrine of providence presents a decisive revolution and improvement on the Greek conception of rational governance, extending reason's rule from the realm of nature into the realm of spirit.[26] In this respect, Hegel is willing to embrace the Christian doctrine of providence as fundamentally compatible with his own conviction of reason's cosmic rule: the belief in providence is consistent with the first principle that reason directs history to an "absolute, rational, final purpose of the world."[27] However, Hegel does not simply embrace the Christian formulation of providential governance without modification. The second weakness of Anaxagoras' formulation of the conviction that reason governs the world—its abstractness—also plagues the Christian conviction. Hegel styles himself as the Socrates to Christianity's Anaxagoras, bringing concreteness to the conviction of divine providential rule and in so doing finally rendering this conviction perfect.

The inadequacy of the Christian doctrine of providence lies in the traditional Christian assertion that the particulars of God's providential rule remain hidden from humanity in mystery. Hegel suggests that Christianity has been too content to embrace an overly abstract and general belief in God's cosmic governance in the name of protecting and respecting God's transcendence.[28] This epistemological humility may have been acceptable at earlier stages in the progressive revelation of the divine in history. However, European humanity now inhabits an epoch of world history in which the divine has revealed itself in history clearly enough to have rendered this conviction obsolete. The time has come, Hegel believes, to trace the hand of providence in history: "We cannot, therefore, be content with this petty commerce, so to speak, on the part of faith in providence."[29] Three features of Hegel's case for a more robust application of the doctrine of providence to human history stand out as particularly important for understanding the nature of his modulation of the Christian doctrine of providence.

First, as is evident above, Hegel wants to use the doctrine of providence as a tool for interpreting particular events in history. Hegel believes modern humanity can dispense with the Christian tradition's unnecessary distinction between general and particular providence.[30] In other words, Hegel wants to make the doctrine of providence do political and historical work. He wants to leverage the doctrine as a means for coming to interpretive judgments about the relationship between particular historical happenings and the metahistorical movement of the divine toward self-consciousness.

Second, Hegel believes that the subject to which this particular, concrete providential analysis ought to be applied is most properly collective individuals—states or peoples. He notes that in the rare cases when Christians in the past have embraced belief in God's particular providence it has almost always been related to isolated instances of direct divine intervention in the life of an individual, usually in the form of unexpected aid in a moment of dire need—perhaps a lost tax refund that arrives in the mail on the day the rent is due. By contrast, when it comes to world history, Hegel is interested in peoples or states, rather than individuals.[31] Hegel's renovation of the doctrine of providence is characterized not only by a movement from the general to the particular but also by a movement from the private/personal to the public/political.

Finally, and—for the purposes of the present investigation—most significantly, Hegel frames his transformation of the doctrine of providence as an internal critique of the Christian tradition, rooted in a development of Christianity's own best insights, rather than as a departure from or rejection of Christianity. Indeed, Hegel cites the central truth of Christianity as the warrant for his intensification and particularization of the doctrine of providence into a rational theory of history:

> The previously concealed God has become manifest. Thus as Christians we know what God is; God is no longer an unknown. . . . God does not desire narrow-minded hearts and empty heads but rather children who are rich in the knowledge of God and put their merit in it alone. Thus Christians are initiated into the mysteries of God. Because the essential being of God is revealed through the Christian religion, *the key to world history is also given to us*.[32]

Hegel defends his desire to trace the movement of the divine in history through particular events and peoples as the dutiful Christian response to God's self-revelation in the incarnation. Yet, significantly, Hegel expands the scope of divine incarnation to include all of world history. As Andrew Shanks has argued, "Hegel places the Incarnation into a world-historical context. . . . For him, God is to be grasped as being present throughout the whole length and breadth of human history."[33] He does not exhaustively identify the incarnation with the appearance of Jesus of Nazareth in human history. Rather, the particular incarnation of Jesus of Nazareth is but one—albeit significant—moment in a much wider process of divine incarnation that unfolds progressively throughout world history and culminates, not in the humanity of a first-century Jew, but rather in modern European humanity.

Hegel thus sees himself as the herald of a new age in which the progressive and self-revelatory incarnation of the divine has reached such a point that providence can be deciphered by rational thought.[34] The doctrine of providence does not provide a conceptual analogue or metaphor for Hegel's core conviction that reason governs the world. At least in these lectures, Hegel locates his philosophical project as a continuation and development of the Christian theological tradition itself—going so far as to suggest that his philosophy in facts *reclaims* the Christian religion from theology itself.[35]

In the light of such passages, it is extremely difficult to argue, as some have, for a purely "secular" or nontheological interpretation of Hegel's philosophy of history without leaving Hegel behind.[36] In the end, the core grammar of

Hegel's philosophy of history is a doctrine of providence modified in light of Hegel's understanding of God, the world, and the relationship between them. Having laid this general theological foundation in his articulation of "The General Concept of World History" in the lectures of 1830/1831, Hegel goes on to elaborate the distinctive theological shape of his modified account of providence as "The Actualization of Spirit in History."

Providence and the Actualization of Spirit in History

The specific theological contours of the philosophy of history that Hegel develops as a reconstruction of the doctrine of providence at the level of pure thought can be summarized as a slight alteration of 2 Corinthians 3:17b: "Where the Spirit is, there is freedom." The "where," for Hegel, is "here," in history: "World history is the progress of the consciousness of freedom."[37] This is the specific content that follows from the general conception of reason's cosmic rule and—like that general conception—it is structured by a theological grammar drawn from a heavily modified doctrine of providence. History, as Hegel reads it, is a progressive, teleological incarnation of the divine in the world, which is itself structured around three further interwoven theological themes: revelation, reconciliation, and consummation. As the site of divine incarnation, world history unfolds as the progressive *revelation* of the divine, accomplished by means of the *reconciliation* of the divine and the created, the infinite and the finite, the transcendent and the immanent, which progresses toward its final *consummation* in the realization of a state of perfect freedom. The processes of revelation, reconciliation, and consummation cannot be strictly separated from one another, but for purposes of clarity, I treat them here in distinction from one another in relationship to the three major subsections of Hegel's treatment of "The Actualization of Spirit in History" in the manuscript for the introduction to the 1830/1 lectures: the general definition of spirit, the means of spirit's actualization, and the material of spirit's actualization.

World history is first of all the providential process of divine revelation. It is the stage upon which the absolute comes both to be known and to know itself. This dynamic, relational conception of divinity that reveals itself and comes to full consciousness of itself in history Hegel identifies as "spirit." However, spirit denotes more than just the revelation in history of an already perfectly constituted divine life. In fact, Hegel bases his concept of spirit in the idea that the process of revelation is constitutive of the divine life itself. As O'Regan suggests, "The self-revealing God of Christianity finds its adequate discursive expression in the term *Spirit*. For Hegel, Spirit does not denote a particular aspect of the divine . . . but rather the divine considered in its entirety. . . . Spirit is the title Hegel gives to the divine considered as an encompassing act or process of revelation."[38] Hegel's concept of spirit does not simply embody the divine-made-known-in-revelation, but also the divine-as-constituted-through-revelation.

As Peter Hodgson has pointed out, because of this dynamism in Hegel's conception of the life of the divine, spirit operates in multiple senses in Hegel's understanding of history. There is spirit considered in its logically independent or pretemporal aspects, absolute spirit (*absoluter Geist*); there are varieties of spirit in partial consciousness of itself that emerge in particular peoples, national spirits or spirits of peoples (*Volksgeister*), and in individual humans, individual spirits (*Geister*). However, all of these are finally subsumed within spirit as the substance and subject of history, the ongoing, dynamic revelation of the divine, which is simultaneously the development of divine self-consciousness: world spirit (*Weltgeist*).[39] World spirit surpasses absolute spirit as the highest form of the divine life because where absolute spirit exists as immediate, and, therefore, abstract, divine consciousness, world spirit exists as fully actualized and particularized divine self-consciousness—that is to say, divine consciousness that has first recognized itself in distinction from itself and then been reconciled to itself.[40] Thus the process of revelation is simultaneously a process of reconciliation, and both of these historical processes function to constitute the nature of the divine itself.

If the nature of the divine is to be known as it comes to consciousness of itself in history, then something must be done to make sense of the seeming chaos that characterizes the passage of time. If history is a divine, teleological process, one certainly wouldn't know it from the appearance of world events. At first glance, the only ordering principle of human historical action seems to be a disorderly chorus of subjective and competing human desires.[41] Therefore, Hegel's account of the revelation of the divine-in-and-as-history is logically dependent upon an account of the reconciliation necessary to close the gap between the chaos, suffering, and evil that mark historical existence and the spiritual goal toward which that existence is supposed to be marching.

Hegel's concept of reconciliation—at least on its surface—echoes many of the familiar themes of the Christian theological tradition's reflection on the incarnation of Christ. However, Hegel redeploys these Christological tropes as an abstract framework for a providential theory of reconciliation-as-historical-progress. The means of spirit's self-actualization are the passions, interests, and ideals of the manifold individuals who pour themselves out as an atoning sacrifice on the altar of history. Hegel is under no illusions about the character of historical events. His historical progressivism is not an optimistic idealism that glosses over or suppresses history's chaotic brutality. History, for Hegel, is a slaughterhouse, which presides over "the destruction of the noblest constructs of peoples and states, the downfall of the most flourishing empires."[42] Therefore, for Hegel to be able to offer a convincing account of spirit as the revelation of the divine-in-and-as-the-created, of the infinite in and as the finite, of the transcendent in and as the immanent, he must make sense of how spirit manipulates these seemingly ill-suited means to its purposeful goal.

Hegel's response to this conceptual puzzle once again draws upon a central trope of Christian reflection on providence: that divine providence works in and through humanity's passions and individual wills, even redirecting evil deeds toward a good outcome. It receives its paradigmatic formulation from Joseph in Genesis 50:20: "Even though you intended to do harm to me, God intended it for good." On Hegel's account, world spirit accomplishes its purposes in and through the very passions, interests, and ideals that seem to run wildly and recklessly across the canvas of history.[43] Hegel famously labels the world spirit's creative and subversive instrumentalization of human passions as "the cunning of reason" (*die List der Vernunft*).[44] He appeals to the case of Julius Caesar for an example of this phenomenon. While Caesar's opposition to his enemies grew out of his individual self-interest and thirst for personal honor and security, the outcome of his actions was the unification of sovereignty in Rome under a single figure, which was itself an important positive development in the overall progress of world history.[45] World-historical individuals are those people whose individual desires and self-interest move history toward its final rational end.

In articulating this concept of reconciliation, Hegel draws deeply on the language and concepts of Christian theology. The power of reason's cunning operates as the philosophically modulated version of the power of the cross.[46] Hegel's world-historical individuals embody familiar themes of Christ's incarnation: they are human beings whose individual and finite desires are in sync with the movement of the divine in history, and it is through their lives and, in the end, their deaths that reconciliation is conceivable. But unlike the main currents of the Christian tradition, Hegel does not exclusively identify the work of reconciliation with the particular historical events of Christ's incarnation, but rather inscribes that work within the *long durée* of world history. For Hegel, world spirit comes to self-consciousness through the work of reconciliation, weaving a divine tapestry of freedom by running the shuttle of the divine idea back and forth across the loom of human passions.[47] Reason cunningly redirects the chaotic suffering that marks human history, channeling it toward an intrahistorical eschaton and history's final rational end: the *state* of perfect freedom.

While Hegel does not blindly divinize the state such that whatever political order establishes itself can claim divine right—one misreading of Hegel's (in)famous claim that "what is rational is actual; and what is actual is rational"—he does develop a theologically inflected vision of human politics in his lectures, which grows out of his commitment to the framework of divine providence.[48] In addition to being the site of divine revelation and reconciliation, world history is also the location of the eschatological consummation of spirit through its full self-consciousness, which takes the form of human freedom. More specifically, history aims at humanity's conscious realization of the freedom that has always been its intrinsic possession in principle.[49] The realization of freedom is the intrahistorical eschaton toward which the world spirit drives.

However, this freedom must have a particular character. It is not a negative freedom, the individual's arbitrary will exercised in the absence of restraint. This freedom is too abstract and not objective, substantial, or concrete enough to represent the culmination of the divine life in history.[50] Hegel understands true freedom, as John Plamenatz has argued, "not as mere absence of constraint but also and above all as the ability to live by principles and in pursuit of aims willingly and deliberately accepted."[51] This account of freedom leads Hegel to create a prominent place for the state within his eschatological schema of the final purpose of the divine in history.

For world history to realize the final actualization of spirit through full consciousness of freedom, that freedom must be concretely instantiated in positive forms of communal life. The state is, therefore, the literal *material* of spirit's actualization, in that it allows spirit to take up concrete, objective form within history.[52] By state, Hegel does not mean strictly "the government" or the institutional mechanisms of political authority and rule, but rather the spiritual totality of a people's laws, institutions, land, history, culture, and morality. The state expresses the particular spirit of a people—the *Volkgeist*.

Hegel treats the concept of the state most fully in the lectures of 1822/1823. There he makes clear that the state he imagines is not based upon a contract that negates freedom, in which individuals trade freedom for security. Rather, the state is the *actualization* of freedom—it provides the conditions and possibilities for humans to be truly free.[53] The state has an objective meaning and purpose because it is drawn into the divine movement of spirit in history: "The state does not exist for the sake of its citizens; rather it is the end in and for itself."[54] Hegel articulates the state, not as a subjective human construct, but as the concrete form through which the divine providential governance of history is carried out. Even Alan Patten, a committed proponent of a nontheological, "humanistic" reading of the lectures, admits that the Hegelian vision of the state makes little sense apart from its place within Hegel's wider spiritual meta-narrative: "Human freedom and subjectivity are the correct ideals for thinking about social and political questions ultimately because God wants, or even needs, to be freely known and worshipped."[55] The eschatological goal of history is the state that enables perfect freedom.

The purpose of the foregoing analysis of the conceptual framework of Hegel's *Lectures on the Philosophy of History* was to establish the presence and shaping influence of a Christian theological grammar at the heart of Hegel's approach to world history. As should now be clear, Hegel models this framework on the Christian doctrine of providence, imagining his own reading of world history as finally realizing the potential of the doctrine of providence to provide a lens through which to read the development of the incarnation of the divine in history.[56] In these lectures, Hegel articulates a philosophically revised doctrine of providence structured around divine-historical processes of revelation, reconciliation, and consummation.

However, the articulation of this providential construct is of secondary importance for Hegel. Hegel's chief aim in these lectures is to put this construct to work, using it as a lens through which to read history with unprecedented clarity as the stage upon which the divine comes to self-consciousness. The majority of the lectures is actually dedicated to this latter task of coming to specific interpretive judgments about the relationship between particular events, movements, and peoples and the meta-historical trajectories of revelation, reconciliation, and consummation that constitute the incarnation of the divine in history.

The sacralization of history is, therefore, one of the central tropes of Hegel's lectures. As Cyril O'Regan suggests, "The eschaton for Hegel is an intrahistorical gestation. If everything is under providential sway, then *everything*, for Hegel, is sacred or holy."[57] Yet O'Regan's conclusion is only partially accurate. For while it is true that Hegel enfolds eschatology into divine providence, rendering history sacred, not *everything*—or, more importantly, *everyone*—participates equally in history. Rather, Hegel's providential reading of history enables the construction of a very particular divine-historical subject: European man.

TIME, SPACE, AND RACE: HEGEL, HISTORY, AND GLOBAL HUMANITY

In the hands of Hegel, the doctrine of providence became a powerful tool for interpreting world history. As I have argued, in the opening sections of the *Lectures on the Philosophy of World History*, Hegel constructs the doctrine of providence as a lens through which to read the movement of the divine in history with—what he believes to be—unprecedented clarity. However, given that Hegel fashions providence as a hermeneutical lens in this way, what does he actually see when he peers through it?

In his lecture cycles, Hegel calibrates his providential interpretation of world history around a vision of European man as simultaneously the contemporary site and teleological goal of the intrahistorical processes of revelation, reconciliation, and consummation that constitute the incarnation of the divine in the world. In order to see that this is the case, one must first understand that Hegel imagines world history as unfolding in three dimensions. For Hegel, the *temporal* progress of the consciousness of freedom, which defines the trajectory of spirit's movement through world history, is also organized along *spatial* and *anthropological* lines. Indeed, Hegel correlates the progressive unfolding of the divine life in history not just with different historical epochs or *times*, but also with different geographical *spaces*—and the *peoples* that inhabit them. Thus, he can just as easily speak of history progressing from east to west as from past to future.[58]

When interrogated in light of this multidimensional conception of world history, it becomes clear that, while Hegel's philosophy of history does indeed sacralize history and humanity, it is in fact a *selective* sacralization. Specifically, Hegel exclusively envisions *European* humanity as the bearers of divine presence in history, viewing European Christian civilization as both the site of complete divine revelation and the site of the eschatological consummation of the divine life on earth—or, both the condition of possibility for genuine knowledge of the divine and the final, eschatological end at which history has finally arrived. In short, Hegel looks through his providential lens and sees European man as the divine subject of sacred history.

Considering that his topic is self-avowedly *history*, Hegel spends a surprising amount of time discussing *geography* and *anthropology* in his lectures. Editors of the *Lectures on the Philosophy of World History* have not always known what to do with this expansive material, which can understandably seem somewhat out of place. More often than not, the editors of the lectures have chosen to separate these portions of Hegel's lectures from the main body of the text—either placing it between the introduction and the division of subjects, as found in the editions of Eduard Gans and Karl Hegel, or attaching it as an appendix, as in the editions of Lasson and Hoffmeister.[59] Unfortunately, this decision functionally solidifies the appearance of a significant disjunction between the temporal and spatial/anthropological dimensions of Hegel's account of the progress of spirit.

While this disjunction—if genuine—would provide a convenient way to vindicate Hegel's account of historical progress from its guilt-by-association with his account of geographical and anthropological progress, it has become increasingly clear in the wake of the publication of critical editions of the manuscripts and transcriptions of Hegel's lectures that Hegel himself would not have supported such a bifurcation. Rather, Hegel explicitly and systematically connects history, geography, and anthropology into a single, seamless theory of the development of spirit in the succession of world-historical states/peoples.[60]

Hegel defends his decision to systematically treat geography and anthropology as inextricable features of his philosophical account of world history by linking it to his axiom that the historical emergence of spirit is the result of a reconciliation of the divine and the natural: "The natural and the spiritual form one shape, and this is history."[61] Because world history results from the confluence of spirit *and* nature, Hegel argues that a philosophical account of world history would be incomplete without some account of the latter's world-historical role. Precisely to avoid this would-be lacuna in his theory, Hegel offers an account of the geographical basis of world history—the external natural setting of the state. Historical progress is not only about successive periods of time but also registers through "concrete *spatial* specificity" or geographical positions.[62] Hegel indexes the successive principles of spirit—which appear on the stage of world history incarnate in particular peoples—both temporally and spatially, as a function of both spirit and nature. As Hodgson notes, "Geography adds a spatial coordinate to the temporal coordinate by which each people is analyzed."[63] Hegel suggests that this method of triangulation—a spiritual GPS of sorts—enables him to chart a complete picture of the differential relationship of the divine to the various peoples that make up global humanity.

In Hegel's account, geography functions as the natural baseline of spirit's development. Spirit takes its first step on the journey to self-consciousness by positing itself over and against the immediacy of nature. Nature's role in the process of world history is both relatively preliminary and vital. Nature provides the original basis—the preliminary conditions and possibilities—for the development of spirit in world history. Hegel adopts an agricultural metaphor to clarify his point: "History indeed lives on the soil of the natural; but this is only one aspect, and the higher aspect is that of spirit."[64] Nature functions like the soil in which spirit grows—either hampering or encouraging spirit's growth depending on its quality. Just as the quality of the soil is only one factor influencing the growth of crops, so nature does not exert a particularly strong influence upon the growth of spirit.

However, Hegel qualifies this point immediately after making it, noting that, in extreme cases, nature plays a limiting function in relationship to spirit. These exceptions occur when extreme natural conditions amplify nature's strength to the point at which a people cannot separate themselves from their immediate natural existence. For these peoples, spiritual development is simply not possible. To extend Hegel's agricultural metaphor, there are certain soils that are so poor that no seed, no matter how well cared for, can grow. Hegel identifies climate as the independent variable that determines the relative strength of nature in relationship to spirit: "Neither the frigid nor the tropical zones create world-historical peoples, for these extremes constitute such a powerful natural force that human beings are unable to . . . pursue higher spiritual interests."[65] The peoples who inhabit these geographic regions are unable to make spiritual progress because the force of nature is too great. According to Hegel, these peoples who are oppressed by nature cannot participate in world history. Thus, ironically, world history is not actually *world* history.

Hegel's mapping of world history onto global space excludes Africa from history entirely, locates Asia at the sparse beginnings of history, identifies the progress of history with the geographical movement from Asia to Europe, positions the climax of history in Western Europe—the land of the Reformation and the Enlightenment—and, revealingly, equivocates about the significance of the New World for world history. However, a close inspection of these portions of Hegel's lectures reveals that Hegel attempts to correlate historical progress, not simply with certain geographical spaces, but more specifically with the peoples who inhabit them. Indeed, Hegel's spatial indexing of the temporal is simultaneously an endeavor in comparative anthropology. Reading Hegel's exploration of the geographical basis of world history in light of his assessment of different peoples' fitness for participation in world history reveals that Hegel envisions a global-historical and sociopolitical order calibrated around a particular kind of human being: European man.

Hegel entirely excludes sub-Saharan Africa from world history.[66] In Hegel's judgment, Africa has minimal contact with world history. Africa is a fundamentally static space, standing entirely apart from the dynamic flow of world history. It "remains in its placid, unmotivated, self-enclosed sensuality and has not yet entered into history."[67] For this reason, Hegel concludes that Africa "has no history . . . and need not be mentioned again. For it is an unhistorical continent, with no movement or development of its own."[68] Africa—which Hegel repeatedly calls a "continent," despite the fact that he does not include Egypt and North Africa within its bounds—simply lies outside the threshold of world history itself.[69]

It is only in Asia, therefore, that one encounters the primitive beginnings of world history. Hegel calls it the "world of dawning (*Aufgang*)," which connotes both its association with the rising of the sun in the east and the beginning point of the world-historical process.[70] In Asia, spirit is first able to posit itself in distinction from the immediacy of nature, and thus the first step toward spirit's self-consciousness occurs with the emergence of the first state.[71] However, this first state reflects only history in its infancy, because the ethical life (*sittlichkeit*) of the imperial state exists in antithesis to the individual subjectivities of its citizens: in Asia, only one person is free: the emperor.[72] Hegel verges on ruling the "Far East" out of history entirely, settling on the judgment that these earliest dawnings of history constitute an "unhistorical history."[73] World history then progresses eastward across the Asian continent through the Middle East to Europe.

Europe, for Hegel, is both the center and the end goal of world history.[74] It is here, among the Germanic peoples of Western Europe, that one can find free spirit subsisting finally for itself in full maturity.[75] Revealingly, however, Hegel is unsure of what to make of the New World in relationship to world history—particularly with respect to North America. On the one hand, the New World "has shown itself to be much feebler than the old world."[76] Yet at the same time, America also has the aspect of "a land of the future."[77] On a first reading, Hegel seems unsure of whether to locate the New World outside of history, with Africa, or to see it as the land of the future. His ambivalence has everything to do with the types of human beings that one identifies with this geographic space. As Michael Hoffheimer argues, "Whatever Hegel meant by calling America 'the land of the future,' this future did not include American Indians."[78] Hegel does not confine his mapping of world history simply to geographical space in accord with climate, but bases his analysis on a comparative anthropological vision of global humanity.

In Hegel's account, the *land* or *geographical space* of the Americas does not have a fixed position in relationship to spirit. He speaks of it, on the one hand, as lying outside of history entirely, with Africa, and, on the other hand, as the land of the future. Instead, Hegel ties his analysis of the Americas to their inhabitants: the indigenous peoples of the Americas lie outside of history, while the rising Euro-American civilization of North America earns the title of land of the future. Hegel notes: "Some of the tribes of North America have disappeared and some have retreated and generally declined, so that we see that the latter lack the strength to join the North Americans in the Free States."[79] The original inhabitants of North America, unable to join the fledgling project that is the United States, do not participate in world history in Hegel's estimation. Indeed, in some manuscripts, Hegel goes so far as to justify the genocide of the indigenous populations of the Americas as an outworking of the extreme differential in spiritual development between themselves and the Europeans. Native culture, suggests Hegel, "had to perish as soon as the spirit approached it."[80] While Hegel is under no illusions about the fact that contact with Europe proved deadly for these populations, his explanation exonerates European colonial practices of all responsibility for the mass suffering of the indigenes: "Few descendants of the original inhabitants survive, for nearly seven million people have been wiped out. . . . Their degeneration indicates that they do not have the strength to join the independent North American states. Culturally inferior nations such as these are gradually eroded through contact with more advanced nations."[81] The European colonists were simply unable to "amalgamate" with them.[82]

However, while the indigenous peoples of the Americas embody the New World's pre- or a-historical existence, the presence of peoples of European descent in the New World is the principal piece of evidence for Hegel's speculation that America may be the land of the future: "They bring with them the whole treasure of European culture and self-awareness."[83] In short,

Hegel describes the world-historical location of the same geographic region in nearly opposite ways, depending upon the type of people who call it home. Hegel's *anthropological* commitments provide the determinative variable which fixes America's place in Hegel's global economy of spirit.

While it reveals itself most clearly in his treatment of the New World, Hegel's deep interest in comparative anthropology manifests itself throughout the portion of his lectures concerned with geography. In his treatment of Africa, Hegel boldly asserts, "Anyone who wishes to study the most terrible manifestations of human nature will find them in Africa."[84] Africans are determined by nature so completely that they have no place in the story of spirit's progress in history: "He is still at the first stage of development: he is dominated by passion, and is nothing more than a savage."[85] Hegel's account of African peoples defines them principally in terms of supposedly rampant and unrestrained practices of cannibalism, fetishistic religion, and human slavery.[86]

As those peoples most thoroughly dominated by nature, Africans provide the anthropological baseline or "control group" against which other peoples can be evaluated to discern their position relative to spirit.[87] It is not just African *space*, but African *people*, that Hegel positions outside of history. Indeed, like his treatment of North America, Hegel undermines the idea that he is engaged in a strictly geographical mapping of the trajectory of spirit. This becomes clear from the way that he ties hope for African progress to contact with European peoples. In his Berlin lectures on the *Philosophy of Spirit*, Hegel notes that Africans have surprisingly demonstrated a capacity for culture through the reception of European Christianity, which has given them at least preliminary access to the consciousness of freedom that is the content of spirit's incarnation in the world.[88] Thus it is contact with European people through which the divine is mediated to peoples of sub-Saharan Africa, Hegel's iteration of the white man's "spiritual" burden.[89]

While Hegel fixes the original inhabitants of Africa and the Americas as the negative limit of his global anthropological vision, he envisions European humanity as its apex. He is quite explicit about the Christian eschatological significance of European civilization: "Up to now, the periods [of world history] involved relating to an earlier and a later world-historical people. But now, with the Christian religion, the principle of the world is complete; *the day of judgment* has dawned for it."[90] The Christian world of Western Europe is, according to Hegel, the exclusive site of any further developments in the life of the world spirit. Just as history moves spatially—from east to west—in Hegel's account, so Hegel's eschaton is not only a *time* but also a *place*.

The fact that history attains its spatial-anthropological eschaton prior to its temporal endpoint leaves Hegel with an untidy theoretical loose end to tie up. Hegel attempts to explain this disjunction between the temporal and spatial endpoints of history by suggesting that all relationships between Europe and the outside world that occur after spirit comes to rest upon the former can only be ones in which that outside world is overcome by Europe.[91] For Hegel, spirit has come to full maturity and perfection in Western European civilization in such a way that European peoples are now the mediators of divine presence to the rest of humanity: "The Christian world has circumnavigated the globe and dominates it. For Europeans the world is round, and what is not yet dominated is either not worth the effort, of no value to rule, or yet destined to be ruled. Outward relationships no longer constitute epochs, are no longer the determinative factor; the essential revolutions occur inwardly."[92] While the divine becoming of spirit in history continues to unfold temporally, world history's geographic and anthropological trajectories have reached their eschatological *telos* in Western Europe. European Christian civilization becomes the final bearer of the incarnation of the divine in the world.

In summary, Hegel conceptualizes world history as a progressive, teleological process of the revelation, reconciliation, and consummation of the divine life in and as history, which unfolds along three axes: the temporal, the spatial, and the anthropological. Hegel thus exemplifies a phenomenon that Judith Butler has diagnosed elsewhere, in which certain conceptions of "temporality" are "organized along spatial lines" in such a way that "Europe and its state apparatus" become "the avatar of both freedom and modernity."[93] Butler argues that European conceptions of freedom—the very subject of Hegel's account of world history—are often parasitic upon an implicit cultural ground, which functions for those concepts "as both transcendental condition and teleological aim."[94] In *The Lectures on the Philosophy of World History*, Hegel traces the hand of providence across time, space, and humanity, mapping the movement of the divine in and through history, geography, and humanity until it comes to rest on the Christian peoples of Western Europe.

CONCLUSION

Hegel formulates an understanding of divine providence calibrated around a vision of European humanity as the divine subject of history—the final manifestation of divine presence in history and the mediator of that presence to the rest of the world. Hegel reads the movement of the divine in history as a rational, teleological operation of historical, geographical, and anthropological progress, imagining Western Europe as an eschatological state of freedom in opposition to those places and peoples who remain trapped in mere nature and deprived of relationship to the divine. Simply put, Hegel resources the doctrine of providence as a global hermeneutical lens through which he conceptualizes European humanity as the center and endpoint of the world-historical drama, enabling him to quite literally rationalize the genocide of the indigenous populations of the Americas and render an apology for the African slave trade as having had a civilizing effect upon African peoples. Three particular features of Hegel's understanding of providence enable him to press the doctrine into service to aid in the construction of a vision of European man as the divine subject of providential history.

First, Hegel inscribes his understanding of divine providence within a heavily revised understanding of the relationship of creation, fall, and redemption, leading him to misidentify the condition of creaturely human existence as a temporary condition to be overcome through the world-historical process. As has been already established, Hegel identifies the Christian theological admonition toward modesty in estimations of humanity's epistemological participation in God's rule over the world as a needlessly self-abnegating expression of humility that is no longer relevant in light of the consummation of the life of spirit in European humanity.[95] For Hegel, providence becomes a way of superseding the finitude of creaturely human historical judgment and vision, enabling certain human subjects—including Hegel himself—to acquire a divine perspective on history.

Second, Hegel collapses the history of creation into the history of salvation, thereby constructing an account of humanity's journey through world history as a soteriological process of progressive divinization that enables humanity to overcome the previously identified limits of creaturely finitude. In so doing, Hegel effectively collapses the theological boundaries between providence and soteriology—infusing the latter directly into the former. As Patricia Altenbernd Johnson suggests, for Hegel, "An eternal history of Absolute Spirit is not a separate history that falls into another world. It is not the history of a divine world that has a distinct temporal and spatial framework, separate from the world of historical experience."[96] Hegel radically closes the distance between providence and eschatology, making possible a sacralization of the historical and political as bearers of ultimate significance. This sets the stage for a soteriological interpretation of world history that correlates the movement of the divine with conceptions of temporal, spatial, and anthropological progress.

Finally, Hegel displaces Jesus of Nazareth from the center of the doctrine of providence, relativizing the significance of the incarnation as the paradigmatic instance of God's action in world history. Divine providence thus becomes little more than a formal teleological construct, which can be calibrated to a vision of a divine subject of history who is not the Jewish human being Jesus of Nazareth. In Hegel's hands, European humanity replaces Jesus as the paradigmatic site of divine revelation, reconciliation, and consummation. Joseph McCarney describes—albeit approvingly—the theological operation that I am suggesting lies at the heart of Hegel's elevation of European man as the subject of the incarnation:

> [Hegel] conspicuously fails to endorse what is surely the simple essence of the matter for ordinary Christians, the unique status of Jesus as the incarnate second person of the Trinity. . . . A shift of perspective on the traditional Christian doctrine of incarnation may be said to have taken place, one that subverts it utterly. Instead of being a doctrine of God taking on human form, it becomes the revelation of humanity as the highest form of expression of the divine, thus turning the central drama of Christian theism against its origins.[97]

McCarney's account, while helpful, fails to fully identify what is at stake in Hegel's theological transformation of the doctrine of the incarnation because he sees Hegel replacing Christ with an abstract general humanity. Yet as I have argued, Hegel's understanding of the incarnation of the divine in history does not culminate in an *abstract* vision of humanity, but rather in a *racialized* one. Hegel identifies one particular figuration of humanity to replace Jesus Christ at the apex of the Christian theological system: European man—the center and telos of the divine world-historical drama.[98] Hegel's interpretation of divine providence inserts modern European man in the place of Jesus of Nazareth, as the highest expression of the divine incarnate in world history.

In sum, Hegel's transformation of the doctrine of providence into a global hermeneutic of temporal, spatial, and anthropological progress pivots around his reconfiguration of the relationship between providence and the incarnation, resulting in a Christological vision of European humanity as the paradigmatic incarnation of the divine in world history. In his lectures, Hegel constructs European humanity as the site of divine revelation, reconciliation, and eschatological consummation, binding the incarnation of the divine in the world to white, European peoples. Hegel understands himself to be bringing the Christian theological concept of divine providence to its final destiny by rearticulating it as a philosophical account of the rational unfolding of spirit in world history in which, as Denise Ferreira da Silva suggests, "reason finally displaced the divine ruler and author to become the sovereign ruler of man."[99]

Indeed, *The Lectures on the Philosophy of World History* provide a paradigmatic example of what Ferreira da Silva describes as "the productive role the racial plays in post-Enlightenment conditions."[100] In Hegel's construction of a global anthropological hierarchy, it is the active, positive movement of a teleological reason/providence in the world that culminates in the production of European identity as the site of universality and freedom. Thus, it is not the case that Hegel harbors a crude racial prejudice that causes him to deviate from his true philosophical commitments in order to maintain his personal prejudice.[101] Rather, the production of a hierarchically differentiated humanity constitutes the process whereby the universal itself is produced—there can be no telos without the teleological apparatus. As Ferreira da Silva argues, "While the tools of universal reason . . . produce and regulate human conditions, in each global region it establishes mentally (morally and intellectually) distinct kinds of human beings, namely, the self-determined subject and its outer-determined others, the ones whose minds are subjected to their *natural* (in the scientific sense) conditions."[102] Racial difference thus emerges as an effect of universal reason itself. Therefore, as Joseph R. Winters concludes, "Hegel's thought demonstrates how the logic of progress operates to establish and justify racial hierarchies."[103] Hegel's lectures exemplify this enactment of differentiation, not as an act characterized by prejudicial exclusion, but as a dangerously "constructive" way of imagining racial difference as the outcome of a providential process that culminates in a vision of the European as the eschatological subject of universality and freedom. Hegel performs Christian theological reflection on providence as an act of intellectual colonialism. The next two chapters examine two different attempts to grapple theologically with this problem.

NOTES

1. Thomas Edward Bowdich, *Mission from Cape Coast Castle to Ashantee, with a Statistical Account of that Kingdom and Geographical Notices of Other Parts of the Interior of Africa* (London: John Murray, 1819). This recapitulation of Bowdich's account conveys his story as it was received by his original audience.

2. Ibid., 43.

3. Susanne Zantop, *Colonial Fantasies: Conquest, Family, and Nation in Precolonial Germany, 1770-1870* (Durham, NC: Duke University Press, 1997), 32.

4. Robert Bernasconi, "Hegel at the Court of the Ashanti," in *Hegel after Derrida*, ed. Barnett (London: Routledge, 1998), 44.

5. Susan Buck-Morss, *Hegel, Haiti, and Universal History* (Pittsburgh: University of Pittsburgh Press, 2009), 115.

6. Zantop, *Colonial Fantasies*, 36.

7. Ibid., 38.

8. Ibid., 38.

9. Ibid., 41, 38, 41.

10. G. W. F. Hegel, *Lectures on the Philosophy of World History: Volume 1: Manuscripts of the Introduction and the Lectures of 1822-3*, ed. and trans. Brown and Hodgson with Geuss (Oxford: Oxford University Press, 2011), 67 (hereafter cited as *LPWH*). Emphasis in the original.

11. Sidney Hook, *From Hegel to Marx* (New York: Humanities Press, 1950), 36. For other important examples of theological interpretations of Hegel, see Nicholas Adams, *Eclipse of Grace: Divine and Human Action in Hegel* (Oxford:

Wiley-Blackwell, 2013); Cyril O'Regan, *The Heterodox Hegel* (Albany, NY: State University of New York Press, 1994); Emil Fackenheim, *The Religious Dimension in Hegel's Thought* (Bloomington, IN: Indiana University Press, 1967); Peter Hodgson, *Hegel and Christian Theology: A Reading of the* Lectures on the Philosophy of Religion (Oxford: Oxford University Press, 2005); Martin J. De Nys, *Hegel and Theology* (London: T&T Clark International, 2009); Ivan Ill'in, *Die Philosophie Hegels als kontemplative Gotteslehre* (Bern: A. Francke, 1946); Jörg Splett, *Die Trinitätslehre G.W.F. Hegels* (Freiburg: K. Alber, 1965); Albert Chappelle, *Hegel et la religion* (Paris: Éditions Universitaires, 1967); James Yerkes, *The Christology of Hegel* (Albany, NY: State University of New York Press, 1983); Emilio Brito, *La Christologie de Hegel: Verbum Crucis*, trans. B. Pottier (Paris: Beauchesne, 1983); Dale M. Schlitt, *Hegel's Trinitarian Claim: A Critical Reflection* (Leiden: E. J. Brill, 1984); Andrew Shanks, *Hegel's Political Theology* (Cambridge: Cambridge University Press, 1991); Glenn Alexander Magee, *Hegel and the Hermetic Tradition* (Ithaca, NY: Cornell University Press, 2001); William Desmond, *Hegel's God: A Counterfeit Double?* (Burlington, VT: Ashgate Publishing Co., 2003); Martin Wendte, *Gottmenschliche Einheit bei Hegel: eine logische und theologische Untersuchung* (New York: Walter de Gruyter, 2007); Cyril O'Regan, *The Anatomy of Misremembering: von Balthasar's Response to Philosophical Modernity: Volume 1: Hegel* (New York: The Crossroad Publishing Company, 2014); Rowan Williams, "Hegel and the Gods of Postmodernity" and "Logic and Spirit in Hegel," in *Wrestling with Angels: Conversations in Modern Theology*, ed. Mike Higton (Grand Rapids, MI: William B. Eerdmans Publishing Co., 2007); Andrew Shanks, *Hegel Versus 'Inter-Faith Dialogue': A General Theory of True Xenophilia* (Cambridge: Cambridge University Press, 2015).

12. *LPWH*, 79.

13. Augustine, *The City of God*, trans. Babcock (Hyde Park, NY: New City Press, 2012), 30; Calvin, *Institutes of the Christian Religion*, 199, 208, 213. Emphasis in original. In *The City of God*, Augustine asserts the mysterious nature of divine providence in response to questions about why the wicked often prosper while the righteous suffer in this temporal life: "Deep is the providence of the creator and ruler of the world, *and his judgments are inscrutable, and his ways past finding out* (Rom. 11:33)." Calvin similarly emphasizes the incapacity of humanity to attain knowledge of God's providential rule in his account of divine providence in Book I of the *Institutes of the Christian Religion*, speaking of "God's secret plan," asserting that "the sluggishness of our mind lies far beneath the height of God's providence," and maintaining that "his wonderful method of governing the universe is rightly called an abyss, because while it is hidden from us, we ought reverently to adore it."

14. *LPWH*, 145.

15. Ibid., 201.

16. Thus, Hegel can describe the New World as either a land lying outside of world history entirely or the land of the future, depending on whether he locates it in relationship to the "disappearing" indigenous inhabitants of the Americas or the emergent Euro-American civilization springing up in the United States. I explore this discrepancy in Hegel's account at further length below.

17. The use of the masculine pronoun "man" is intentional. The divine subject of history that resides at the apex of Hegel's philosophical account of world history is gendered as male. While Hegel does not address gender explicitly in the lectures, his grounding of world history in the publicity and universality of the state must be read in light of his relegation of women to the private and particular realm of the family in his *Elements of The Philosophy of Right*, trans. Nisbet (Cambridge, Cambridge University Press, 1991), 206–207: "Man therefore has his actual substantial life in the state, in learning, etc., and otherwise in work and struggle with the external world and with himself. . . . Woman, however, has her substantial vocation in the family. . . . When women are in charge of government the state is in danger, for their actions are based not on the demands of universality but on contingent inclination and opinion." For Hegel, world history is concerned with the state and is, therefore, on his own understanding of gender roles in society, a thoroughly masculine phenomenon. For more on this point, see Genevieve Lloyd, *The Man of Reason: "Male" and "Female" in Western Philosophy* (Minneapolis: University of Minnesota Press, 1984), 80–85.

18. Fackenheim, *The Religious Dimension in Hegel's Thought*, 9.

19. Robert Bernasconi, "'The Ruling Categories of the World': The Trinity in Hegel's Philosophy of History and the Rise and Fall of Peoples," in *A Companion to Hegel*, ed. Houlgate and Baur (Oxford: Blackwell Publishing Ltd., 2011), 328.

20. It is important to bear in mind that the texts of the *Lectures on the Philosophy of World History* that we possess today are mostly patchwork documents, combining fragments from Hegel's own manuscripts with transcriptions of the lectures made by Hegel's students. However, while for many years the lack of a critical edition of the texts of the lectures on world history—comparable to the critical edition of his *Lectures on the Philosophy of Religion*, for instance—proved to be a significant obstacle to sure-footed interpretation and analysis, recent years have seen the publication of the beginnings of a critical edition of the lectures, allowing for a higher degree of certainty about their original structure and content. Whereas the editions of Hegel's lectures published by Eduard Gans (1837), Karl Hegel (1840), George Lasson (1917), and even Johannes Hoffmeister (1955) were compiled with significant editing that makes their relationship to the original lectures somewhat unreliable, a complete transcription of the lectures of 1822/23 was published in 1996, providing a new foundation for analysis of the lectures. This edition has recently been translated into English by Robert F. Brown and Peter C. Hodgson, along with fragments of Hegel's manuscripts from the introduction to the lectures of 1822 and 1828, a lengthy manuscript from Hegel's introduction to the lectures of 1830-1, and loose sheets written in Hegel's hand that relate to the lectures of 1830-1. Wherever possible, I engage the texts from the critical editions of Jaeschke and Ilting, Brehmer, and Seelmann (translated by Brown and Hodgson), cautiously supplementing these when necessary with Hoffmeister's edition of the introduction (translated by Nisbet), which is the best of the previous editions. For these critical editions, see G. W. F. Hegel, *Vorlesungen über die Philosophie der Weltgeschichte (Berlin 1822/23)*, ed. Ilting, Brehmer, and Seelmann, *Vorlesungen: Ausgewählte Nachschriften und Manuskripte*, xii (Hamburg: Felix Meiner Verlag, 1996) and the translations of Brown and Hodgson. The German source for the manuscript materials

is *Vorlesungsmanuskripte II (1816-31)*, ed. Walter Jaeschke, *Gesammelte Werke*, xviii (Hamburg: Felix Meiner 1995). For a comprehensive discussion of the various editions of Hegel's lectures see Bernasconi, "The Ruling Categories of the World," 316–318 and the editorial introduction to Brown and Hodgson's translation of the lectures.

21. The material that Hegel uses in this section of the 1830/1 on "The General Concept of World History" has significant parallels in his account of philosophical world history as the third of three possible types of history in the 1822/3 lectures transcribed by Griesheim and Hotho which will be cross-referenced where appropriate.

22. *LPWH*, 78. Emphasis in original. See Frederick C. Beiser, "Hegel and Ranke: A Re-examination," in *A Companion to Hegel*, ed. Houlgate and Baur (Oxford: Blackwell Publishing Ltd., 2011), 332–350. Beiser suggests that the historical methodologies of Hegel and Ranke are considerably more similar than has been traditionally acknowledged.

23. Ibid., 81.

24. Burleigh Taylor Wilkins, *Hegel's Philosophy of History* (Ithaca, NY: Cornell University Press, 1974), 48–49.

25. *LPWH*, 82–83.

26. Wilkins, *Hegel's Philosophy of History*, 48.

27. *LPWH*, 83. Emphasis in original.

28. Ibid., 85. While Hegel does not mention Kant by name here, it is obvious that this entire line of argument is a direct refutation of Kant's own position on the possibility of knowledge of God in relationship to history. See, for example, Kant's comments on the pretentiousness of claims to have access to cognitive knowledge of God's providence in "To Perpetual Peace: A Philosophical Sketch," 120–121.

29. Ibid., 84.

30. The distinction between general and particular providence, which rests on the division between God's care for the entire universe and God's care for individual creatures, should not be mistaken for the distinction between general, special, and most special providence, which addresses God's relationship to different classes of creatures (usually nonhumans, all humans, and Christians). See Charles Wood, *The Question of Providence*, 36 n. 13.

31. *LPWH*, 84. For a critique of the internal consistency of this position with respect to Hegel's wider philosophical commitments, see George Dennis O'Brien, *Hegel on Reason and History: A Contemporary Interpretation* (Chicago: The University of Chicago Press, 1975), 58–59.

32. Ibid., 145. Emphasis added.

33. Shanks, *Hegel's Political Theology*, 16.

34. *LPWH*, 85.

35. Ibid., 85. "In opposition to certain kinds of theology, philosophy has to take on the content of religion."

36. O'Brien, *Hegel on Reason and History*, 53.

37. *LPWH*, 88.

38. O'Regan, *Heterodox Hegel*, 29–30.

39. Hodgson, *Shapes of Freedom*, 25.

40. Walter Jaeschke, "World History and the History of the Absolute Spirit," in *History and System: Hegel's Philosophy of History*, ed. Perkins (Albany, NY: State University of New York Press, 1984), 115.

41. *LPWH*, 89.

42. Ibid., 90.

43. Ibid., 93–94.

44. Ibid., 96 n. 44.

45. Ibid., 95.

46. Hodgson, *Shapes of Freedom*, 45–46. "Because cunning has the power of apparent weakness, the metaphor can be stretched further to suggest that the power of cunning is like the power of the cross, where God in human shape dies at the hands of human violence but where God's purpose prevails nonetheless. God 'lets' human beings do as they please, but God's will prevails. The cross represents the great reversal, the counterthrust to the idea. . . . The cross is a negative sign of God's power in the world, and it is by the negation of negation that spiritual power prevails."

47. *LPWH*, 147. This is Hegel's preferred metaphor for explicating the means of spirit's self-actualization in the lectures of 1822/3: "Thus we have here the idea as the totality of ethical freedom. Two elements are salient: first, the idea itself as abstract; and second, the human passions. The two together form the weft and warp in the fabric that world history spreads before us."

48. Hegel, *Elements of The Philosophy of Right*, 20.

49. Hodgson, *Shapes of Freedom*, 9.

50. Hegel, *Elements of the Philosophy of Right*, 48. "When we hear it said that freedom in general consists in *being able to do as one pleases*, such an idea can only be taken to indicate a complete lack of intellectual culture; for it shows not the least awareness of what constitutes the will which is free in and for itself."

51. John Plamenatz, "History as the Realization of Freedom," in *Hegel's Political Philosophy: Problems and Perspectives*, ed. Pelczynski (Cambridge: Cambridge University Press, 1971), 45.

52. *LPWH*, 100.

53. Ibid., 178. For Hegel's full exposition of the state as the realm of objective freedom, see *Elements of the Philosophy of Right*, 275–282.

54. *LPWH*, 179.

55. Alan Patten, *Hegel's Idea of Freedom* (Oxford: Oxford University Press, 1999), 204. Cited in Peter C. Hodgson, *Shapes of Freedom: Hegel's Philosophy of World History in Theological Perspective* (Oxford: Oxford University Press, 2012), 71.

56. It should be noted that for Hegel this reading is always *retrospective*. That is to say, Hegel had no pretensions to be able to leverage his reading of history in order to predict the future—thus, his assertion in the *Philosophy of Right* that "the owl of Minerva begins its flight only with the onset of dusk" (23). Nevertheless, Hegel does seek to exercise the power of philosophy to interpret the past and the present and his particular approach to these tasks carries with it enough trouble of its own, as I shall demonstrate below. Shlomo Avineri aptly captures the ambiguity of Hegel's disavowal of philosophy's relationship to social criticism and the future: "To borrow

and invert a phrase from Marx, philosophy cannot change the world, only interpret it; but by its very act of interpretation it changes it, it tells the world that its time is up." Shlomo Avineri, *Hegel's Theory of the Modern State* (Cambridge: Cambridge University Press, 1972), 130.

57. O'Regan, *The Heterodox Hegel*, 274. Emphasis added.
58. *LPWH*, 201.
59. Hodgson, *Shapes of Freedom*, 80.
60. For a similar argument, see Robert Bernasconi, "With What Must the Philosophy of World History Begin? On the Racial Basis of Hegel's Eurocentrism," *Nineteenth-Century Contexts* 22 (2000): 172. "[Hegel] does not simply append his views about non-European peoples to his philosophy; these views are elevated above the level of mere prejudice by the logical framework which helps sustain them and to which they in turn lend support."
61. *LPWH*, 198.
62. Ibid., 191. Emphasis added.
63. Hodgson, *Shapes of Freedom*, 81.
64. *LPWH*, 191.
65. Ibid., 191.
66. Ibid., 196.
67. Ibid., 197.
68. Hegel, *Lectures on the Philosophy of World History: Introduction*, trans. Nisbet (Cambridge: Cambridge University Press, 1975), 190.
69. Bernasconi, "Hegel at the Court of the Ashanti," 43; Hegel, *Lectures on the Philosophy of World History: Introduction*, 190. Hodgson confirms the presence of these sentiments in the critical texts of 1830–1831, which have not yet been published, in *Shapes of Freedom*, 85.
70. *LPWH*, 198.
71. Ibid., 205.
72. Ibid., 87.
73. Ibid., 206.
74. Ibid., 201.
75. Ibid., 208.
76. Ibid., 193.
77. Ibid., 194.
78. Hoffheimer, "Hegel, Race, Genocide," *The Southern Journal of Philosophy*, 39 (2001): 37.
79. *LPWH*, 193.
80. Hegel, *Lectures on the Philosophy of World History: Introduction*, 163.
81. Ibid., 163; Hoffheimer, "Hegel, Race, Genocide," 37–38.
82. Hegel, *Lectures on the Philosophy of World History: Introduction*, 163.
83. *LPWH*, 193.
84. Hegel, *Lectures on the Philosophy of World History: Introduction*, 190.
85. Ibid., 177.
86. Ibid., 174–190.

87. Bernasconi, "Hegel at the Court of the Ashanti," 51: "Hegel's account of Africa served as a null-point or base-point to anchor what followed."

88. Cited in Bernasconi, "Hegel at the Court of the Ashanti," 61 n. 83.

89. Rudyard Kipling, "The White Man's Burden," in *100 Poems Old and New* (Cambridge: Cambridge University Press, 1997), 111–113; Bernasconi, "Hegel at the Court of the Ashanti," 61.

90. *LPWH*, 463. Emphasis added.

91. Ibid., 463–464.

92. Ibid., 464.

93. Judith Butler, "Sexual Politics, Torture, and Secular Time," *The British Journal of Sociology* 59, no. 1 (2008): 1–2.

94. Ibid., 2.

95. *LPWH*, 85.

96. Patricia Altenbernd Johnson, "Comment for Walter Jaeschke," in *History and System: Hegel's Philosophy of History*, ed. Perkins (Albany, NY: State University of New York Press, 1984), 117.

97. Joseph McCarney, *Hegel on History* (London: Routledge, 2000), 48.

98. *LPWH*, 198.

99. Denise Ferreira da Silva, *Toward a Global Idea of Race* (Minneapolis: University of Minnesota Press, 2007), 2.

100. Ibid., xiii.

101. For an example of this kind of argument, see Hodgson, *Shapes of Freedom*, 92: "Much can be faulted in his approach, especially his account of the Asian world in its *ancient* manifestation only, not as a contemporary phenomenon, but also his neglect of Africa and the Americas. The Hegelian story would have to be written very differently today, but the central plot concerning 'shapes of freedom' remains compelling." Emphasis in original. See also, Joseph McCarney, "Hegel's Racism?: A Response to Bernasconi," *Radical Philosophy* 119 (2003): 34: "The point may be put in a more general form. This involves the view that, however hard to articulate, there is an indispensable distinction of some kind to be acknowledged between what belongs to the structure of a philosophy and what does not, between contingent facts about the lives and opinions of some Enlightenment thinkers and what is of the essence of Enlightenment philosophy. . . . The distinction in question is needed because without it, disreputable opinions, or even incidental remarks, instead of being judged to be incompatible with the logic of a philosopher's position, a sad decline from her best insights, are liable to engulf the whole."

102. Ferreira da Silva, *Global Idea of Race*, xiii.

103. Joseph R. Winters, *Hope Draped in Black: Race, Melancholy, and the Agony of Progress* (Durham: Duke University Press, 2016), 10.

Chapter 3

Karl Barth

Providence between East and West

By 1945, just over a century after Hegel delivered his *Lectures on the Philosophy of World History* for the last time, the providential world-historical order that he had envisioned therein lay in ruins in the aftermath of two world wars. European humanity, who was supposed to have embodied the consummation of the divine life in human history, had instead spent three decades destroying itself. With the detonation of the first nuclear weapon on July 16 of that year—in a test that was ironically code-named "Trinity"—the eschatological day of judgment that Hegel had heralded seemed more likely to manifest itself in the final annihilation of human civilization than in its consummation. If, as Hegel had thought, spirit had reached its full maturity in Europe, then it seemed that it might well have been a demonic spirit, intent on ushering in the end of history by condemning global humanity to nuclear obliteration.

Furthermore, by the middle of the twentieth century it had become clear that Hegel had also misjudged the supposedly "ahistorical" peoples of Africa, Asia, and the Americas, who had refused to be confined to the position outside of world history that Hegel had assigned them. Hegel's verdict that European humanity had definitively "dominated" and "overcome" the rest of the globe had proven premature, as an increasing chorus of revolutionary voices emerging from global anti-colonial movements were willing to testify.[1] As the first half of the twentieth century drew to a close, the world order that Hegel had confidently identified—barely a century earlier—as the absolute, rational, final, and *divine* purpose of history seemed to have collapsed.

Yet no sooner had the old European world order been eulogized than new candidates emerged to replace it from the East and the West. Following the cessation of hostilities in 1945, Soviet Russia and the United States—each trumpeting its own providentialist rhetoric—competed for the right to oversee the establishment of a new world order. The experience of Hungary in the 1940s bears particularly clear witness to this final collapse of the old order and the consequent struggle over the new that dominated European politics in that decade.[2]

Barely two and a half decades after the collapse of the Austro-Hungarian Empire, Hungary found itself suffering through the final months of the Second World War as the last ally of Nazi Germany. Hungary paid the price for its loyalty to the Germans through the death and destruction of its peoples, infrastructure, and lands during Hitler's increasingly desperate attempts to stave off defeat. As the Soviet army slowly advanced west toward Budapest in the last months of 1944, the retreating German and Hungarian militaries destroyed much of the country's industrial, commercial, and transportation infrastructure in order to prevent it from falling into Russian hands. In early 1945, both Hitler and Stalin became personally invested in the siege of Budapest, as victory became as much a political objective as a military one. Hitler in particular became increasingly stubborn in his desire to hold the city at all costs, repeatedly ignoring the pleas of his commanders to retreat.[3] His obstinacy produced catastrophic results: 23,624 civilians died in the siege. When Budapest fell, its German and Hungarian defenders sustained 90 percent casualties in just five days.[4] Following the war, Hungary's woes continued. With the death of nearly one million Hungarians out of a total population of less than ten million and the loss of another half a million of the country's skilled laborers and bureaucrats to emigration, the country was ill-suited for the task of reconstruction. Massive reparation payments collided with skyrocketing inflation, leaving the country destitute.[5]

With the cessation of armed conflict, the battle for control over Hungary moved to the ballot box. Underestimating Hungarian resentment of the brutal Soviet conquest, Stalin allowed democratic elections to take place in October and November of 1945. The Communist party won only 17 percent of the vote and was awarded just four of the eighteen cabinet posts in the subsequent coalition government.[6] On February 1, 1946, Hungary became a republic and elected Zoltán Tildy, a Calvinist minister, as president.

The Communists, however, were undeterred by their electoral defeat. Backed by the Hungarian military and police—and supported by the Soviet occupiers—they quickly began eliminating their political opponents through forced deportations.[7] New elections were held in August of 1947. Helped along by Communist interference, they yielded a second coalition government tilted decisively in favor of the Communists. Following the election, the Communists consolidated full control of the country, nationalizing the banks in September 1947, all factories employing more than one hundred workers in the spring of 1948, and the schools in June 1948.[8] By the elections of 1949, voters were presented with a single list of Communist candidates and the Communists, not surprisingly, won 95 percent of the vote. In August of 1949, a near duplicate of the Soviet constitution was adopted, and the country became the People's Republic of Hungary.

Given all that took place in Hungary from 1944 to 1949, one could be forgiven for overlooking a comparatively minor event that occurred in the midst of the violent collapse of the old order and the struggle to establish its successor during these tumultuous postwar years: the visit of a Swiss theologian during the spring of 1948. At the invitation of the Hungarian Reformed Church, Karl Barth, along with his colleague Charlotte von Kirschbaum, spent several weeks traveling throughout the struggling, conflict-torn country, delivering lectures, preaching sermons, and meeting with leaders from the church and theological academy. As they traveled and worked, Barth and Kirschbaum were surrounded by evidence of the devastation of the war and the rapidly deteriorating political situation. Barth preached on Good Friday in the "Great Church" in Debrecen, which, he noted, "had just been restored after sustaining heavy bomb damage."[9] He met with President Zoltán Tildy, the former Calvinist minister, mere months before Tildy was forced to resign from office and placed under house arrest for virtually the remainder of his life. He spent an entire morning in Budapest holding a public question and answer session, during which he responded to questions about the concept of the constitutional state, the relationship between Romans 13 and Revelation 13, the proper Christian attitude to a State that pretends to tolerate the church for purely instrumental reasons, and the permissibility of joining a political party in order to keep one's job. As Barth noted afterward, some of the questions were "uncannily specific."[10]

Fresh from this experience in Hungary, Barth returned to Basel in the early summer of 1948 and immediately began work on the next installment of the *Church Dogmatics*—volume III/3—which prominently featured Barth's account of the doctrine of providence in §48, "The Doctrine of Providence, Its Basis and Form," and §49, "God the Father as Lord of His Creature." It took Barth almost exactly a year to finish *Church Dogmatics* III/3, which included, in addition to the doctrine of providence, his discussions of Nothingness and of angels, demons, and the kingdom of heaven.

While working on this part-volume between the summers of 1948 and 1949, Barth found himself engaged in high-profile discussions of the new world order beginning to take shape through the tug of war between the Eastern and Western superpowers. He gave the opening address at the inaugural meeting of the World Council of Churches, became embroiled in heated public disputes with both Reinhold Niebuhr and Emil Brunner over his refusal to condemn Communism more strongly, and composed his famous essay on the church's response to Cold War politics, "The Church Between East and West," which made him a persona non-grata in many theological and political circles in Europe and the United States. I recount this historical background at the outset of this chapter because, as will become evident, the significance of Barth's doctrine of providence can only be understood when it is placed within this specific context.

In this chapter, I will argue that Barth composed his doctrine of providence in *Church Dogmatics* III/3 as a means of engaging with a European world that was only just beginning to grapple with the historical and cultural ramifications of the Holocaust and the Second World War as it found itself caught up in a new ideological conflict of global proportions.[11] Barth, like Hegel before him, deploys the doctrine of providence as a conceptual lens through which to interpret his own historical moment in light of an understanding of the nature and shape of God's relationship to the history of the cosmos between creation and eschaton. Yet the particular accounts of divine providence worked out by Hegel and Barth could scarcely be more different.

As I have argued previously, Hegel articulates a vision of providence as an abstract, teleological theory of the incarnation of the divine through historical, geographical, and anthropological progress, culminating in a vision of European man as the soteriological center and eschatological endpoint of world history—effectively divinizing the white, male European subject. Barth casts his own doctrine of providence in radical antithesis to this Hegelian vision, offering an alternative theological exposition of the relationship between divine providence, history, and humanity centered upon the particular God revealed in the covenant with Israel and the incarnation of the Jewish human being Jesus of Nazareth. While Hegel wields the doctrine of providence as a conceptual resource through which to forge a vision of European man as the divine Subject of history, Barth bases his own doctrine of providence on an alternative vision of Jesus Christ as the center and telos of world history. Barth's doctrine of providence contains a radical critique of the very theological processes by which Hegel was able to theorize the divinization of European man.

This chapter recovers these political dimensions of Karl Barth's doctrine of providence in §48 and §49 of *Church Dogmatics* III/3 by interpreting these texts against the background of his political writings from the same time period.[12] While working on *Church Dogmatics* III/3 between the summers of 1948 and 1949, Barth also produced occasional lectures, letters, and essays that directly and explicitly engaged the political and cultural issues of his day. When contextualized in light of Barth's occasional writings from 1948 and 1949, his account of providence in *Church Dogmatics* III/3 can be understood as a critique of a providential conception of Western, Christian civilization that had made National Socialism bewitchingly appealing to the church in Germany in the 1930s and was threatening to capture the political imagination of Western Christianity in the emerging East-West conflict at the end of the 1940s. Barth's reformulation of the doctrine of providence in *Church Dogmatics* III/3 is an attempt to articulate a radically Christological doctrine of providence that will be able to challenge, interrogate, and subvert the pseudo-Christian providential discourses of world-governance that lay at the heart of National Socialism and which threatened to be reborn in the Western capitalist order's opposition to Soviet Russia.

The first part of this chapter examines Barth's occasional writings from 1948 and 1949, while the second part interprets Barth's doctrine of providence in §48 and §49 of *Church Dogmatics* III/3 in light of that exposition. When read in the context of Barth's occasional writings, these paragraphs appear in a new light. In *Church Dogmatics* III/3, Barth engages in a "radical correction" of the traditional Reformed doctrine of providence.[13] This revision of the doctrine takes the form of a Christological delimitation of the divine Subject of providence.

According to Barth, Christian theologies of providence have too often been content to identify the God who providentially rules over creation with an abstract—and ultimately anonymous—divine being, with the result that the doctrine of providence has functioned as little more than a formal framework for articulating "divine world-governance."[14] Lacking specifically Christian content, this formal framework has been constantly in danger of being ideologically colonized by other interpretations of the meaning and significance of the world-historical process. Over and against this error, Barth's doctrine of providence locates the incarnation of Jesus Christ as the center and endpoint of the entire historical relationship between God and creation. In so doing, Barth attempts to foreclose upon the possibility that an abstract, teleological concept of providence might fall ideologically captive to a vision of European man as the sovereign subject of world history.

THE WORLD OF KARL BARTH, 1948–1949: BARTH BETWEEN EAST AND WEST

In the previous chapter of this study, I argued that a particular construal of the doctrine of divine providence provided the theoretical framework within which Hegel was able to theorize world history as an intrahistorical process of divine incarnation in his *Lectures on the Philosophy of World History*. I suggested that this providential incarnation of spirit in history was, on Hegel's account, an abstract, teleological process of historical, geographical, and anthropological progress, the net effect of which was to sacralize European humanity and its civilization, portraying it in eschatological terms as the apex of anthropological and cultural development and the final site of divine revelation and divine presence in human history. Within Hegel's understanding of divine providence, European man subsumes and surpasses the person and work of Jesus Christ as the final subject of the incarnation and, therefore, as the definitive subject of world history: the human subject around whose flesh all the rest of time, space, and humanity finds meaning and receives its ordered place.

Fittingly, in Barth's occasional writings from the period in which he was composing his own doctrine of providence, he repeatedly identifies almost this exact sublation of divine incarnation within a providential conception of European Christian civilization as the animating principle of the theological imagination that made National Socialism bewitchingly appealing to the church in Germany and was now threatening to help stoke the fires of Western anti-communist sentiment. Barth argues that the National Socialist crisis revealed a powerful and dangerous theological heresy at the heart of European Christianity as a whole: a distorted conception of providence that identifies the content of divine election and incarnation with the person of European man, thereby sacralizing European humanity and rejecting the election of the people of Israel and the incarnation of Jesus Christ. Viewed within this context, Barth's attempt to recast the relationship between providence, the Christian subject, and the incarnation of Jesus Christ in *Church Dogmatics* III/3 takes on politically radical significance.

Barth offers his theological analysis of the political and cultural turmoil in Europe in the late 1940s in a number of texts composed contemporaneously with *Church Dogmatics* III/3. Two particularly important documents serve to bracket Barth's political-theological efforts during this period. First, "The Christian Message in Europe Today," a lecture that Barth delivered repeatedly in the summer of 1946, offers an analysis and critique of the cultural moment in which postwar European humanity found itself after the cessation of hostilities between the Allied and the Axis powers. Second, Barth's major statement on the East-West conflict, "The Church Between East and West," which first appeared in the spring of 1949, contains Barth's argument against taking the side of the supposedly "Christian West" in the rapidly intensifying struggle between the two new global superpowers.

In between the composition of these two pieces, two important events occurred in Barth's life. First, Barth took his previously mentioned trip to Hungary in the spring and early summer of 1948, immediately prior to commencing work on his doctrine of providence. He produced a number of written pieces during his Hungarian voyage, the last of which led to a high-profile dispute with Emil Brunner. Second, in August 1948 Barth delivered a controversial opening address at the founding of the World Council of Churches in Amsterdam, the text of which drew heavily on the themes of his then in-progress doctrine of providence as it warned the newly formed council against embracing a certain sociopolitical posture in the midst of the uncertain times in which it found itself.[15] In what follows, I will examine these written materials in order to outline Barth's theological analysis of the emerging East-West conflict and the apparent "collapse" of Europe in the wake of the Second World War.

1946: "The Christian Message in Europe Today"

In the summer of 1946, Barth and Charlotte von Kirschbaum traveled to Bonn to contribute, in their own way, to the task of reconstruction in Germany. Traveling via a freighter on the Rhine, Barth and Kirschbaum "saw sunken ships, broken bridges, bombed cities one after the other" as they made their way back to the university from which Barth had been dismissed at the end of 1934 for his refusal to give the oath of loyalty to Hitler. In Bonn that summer, Barth held class "in the semi-ruins of the once stately Kurfürsten Schloss," lecturing over "the noise of the demolition crane which was breaking up the ruins."[16] When he was not teaching, Barth traveled throughout West Germany, offering public lectures to large audiences. In one of these lectures, later published under the title "The Christian Message in Europe Today," Barth attempted to help the church in Europe grapple with the significance of the Second World War and the Holocaust and their consequences for Christian identity and proclamation in relationship to the new, seemingly perilous cultural moment in which European humanity found itself.

Barth opens the essay with his own description of the postwar European cultural moment. He refuses to endorse the popular notion of a twentieth-century European collapse, arguing that it is only an equal and opposite reaction to prior narratives of European progress and cultural supremacy. Instead, Barth argues that the greatest threat to European Christianity is not Europe's cultural decline, but the colonization of Christian proclamation in the service of a providential narration of the place of Europe in world-historical time and global space. For hundreds of years, Barth asserts, "the European was left to believe that his idea of might and right, science and education, religion and the moral code must necessarily be the right one."[17] However, after two world wars were birthed from the heart of Europe, this idea has seemingly collapsed under its own weight.

How can this upheaval in Europe's self-understanding be explained? Barth writes, "At the height of European development, here in the heart of Europe, an unparalleled revolutionary movement arose—called the revolution of nihilism."[18] Barth argues that this revolution of nihilism—National Socialism—was not an aberration from European development, but its logical conclusion. Indeed, this revolution revealed something that was true of Europe as a whole. As Barth sees it, Hitler's Germany was the logical and final telos of the project of modern Europe as a whole. All of Europe was implicated in the National Socialist project. Consequently, having been rescued from itself by the Soviets and the Americans, Europe now finds itself dethroned, pushed to the sidelines, and increasingly crushed between the two emergent superpowers.

Having framed the contemporary European moment in this way, Barth moves on to discuss the place and role of the church in it. Barth outlines three concrete prescriptions for the church in Europe, intended to help the church extricate itself from its relationship with the problematic constructions of European identity that helped to bring about Europe's near self-immolation on the altar of National Socialism.

First, Barth asserts that the church must disentangle its *Christian* identity from its *European* identity: "The Christian message cannot and may not rely upon the fact that it is surrounded and sustained, as it was previously, by the glory and the pathos of the culture and the politics of a Europe rapidly rising to prominence and power."[19] For Barth, Nazi anti-Semitism was the flower that finally bloomed from the stem of European Christian civilization, revealing as its true content that which had been suppressed for centuries: the rejection of the God revealed in the election of Israel and the incarnation of Jesus Christ. By bringing this hidden truth to the surface, National Socialism bore witness to the stark contradiction between the project of constructing European civilizational identity and the content of Christian proclamation—a contradiction that the Christian church in Europe had proven itself mostly incapable of grasping up until that point. Thus, for Barth, National Socialism offered the Christian church the possibility of a moment of chilling clarity, an opportunity to free itself from its self-imposed captivity and bewitchment.

Second, Barth argues that the church must eschew all abstract, teleological narrations of the direction of history. It must not allow its proclamation to be circumscribed by narrations of European historical development—whether positive or negative. The Christian church does not possess the authority to proclaim either a coming rebirth of Europe or its immanent collapse. To endorse either message as a *Christian* message is to perpetuate the church's identification of Europe as the primary referent of Christian proclamation. The church's objective is not Europe, but the kingdom of God.[20]

Third, Barth urges the church to re-center itself upon the person of Jesus Christ as the center of its life and proclamation in order to prevent the identification of the content of the kingdom of God with a providential interpretation of the European future. Where the providential narration of European development climaxed in the rejection of the Jews—and, therefore, the rejection of Jesus—the content of the kingdom of God is nothing but Jesus Christ himself.[21] Barth underlines the contradiction between the Christian proclamation of the kingdom of God and quasi-Christian proclamations of European religious and cultural superiority. At the heart of the latter proclamations, Barth insists, lies a rejection of Israel and Jesus. This contradiction has too often gone unrealized, leading the Christian church to unwittingly proclaim the quasi-Christian good news about European humanity as though it were the gospel of Jesus Christ. This was the mistake of the *Deutsche Christens* under Hitler, a mistake that, Barth insists, must at all costs not be repeated again.

Yet it is precisely the imminent risk of a repetition and continuation of this error that deeply troubles Barth in this essay. Already in 1946, Barth sees a new ideological context emerging that will tempt the Christian church to repeat its past mistakes and once again bind its own proclamation to a quasi-Christian providential narration of world history centered elsewhere than the person of Jesus Christ. While the catastrophic events of the thirties and early forties had powerfully and terribly disabused Europe of the notion that it was the center of world history, new candidates for this role were already emerging from the East and West. Barth's insistence on the freedom and independence of Christian proclamation in Europe is not simply intended as a retrospective analysis of the errors leading to National Socialism. It is also a prospective admonition to the Christian church not to allow its proclamation to once again fall ideologically captive to a powerful narration of the direction of world history that has as its subject anything or anyone besides Jesus Christ: Christianity in Europe must be free, "not dependent on the alternatives of revolution or tradition, optimism or pessimism, *West or East*."[22]

1948: The Hungarian Voyage and the World Council of Churches

After two summers spent in Bonn, Barth stayed in Basel for the summer semester of 1948 where he began lecturing on the doctrine of providence while composing *Church Dogmatics* III/3. Just prior to this, Barth visited Hungary, touring the country at the invitation of the Hungarian Reformed Church just as the Communists were consolidating control of the government and expelling the last of their political opponents from the country. Needless to say, his Hungarian hosts expected Barth to have something to say about these matters: how would the great opponent of German National Socialism respond to the rise of Hungarian Communism? In a series of lectures delivered throughout the country, Barth reiterated many of the central themes from "The Christian Message in Europe Today," reminding the Hungarian church that its freedom and independence in Christ meant that it had to resist any and all attempts made to ideologically colonize its proclamation.

However, in the materials from Hungary, Barth adds a further level of specification to this thesis in light of the development of East-West hostilities. This is his judgment that the greater threat of such an ideological colonization of Christian discourse lies in the West as opposed to the East. As Barth sees it, Communism's open hostility toward Christianity makes it an unlikely candidate to pose this type of threat. Yet this is not to say that Barth in any way embraces Communism. As far as Barth is concerned, Communism may very well be a wolf, but it is at least not a wolf in sheep's clothing. The latter figure seemed much likely to emerge from the West, where Christian and anti-communist forces were rapidly uniting into an ideological front: the forces of the Christian West arrayed over and against the "godless" Soviets.

In his first lecture of the tour, a talk given in Sarospatak and Budapest entitled "Modern Youth: Its Inheritance and Its Responsibility," Barth repeats more forcefully the indictment of European Christian civilization that featured centrally in his lecture on the Christian message in Europe from 1946. The belief in European progress has been dealt a fatal blow by the millions and millions of lives destroyed by the two world wars: "We have seen how the morality of modern civilized man has turned out to be a terribly thin covering of ice over a sea of primitive barbarity." Indeed, "The whole conception of a Christian civilization in the West has been pitilessly exposed as an illusion."[23] As he did in 1946, Barth quickly pivots to make clear that the demise of the illusion of a "Christian civilization" should be seen, not as a threat to the Christian church, but as a liberating opportunity to free itself from ideological entanglement in the project of Western civilization.[24] Barth reaffirms his opposition to narrations of Christian identity and Christian temporal existence that are enfolded within accounts of the providential progress or decline of European civilization.

Barth offers his definitive response to the question of the proper Christian attitude toward the political upheaval then being experienced in Hungary in a second essay entitled "The Christian Community in the Midst of Political Change." Here Barth turns to the doctrine of providence as a resource for understanding contemporary political events, deploying it as a theological framework for thinking about the place of the church in relationship to the political order from the perspective of God's action in world history.

Barth argues that any attempt to think about God's relationship to contemporary political events must begin with the definitive instance of God's activity in history, the incarnation of Jesus Christ. One does not begin with a general theory of God's providential relationship to historical events, but with the particular reality of God's specific relationship to history in Jesus Christ. Barth approaches the question of political change from this Christological starting point: "The alternation and the changes of political systems stand in the light of this great change which is called Jesus Christ."[25] In a preview of one of the central themes of *Church Dogmatics* III/3, Barth asserts that, in Jesus Christ, world history is definitively determined by salvation history.

Barth goes on to argue that locating world history in relationship to and distinction from salvation history both increases the seriousness of Christian political participation and relativizes the stakes involved in earthly politics. Because world history is not independent from, but related to, salvation history, the church has a vested interest in the political life of humanity. It is a realm of serious concern for the church because it is a realm integrally related to God. Yet because world history is distinct from salvation history, human political activity is relieved of any messianic pretensions. The church is, therefore, called to serious, but critical participation in political life, marked by both a sincere commitment to politics rooted in the connection between world history and salvation history and a perpetual readiness to engage in critique and protest in recognition of the distance between world history and salvation history.

Barth's understanding of the relationship between providence and politics enables the church to remain free and independent in the midst of political change. Because world history is not salvation history, the stakes involved in political change are lessened: it is a temporal human matter, not an eternal divine one. The church is "grounded in the Word of God and committed to Him alone. . . . It cannot therefore ally itself with any political system."[26] This rejection of ideological entrapment is not an excuse for the church to withdraw from political participation, but the starting point of true concern and interest in politics.

Rather than fusing providence with either of two opposed ideological frameworks in a moment of political conflict, the church is freed to make discrete judgments about particular political issues in light of the good news revealed in Jesus Christ: "It cannot make itself responsible either for any—ism or for rejecting it." When confronting any political issue, the church will actively undertake the task of discernment and action, taking Jesus Christ as its criterion of judgment: "The question the Church asks is what difference will these things make to the men on whom God has bestowed His grace in Jesus Christ, for whom Christ died and rose again?"[27] In sum, Barth's Christological conception of divine providence provides him with critical resources to protect the political activity of the church from ideological capture while also enabling the church to embrace rigorous and critical political participation.

Barth's theological position led him to some unpopular conclusions about the Communist takeover in Hungary. In "The Reformed Church behind the 'Iron Curtain,'" a report on his Hungarian journey published upon his return, Barth made these conclusions explicit. As Barth remarked in a letter to Alphons Koechlin, the report was met with a "shower of rotten eggs and dead cats" from the Swiss press.[28] The most notable response to Barth's views on the Hungarian situation came from Emil Brunner, who wrote an open letter to Barth sharply criticizing him for not opposing Communism in the way he had opposed National Socialism. In his letter, Brunner rehearsed a harsh indictment of Barth's political position, accusing him of showing deference to Communism by minimizing and overlooking its necessary commitment to totalitarianism. As Brunner saw it, Barth—the great critic of the church's collaboration with Hitler—had made himself the "spokesman" of the collaborationist position with respect to another, equally dangerous variety of anti-human, anti-Christian totalitarianism.[29]

In his response dated June 6, 1948, Barth wastes no time in getting to the point: "Dear Emil Brunner,—You do not seem to understand."[30] The bulk of Barth's defense rests upon the distinction he makes between the situation with National Socialism in the 1930s and the present situation with Communism. Where Brunner wants to minimize any difference between them, Barth emphasizes the uniqueness of the two moments. In order to do so, Barth draws a distinction between the political problem of totalitarianism and the theological problem of the colonization of Christian discourse by a political ideology.

As a theologian, Barth approaches these issues in light of this latter perspective, which leads him to offer two very different verdicts about Communism and National Socialism. Barth first explains the logic of his determined resistance to National Socialism: "What made [National Socialism] interesting from the Christian point of view was that it was a spell which notoriously revealed its power to overwhelm our souls, to persuade us to believe in its lies and to join in its evil-doings."[31] When one understands the true danger of National Socialism in this way, Barth contends, it becomes clear that Communism does not come close to posing the same sort of threat, as Communism has met with widespread rejection and disapproval from the Christian church.[32] The difference between Communism and National Socialism is not, as Brunner suggests, merely the difference between two different shades of totalitarianism. Rather, it is the difference between a political ideology that has aroused widespread Christian opposition and one that proved itself to be incredibly effective at colonizing, subjugating, and systematically distorting Christian belief and practice in support of an anti-Christian agenda.

Furthermore, in addition to asserting the fundamental *dissimilarity* between the dangers posed by Communism and National Socialism to the Christian church, Barth hints at a worrying *similarity* between the bewitchment of the German church by National Socialism and the ease with which the Christian church in the United States and Western Europe has been swept up inside of "Western Christian" civilization's opposition to Communism.[33] Barth would articulate this second point more explicitly just a few months later when he gave the opening address at the inaugural assembly of the World Council of Churches.

In August 1948, Barth traveled to Amsterdam to deliver his address to the World Council of Churches on the theme "Man's Disorder and God's

Design."[34] In a speech that Barth could not have expected to garner much praise, he presented a critique of the conference theme—arguing that it should instead be "God's Design and Man's Disorder"—and called into question the mission and work of the newly formed ecumenical body on theological grounds. Barth feared that the council had insufficiently guarded itself against the temptation to envision God's providential rule of the cosmos as bound to, and, therefore, controlled by, the Christian church. This address provides yet another example of how Barth engaged the doctrine of providence as a key resource for negotiating sociopolitical existence in the very moment at which he was composing the volume on providence in the *Church Dogmatics*. Once again, his understanding of the relationship between providence and Christology proves to be the critical center that fuels his theological critique.

Barth opens his address by informing his audience that the conference theme "the world's disorder and God's design" was a non-starter. Nothing can be gained by beginning with an account of the present moment of cultural, political, and economic crisis and then turning to God's design for some sort of solution. To attempt to build up from certain conceptions of the world's disorder—and various proposals for ameliorating that disorder—to a picture of God's order can only be an idolatrous Babel-like endeavor. Barth insists that the starting point for the conference proceedings must be "God's design" and not "Man's Disorder."

However, not content simply to invert the conference theme, Barth also suggests that the theological meaning and significance of "God's design" must itself be carefully and critically examined. His remarks on this point take the form of an explication of the doctrine of providence in which Barth draws out the political stakes involved in the accurate formulation of the doctrine.

Barth's central thesis is that the person of Jesus Christ is wholly determinative of God's providential design: "'God's design' really means his plan; that is, his already come, already victorious, already founded Kingdom in all its majesty—our Lord Jesus Christ." This rules out an otherwise tempting, but deeply distorted, interpretation of God's providence: "'God's design,' therefore, does not mean the existence of the church in the world, its task in relation to the world's disorder, its outward and inward activity as an instrument for the amelioration of human life, or finally the result of this activity in the Christianization of all humanity and, consequently, the setting up of an order of justice and peace embracing our whole planet."[35] This latter account of providence is not only theologically inaccurate but politically dangerous.

By construing the church as "a continuation of the incarnation of the Word of God," Christians are tempted to imagine that "the power of God's providence would have fallen under the sovereign power and administrative control of Christendom and enslaved mankind would have to expect its salvation from us—from our clear grasp of the world-historical situation." This opinion is "the root and ground of all human disorder: the dreadful, godless, ridiculous opinion that man is the Atlas who is destined to bear the dome of heaven on his shoulders."[36] If the church's understanding of God's providential design is not thoroughly determined by the authoritative revelation of that design in Jesus Christ, then "it might turn out that what we think we ought to show the world under the authority of God's word is a program like other programs, and—who knows?—only too closely related to the programs of particular parties, classes, and nations." Barth issues a pointed warning: "We must be very sure that in carrying out our prophetic task we really point to *God's* Kingdom, and not, though in the best of faith, to some other kingdom."[37] Any attempt to understand God's providential design and activity in the world apart from the paradigmatic instance of that design and action in the incarnation of Jesus Christ opens the door to precisely the kind of ideological colonization of Christian proclamation that the church in Germany embraced under National Socialism. In the present conflict between East and West, Barth worries that the church will repeat this exact same error.

1949: "The Church between East and West"

First published on February 6, 1949—just as Barth was pressing toward the end of *Church Dogmatics* III/3—"The Church Between East and West" was Barth's attempt to draw together the various lines of argument that had appeared in his letters, lectures, and essays over the past several years into a cohesive statement on the East-West conflict. In this essay, the close connections between Barth's political and dogmatic views are on full display, as the core theological rationale that Barth presents for his position on the East-West conflict is an almost exact reproduction of the fundamental theme of his doctrine of providence in *Church Dogmatics* III/3: world history and salvation history are bound together in Jesus Christ.

Barth's argument about the East-West conflict directly follows from this dogmatic position. Because world history and salvation history are *bound together* in Jesus Christ, the church is called to vigorous engagement with worldly politics and is obligated to take the risk of judgment and action in the political realm. However, because world history and salvation history are bound together *in Jesus Christ*, the church must remain free and independent in its political work and witness, making Jesus Christ the sole criterion for its judgment and action. This necessarily rules out the possibility that the church can rely on any human program, philosophy, or ideology as an alternative criterion. For this reason, Barth refuses to take sides in the East-West conflict, and is sharply critical of those who want to align Christian judgment and action with anti-communist ideology.

In the opening two paragraphs of the essay, Barth lays the theological groundwork upon which he will build his argument. First, he asserts that the church is called to serious engagement with the East-West situation. Barth is not in any way a quietist.[38] God is concerned about the unfolding of human political life within world history because that history has been joined to God's own history in the incarnation of Jesus Christ. Second, Barth contends that, in its serious engagement with the East-West problem, the church must measure any answer it might wish to formulate against the one true criterion of judgment: Jesus Christ.[39] For Barth, world history is illuminated by God's eternal history at the single point at which God Godself entered into it in Jesus Christ. To see any event in world history clearly, Christians must view it in the light of Christ. Having laid this theological foundation, Barth proceeds to engage the world-historical matter at hand.

Barth outlines two distinct aspects from which the East-West conflict must be viewed. Considered from the first aspect, it is a political struggle for world dominance between Russia and the United States. It is a struggle between the two offspring of Europe, who have become fully grown and want to take their mother's place.[40] As Barth sees it, the Christian response to this first aspect of the conflict is quite simple: the church must not act out of fear, must not take part in the conflict, and must be there for the victims produced by the struggle. Yet there is, Barth thinks, a higher and more complex form of the conflict than this world-political struggle, the Christian response to which is not so easily discerned.

This second, more complex aspect of the East-West conflict defies concise description. It is a comprehensive dispute about "two textures of life, in which not merely America and Russia, but . . . a great part of the world is involved."[41] Both sides accuse the other of the most severe inhumanity, nourished on the mistruths of a false faith: West charges East with treating humanity like an economic automaton and subscribing to a demonic faith in social progress, while East charges West with hypocritically espousing a spiritual conception of humanity and a faith in democracy which is only ideological camouflage for the reality that Western humanity is dominated by the power of "anonymous capital."[42] Barth uses the theological framework laid out in his introduction to outline a Christian response to this second form of the conflict.

Barth's basic argument is that because world history and salvation history do not connect at any point other than in Jesus Christ—who as a Jew is not a partisan of either East or West—it is impossible to identify the cause of God with the cause of either side. Rather than choosing between East and West, the church must seek a third way.[43]

Barth anticipates that his audience might respond to his assertion with a certain degree of disbelief: how could the man who had written in 1938 that every Czech soldier who fought against the Nazis would "stand and fall not only for the freedom of Europe, but also for the Christian church," now advocate for ecclesial neutrality in the face of Communism?[44] Barth attempts to preempt such criticism with a lengthy comparison of the two situations, arguing for a fundamental continuity between his differing responses to each: "Ten years ago we said that the Church is, and remains, the Church, and must not therefore keep an un-Christian silence. Today we say that the Church is, and remains, the Church, and must not therefore speak an un-Christian word."[45] He cites three major differences between the two situations.

First, National Socialism presented the church with a "single and absolutely clear-cut political and spiritual menace . . . a mixture of madness and crime in which there was no trace of reason." However, the present conflict is different in that the church finds itself torn between two sides, each of which presents its own temptation and threat to the church: "To turn against the wild boar then was not to commit the folly of exposing one's rear to the wolf."[46] Barth shows no love for Communism.[47] Nevertheless, Barth admits that Communism represents a genuine, if failed, attempt to address the social problem that plagues the West. Therefore, Barth suggests, the West's rejection of Communism will smack of hypocrisy so long as the West allows massive social inequality to persist within its own realm. The cause of God—which in Christ is also the cause of genuine humanity—cannot be the cause of the West as long as the East can accuse the West of inhumanity with any degree of truth.[48]

Second, Russian Communism is openly godless, whereas National Socialism was founded upon something far more dangerous: false godliness. The church's true enemy, Barth insists, is not the non-Christian, but the anti-Christ: "Communism, as distinguished from Nazism, has not done, and by its very nature cannot do, one thing: it has never made the slightest attempt to reinterpret or falsify Christianity."[49] If persecuted by godless Communism, Barth argues, the church's duty is not to respond with a call to arms, but to joyfully persevere and fearlessly proclaim the good news of Jesus Christ.[50] Furthermore, the confrontation with godlessness presents the church with an opportunity for self-examination. When the godless reject the Christian message, the church must make sure that the fault does not lie with the truthfulness and consistency of the message it has proclaimed: "Where, then, is the Christian West that could look straight into the eyes of the obviously un-Christian East even with a modicum of good conscience?"[51] In this instance, the church must be sure that its message has not been adulterated by confusing its loyalty to Jesus Christ with an unquestioning identification of itself with Western civilization.

The last difference between the National Socialist and Communist moments is the cost involved in speaking out. While Barth's vehement rejection of National Socialism was almost universally unpopular at the time, to speak a word against Communism today would be to do nothing more than pour one's own small can of gasoline on the West's raging bonfire of cheap and idle slander about the East. Furthermore, to speak out against National Socialism was to oppose the anti-Christ. However, to turn against the East in the present conflict would be in fact to encourage the idolatrous pretensions of the West. If Christians are going to pray for the destruction of the East, Barth argues, then they "should have to pray in the same breath for the destruction of the bulwarks of the Western Anti-Christ as well."[52] Christians should be immediately suspicious when their Christian duty seemingly requires no effort or sacrifice, but seems to flow perfectly in sync with the riptide of Western anti-communist hysteria.

In each of these three distinctions between National Socialism and Communism, Barth appeals to the same theological criterion to demonstrate the fundamental continuity between his differing judgments: Jesus Christ, the Word of God made flesh. First, Jesus Christ's humanity exposes the West's inhumanity with regards to the social problem and prevents the church from identifying the cause of God with the cause of the West. Second, Barth's extreme partisanship against Nazism emerged because it threatened to colonize and subvert the church's one and only criterion of judgment, Christ himself. National Socialism's rejection of the Jews, of Jesus' Jewish human flesh, and, therefore, of the God revealed in that flesh, exposed its anti-Christian core. Therefore, to oppose the Nazis was to oppose the anti-Christ, while to oppose the Russians may very well be to encourage the West's anti-Christic tendencies. Third, Christian political action that centers itself upon Jesus Christ requires speaking the truth of Jesus Christ in the midst of the lordless powers. This is what Barth urged the church to do in the 1930s. However, it is decidedly inconsistent with the cheap, idle, and useless chatter requested of the church in the East-West conflict.

In sum, Barth deploys the central theme of his doctrine of providence—that world history and salvation history are held together in Christ—as a critical lens through which to make visible the differences between National Socialism and Communism, render intelligible his political judgment about the place and role of the church in the East-West conflict, and expose the threat posed to the Christian church and its message by the idea of a "Christian West." Barth argues that a truly Christological politics, which judges world-historical events in the light of the history of salvation revealed in the person of Jesus Christ, must be a politics of genuine humanity. He therefore concludes that the positive task of the church between East and West is to place humanity before ideology.[53]

Barth's doctrine of providence provides the basic theological rationale for his interpretation of the political and cultural situation of Europe at the end of the first half of the twentieth century. World history and salvation history are held together in the person of Jesus Christ in a dialectical relationship. First, the two histories are *distinct*. Therefore, there can be no sacralization or divinization of human politics, culture, or civilization. Yet, second, the two histories are *related* in Christ. Therefore, there can be no independent or natural theological account of human politics, culture, or civilization that can function authoritatively for the Christian church. While world history and salvation history are intimately connected, their point of connection is Jesus Christ alone. Therefore, Christ is the final criterion of Christian political judgment and action. In *Church Dogmatics* III/3, Barth articulates the constructive dogmatic account of providence that underlies this political-theological account of the church's role in the world-historical moment in which it found itself at the mid-point of the twentieth century.

THE WORK OF KARL BARTH, 1948–1949: THE DOCTRINE OF PROVIDENCE BETWEEN EAST AND WEST

Reading §48 and §49 of *Church Dogmatics* III/3 in light of Barth's essays and speeches on the East-West conflict enables a new interpretation of the text, both in terms of its formal significance and its theological content. Recent studies of Barth's doctrine of providence have variously interpreted the text as a "lengthy, theological prayer," as an intervention in the history of Reformed theology, or as a theological experiment in personalist philosophy.[54] While there is a degree of truth in each of these perspectives, all of them heavily sanitize Barth's doctrine of providence, stripping it of any political significance. Given Barth's extensive use of the doctrine of providence in his occasional writings in 1948 and 1949, it would be highly unusual if the dogmatic formulation of that doctrine that he composed at the exact same time as these occasional pieces could be interpreted without substantial attention to its political significance.

Whatever else it may be, *Church Dogmatics* III/3 is also—and, given Barth's own sentiments on the subject, perhaps even first and foremost—an exercise in theological ideology critique which seeks to unmask and oppose the dangerous distortion of the doctrine of providence that allowed European humanity to substitute itself into the place of Israel and Jesus as the center and telos of God's providential activity in world history. Over and against this idolatrous conception of providence—which Barth traces from its roots in early Reformed and Lutheran theology all the way to its flowering in National Socialism—Barth enacts a "radical correction" of the doctrine in *Church Dogmatics* III/3. This correction takes the form of a Christological delimitation and specification of the divine Subject of the doctrine of providence. Where the Christian tradition has too often adopted an abstract and formal account of the identity of the God whose lordship over creation is the subject matter of the doctrine of providence, Barth reconstructs the doctrine of providence in light of the fact that the identity of this God—as well as the nature and purpose of God's sovereignty and providential lordship—has been revealed in the incarnation of Jesus Christ. Barth's Christological specification of the divine Subject of providence prevents the doctrine from becoming an abstract theological framework of divine world-governance whose Subject might just as easily be some other god—or some other human being.[55]

§48: The Doctrine of Providence, Its Basis and Form

In §48, Barth outlines the general theological framework within which he will articulate the four specific aspects of the doctrine of providence in §49. Given the deep confusion about the doctrine of providence that Barth observes in the history of Christian theology, he uses §48 to carefully outline the dogmatic and methodological "rules of engagement" that must be observed when discussing the doctrine.

Barth argues that the Christian tradition has too often identified the divine Subject of the doctrine of providence with an anonymous deity whose chief characteristic is an omnipotent divine will, rather than the triune God revealed in Jesus Christ. Lacking this substantial basis and content, the doctrine has functioned as little more than a formal framework for the articulation of an abstract concept of "divine world-governance," which has been perpetually in danger of being detached from its original content—the triune God revealed in Jesus—and given a new referent. This in fact came to pass, Barth asserts, when modern Christian humanity idolatrously claimed for itself the place previously occupied by the Christian God, fashioning itself as the center of the providential economy, the telos of world-historical development, and the sovereign power who rules over all created time and space.

In §48, Barth outlines a theological approach to providence that rules out such a misappropriation of the doctrine. Rejecting all attempts to abstractly correlate divine history and creation history, Barth develops an approach to providence rooted in the paradigmatic instance of the historical relationship between God and creation: the incarnation of Jesus Christ.[56] Barth outlines this account in three stages in §48, discussing in succession the concept of divine providence, the Christian belief in providence, and the Christian doctrine of providence.

Barth opens *Church Dogmatics* III/3 with his basic definition of providence: "By 'providence' is meant the superior dealings of the Creator with his creation, the wisdom, omnipotence, and goodness with which He maintains and governs in time this distinct reality according to the counsel of His own will."[57] Given that its basic content includes both God and creation, the question naturally follows whether the doctrinal home of providence ought to lie in the doctrine of God or the doctrine of creation. In answering this question, Barth outlines a typology of the various aspects of the relationship between God and creation.

The first aspect of the relationship between God and the world is God's eternal decree concerning his will for creation, which Barth classifies as *predestination*. It rightly belongs to the doctrine of God because it is first and foremost a matter of the eternal election of the Son of God.[58] Because God's election takes place from all eternity, it does not presuppose the act of creation. Providence, however, does presuppose creation. Providence, therefore, exists within the second aspect of the relationship between God and the world: the *execution* of God's eternal decree.[59] Barth, therefore, does not ground the doctrine of providence in the doctrine of God, departing from medieval scholastics like Peter Lombard, Bonaventure, and, to a certain extent, Thomas Aquinas.[60] Providence, as the doctrine of the relation between Creator and creature, must reside within the doctrine of creation.

Providence is not, however, simply identical with the doctrine of creation. The subject matter of providence begins where creation ends: providence concerns the ongoing history of the completed work of creation. However, this history of creation itself is actually two closely related but nevertheless distinct *histories*: the history of the covenant and the history of the creature. The first thing that follows from the act of creation is the history of the covenant, or salvation history, whose content is the intrahistorical execution of God's eternal election of the creature. Running parallel to this first history—but always already determined by it—is the history of the creature. The creaturely covenant partner of God is distinct from God, having its own being that, while determined wholly by God's election, is not exhausted by it.[61] However, the creature is wholly dependent on the Creator for its creaturely life. God must, therefore, be active in accompanying, surrounding, and sustaining the creature in its basic historical existence. Invoking a variation on his doctrine of creation, Barth states that the history of the creature is the external basis of the history of the covenant, and this external basis is the territory of providence.[62] God's providence is not a property of God's own nature. It is not a part of God's eternal decree of election. It is not even primarily responsible for the execution of that decree within created time and space. Rather, God's providence maintains the basic creaturely existence of the covenant partner of God. Providence concerns God's relationship to world history, but only as world history is itself always and already determined by salvation history.

Having externally delimited the place of the doctrine of providence in relationship to the doctrines of God and creation, Barth turns to address the doctrine itself. Providence concerns the Creator's faithful and constant association with the creature "to precede, accompany, and follow it, preserving, cooperating, and overruling, in all that it does and all that happens to it."[63] Barth clarifies this definition by making three strict delimitations regarding the basis, object, and substance of the belief in providence. Each of these seeks to prevent the use of the doctrine as an ideological framework through which to sacralize a certain conception of the human subject.

The basis of the belief in providence is strictly and only faith. The only possibility for rightly affirming belief in God's providential care for creation is when one does so in response to having first received the Word of God. Barth, therefore, sharply rejects any formulation of the belief in providence that would make human judgments about God's providential activity determinative. If belief in providence was grounded in the believing human subject, Barth contends, then it would become dangerously unstable.[64] As Barth goes on to explain, this instability consists in the fact that the doctrine whose content is the lordship of *God* over creation will always threaten to deteriorate into a doctrine whose content is the lordship of the *believing human subject* over creation. The confession of providence, if it is not a confession of faith, stands poised to become "only the believer's confession of himself."[65] The Christian subject then becomes the one who is capable of taking the measure of all things.

To this specification about the basis of the belief in providence, Barth adds a second delimitation of that belief, this time with regard to its object. The object of the belief in providence is simply God Godself. Here too, Barth is concerned to rule out a conception of belief in providence that would reduce God's action in history to a postulate under the control and judgment of the believing human subject. Echoing his warnings from "The Christian Message in Europe Today" and "Modern Youth," Barth points out the danger in binding a conception of divine providence to an abstract theory of the shape and direction of history. Belief in providence can never be allowed to slide subtly into belief in a "human system of history invented by man."[66] If this were to happen, then theological discourse about providence would merely become a way for humanity to cover its own judgments about history with a thin religious veneer.

Having clarified the basis and object of the belief in providence, Barth turns to the final and most significant specification of this belief: its substance.[67] Here Barth initiates the Christological turn in his formulation of the doctrine. The substance of the Christian belief in providence is faith in Christ. The Christological determination of the doctrine of providence definitively rules out the possibility that any other human subject might position itself at the center of God's providential action in history. Belief in providence "is not a general form which might have a very different content."[68] Only at this one point, in Jesus Christ, does the Christian belief in providence have any grounding or merit, because it is the one point at which world history, salvation history, and divine history can be seen to align.[69] All other attempts to illuminate world history with the light of salvation history are doomed to fail, especially those that would attempt to refract the light of salvation history through a human being other than Jesus Christ.

At the end of his discussion of the Christological substance of the belief in providence, Barth offers one of his few explicit reflections on the political stakes involved in his dogmatic formulation of the doctrine of providence. Barth rehearses a genealogy of the concept of providence that runs from John Calvin to Adolf Hitler, in which he identifies the theological error that allowed the church in Germany to fall under National Socialism's spell: the use of an abstract conception of divine lordship as the basis and starting point of the doctrine of providence.

Both Lutheran and Reformed theologians treated God's lordship over the history of creation as one of the central points of Christian doctrine. However, they did so "without attempting to say what is the meaning and purpose of this lordship." Instead, they understood it only as "the act of a superior and absolutely omniscient, omnipotent, and omnioperative being." Without realizing it, they constructed magisterial accounts of divine providence upon this "empty shell."[70] Barth marvels at the fact that entire generations of Protestant theologians seemingly forgot to ask what the doctrine of God's lordship has to do with Jesus. In these older orthodox traditions, the doctrine of providence became a theological Trojan horse, containing a dangerous void at its center that should have been filled only by Christ.

When not specifically tied to the triune God revealed in the human being Jesus Christ, providence became a formal framework for mapping the relationship between God and the world that could just as easily be tied to some other God or some other human being. In this way, Barth asserts, "Belief in history and its immanent demons could replace faith in God's providence, and the word 'providence' could become a favorite one on the lips of Adolf Hitler."[71] Barth concludes that it was the abstract conceptions of the older Reformed theologies of providence that first set the belief in providence on this path. By placing Jesus Christ at the center of the doctrine of providence, Barth fills the divine-human abstraction implanted in the heart of the doctrine by previous generations of theologians. The critical intent of this decision is clear: if Jesus Christ is the subject of world history, no other construction of the human may lay claim to that title.

Barth closes his introduction to the doctrine of providence in §48 with a brief exposition of the content of a truly *Christian* doctrine of providence—meaning one which is founded upon a Christological basis. Here he explicates the fundamental theme of his doctrine of providence which will guide his detailed exposition of the doctrine in §49. This theme corresponds exactly to the theological position from which he was at that very time deriving his political judgments about the East-West conflict in his occasional writings: the history of the covenant and the history of creation—salvation history and world history—are held together in Jesus Christ. The Christian doctrine of providence, for Barth, contains no obscurity about the will and working of God in history, because that God is not a "mere supreme being," but the particular God who acted to fulfill the covenant in Christ through Jesus' lowly death on a cross.[72] The God who preserves, accompanies, and rules over the creature is the same God who has elected that creature to be God's covenant partner. The Christian doctrine of providence begins with the recognition that the history of creation is ordered to and determined by the history of the covenant. World history gains its meaning and purpose from this fact.[73] The significance and value of world history can only be found here in God's covenant faithfulness revealed in the covenant with Israel and in the incarnation of Jesus Christ.

The history of creation, though determined by the history of the covenant, is not identical to it or exhausted by it. Indeed, Barth suggests, the history of the covenant is only one thin line running inconspicuously through the "confusion" of the history of creation, which is composed of a multitude of "apparently much more powerful and conspicuous lines."[74] The doctrine of providence addresses the way in which, despite all appearances, God causes the many lines of world history (the history of the creature) to "cooperate" and be "coordinated" and "integrated," with the one thin line of salvation history (the history of the covenant).[75]

Barth proceeds to lay out two crucial qualifications to his claim about the coordination, integration, and cooperation of the history of the creature with the history of the covenant. First, it is only possible through grace. It is always and only the direct work of God that causes this to happen and never any creaturely possession, property, or potentiality. Creation has no cause for boasting.[76] The history of the creature cannot in any way participate in the history of the covenant apart from God's grace. However, the history of the creature really is the external basis of the history of the covenant as God graciously causes it to be so.

Barth's second qualification about the coordination, integration, and cooperation of creaturely history and salvation history is that this coordination, integration, and cooperation takes place definitively in the incarnation of Jesus Christ. The doctrine of providence does not look to a theory or system for its conception of God's relationship to world history. It looks to a person. The history of the covenant and the history of the creature cannot be abstractly related to each other. They intersect very concretely in the person of Jesus. When the doctrine of providence addresses the cooperation of the creature in God's saving work in history, it can look nowhere else but Jesus.[77] From the light cast by God's self-revelation in Jesus Christ, world history is illuminated—but only by this very particular light. Therefore, human judgments about the activity of God in world history can be made, but only ever falteringly, partially, and fragmentarily, in total dependence on the Holy Spirit. The attempt to abstract God's general activity in world history from God's specific work in Jesus Christ leads, not to a Christian doctrine of providence, but to the elevation of the human subject into the place of Christ as the center and telos of divine action in history.[78]

In §48, Barth gives an account of the Christian doctrine of providence whose starting point is not world history in the abstract, but the very concrete and specific line of salvation history that runs inconspicuously through this larger whole. At the core of Barth's argument is his conviction that knowledge of God's providence is strictly and only possible on the basis of revelation: he argues that the shape and purpose of God's action in history is discernable in no other way than by looking, first, at the covenant with Israel and the incarnation of Jesus Christ, and then back from these events to world history in general. Any other approach to conceiving of God's relationship to world history cannot be called a Christian doctrine of providence.

§49: God the Father as Lord of His Creature

In §49, "God the Father as Lord of His Creature," Barth articulates his constructive account of the doctrine of providence in detail, carrying out the Christological reconfiguration of the doctrine which he outlined in §48. Barth grafts his Christological revision of the material content of providence onto the Reformed tradition's classic scheme of the doctrine, adopting the three-part structure of *conservatio*, *concursus*, and *gubernatio*, while adding a fourth section: "The Christian under the Universal Lordship of God the Father."[79] Barth maintains the formal scheme of the doctrine as it had been developed in Reformed and Lutheran traditions, while revolutionizing its content in light of his steadfast determination to "hold fast at all costs . . . to the Christological thread."[80] In what follows, I will trace this Christological thread as it runs through each of the four major sections of Barth's doctrine of providence, showing at each point how it enables Barth to formulate an account of the doctrine with the critical potential to unmask and critique the ideological distortion and subversion of Christian proclamation and witness in Europe in Barth's day.

In each of the three main aspects of the doctrine of providence, Barth argues that a Christological revision of the content of divine preservation/*conservatio*, accompaniment/*concursus*, and ruling/*gubernatio* resolves a problem that has traditionally plagued each of these aspects of the doctrine, respectively. Thus, with his account of divine preservation, Barth attempts to resolve the seeming contradiction between God's potentially unlimited power to preserve the creature and the reality of the creature's limited preservation. In regards to the divine accompaniment, Barth's Christological reconstrual of the doctrine allows him to articulate a non-competitive account of divine and human agency within the operations of *concursus*. Finally, Barth's Christological account of divine government addresses questions about the nature of divine sovereignty over creation. However, Barth's concerns are not solely dogmatic and philosophical.

At each of these points, Barth's Christological renovation of the traditional conception of providence bears significant political ramifications. Barth's resolution of the contradiction between God's unlimited power and the creature's limited preservation rules out a providential conception of creaturely self-preservation that leads to the "titanism" of the creature.[81] Barth's non-competitive account of *concursus* guards against an account of providence that would blindly stamp creaturely activity with the *imprimatur* of the divine. Finally, his strict Christological delimitation of the divine world-government forecloses upon the possibility that God's divine rule over the cosmos could be articulated as an abstract schema of global governance that could be associated with ruling powers other than the triune God. At each point, therefore, Barth's articulation of the doctrine of providence serves to critique the theological imagination that he identifies in his occasional writings as enabling the church's captivity to National Socialist and anti-communist ideologies: a providential vision of the Christian, Western subject as an incarnation of the activity and cause of God in world history.

The first affirmation of the Christian doctrine of providence is that God preserves the creature. God does this, according to Barth, by sustaining the existence of the creature and providing continuity to its existence.[82] In this formal definition, Barth aligns himself with the Reformed tradition's understanding of the divine *conservatio*.[83] However, he quickly proceeds to offer an important Christological qualification of that formal definition that differentiates him from the tradition. The divine Subject of preservation is not an anonymous deity characterized primarily by an abstract, omnipotent will, but the triune God revealed in the covenant. Therefore, the divine power that preserves the creature is not ambiguous with regards to its basis or purpose: "The power in which He sustains the creature is the mercy with which in His Son Jesus Christ He is revealed and active within creation."[84] Over and against the tendency of the older Reformed thinkers, Barth refuses to separate God's sustaining power and God's loving mercy.[85]

The preservation of the creature by God is not primarily, therefore, a matter of a general and metaphysical causal necessity, but of the particular will of God to be in covenant relation with the creature. Consequently, the doctrinal basis of divine preservation is not an abstract doctrine of God, but Christology. Jesus is the one in whom the preservation of the creature's existence has its foundation.[86] This God, and no other, can claim to be the source of creation's preservation. Therefore, there can be no ambiguity about the character or purpose of God's preserving work. It is, and can only be, an expression of God's love.[87] Barth grounds this reconfiguration of the relationship between God's power and God's mercy and love in the witness of Scripture. When Scripture talks about preservation, Barth argues, it is always tied to the history of the covenant. There is little attention paid to a general, abstract preservation of creaturely existence as such. The Old Testament addresses divine preservation primarily as God's particular preservation of the people of Israel. The New Testament identifies Jesus Christ as the one who preserves the creature so that the creature may participate in the covenant.[88] The basis of the divine preservation of the creature is not the omnipotent power of an abstract deity, but God's self-emptying love revealed in Jesus Christ.

Reading Barth's exposition of divine preservation against the background of his sociopolitical context reveals the critical potential latent within his Christological revision of the concept: a Christological construal of divine preservation enables an account of the *finite* and *limited* preservation of the creature that does not stand as an affront to the power or quality of God's preserving action. If the basis of the divine preservation of the creature were God's unlimited power, then the limitation of that preservation would problematically call into question either the efficacy of that power or the disposition of God toward the creature: if, given God's unlimited power, God could preserve the creature indefinitely, then why does God not do this? Barth's Christological approach to preservation resolves this apparent contradiction. There is no incongruity between the limited, finite existence of the creature and God's eternal preservation of the creature because the two converge in Jesus Christ. As Barth sees it, the creature is preserved in its limited time so that in that time it may come to participate in Christ's eternal life. In that finite preservation the creature truly can participate in eternal life.[89]

Because the preservation of the creature is ordered toward the salvation of the creature in Christ, the creature is free to embrace his or her limits and finitude and has no need to attempt to overcome them through projects of self-salvation.[90] The creature is free to admit its need and to embrace its creaturely finitude, and, therefore, must offer a definitive "No!" to all projects of self-salvation. Therefore, the doctrine of providence cannot provide a pretext for the creature to bind itself to the work of God in the world, making itself the locus of divine activity and presence in history. The creature can resist the temptation to construe itself as the incarnation of the divine in history and the subject of its own world-historical drama of salvation, because it already participates fully in the salvation accomplished through the incarnation of

Jesus Christ. Thus construed, the doctrine of providence becomes a way to affirm creaturely limits, rather than an idolatrous way for the creature to view history from the standpoint of the Creator.[91] Providence is not a framework for articulating immanent processes of creaturely divinization, but for affirming and embracing the finite, limited character of creaturely existence in the knowledge that the God revealed in Jesus Christ will uphold and sustain the creature within those limits and guide the creature to eternal life through participation in Christ.

Barth's Christological delimitation of the nature and shape of God's *accompaniment* of the creature—the second major facet of Barth's account of the doctrine—prevents divine and human agency from being placed in a competitive relationship. As in his account of preservation, the resolution of this problem not only is a matter of dogmatic or philosophical coherence but also bears significant political consequences. For—Barth believes—if creaturely and divine agency are cast in competition, then the doctrine of *concursus* will always be torn between the two poles of synergism and monism. When, in the former case, divine *concursus* becomes a way to articulate an abstract synergy between divine and creaturely historical action, then humanity will always be tempted—as Hegel was—to imagine its own history as "the history of God" and the human being as a "God-man."[92]

The doctrine of divine accompaniment addresses God's lordship in relationship to creaturely agency and freedom. It is the next step beyond the doctrine of preservation. God's providential care of the creature extends past a mere preservation of its existence. God does not preserve the basic existence of the creature and then leave it to its own devices.[93] Instead, God actively coexists and cooperates *with* the creature in the creature's activity, enabling that activity to be free and autonomous. God's accompaniment of the creature coexists with and affirms the autonomous activity of the creature.[94]

Concursus emerged as an alternative to two problematic conceptions of the Creator-creation relationship: one that made creation independent of the Creator after the completion of the act of creation—as in deism—and another that merged Creator and creation into an undifferentiated whole—as in pantheism. Barth's doctrine of providence follows a middle way between these two alternatives, attempting to do justice to both the co-existence of and the distinction between divine and creaturely action.[95]

In the attempt to formulate an account of the divine accompaniment of the creature that respects both God's "majesty" and the creature's "autonomy and dignity," Christian thinkers have overwhelmingly relied upon the Aristotelian distinction between primary and secondary causation to render the distinction between divine and creaturely activity intelligible.[96] Identifying God with the *causa prima* and the creature with the *causa secundae*, older Reformed dogmaticians attempted to place the two in non-competitive relationship, rejecting both a synergistic account that tried to combine the two causes into a *tertium quid* and a monistic account that rejected one in favor of the other.

The problem with these efforts is that they subordinated the particular content of Christian revelation to a formal schema of Aristotelian causality. Thus, while the older dogmatic accounts of *concursus* were formally correct, there was nothing in the content of their visions of God and the creature that made them specifically Christian. As it was predominately formulated, *concursus* could apply just as easily to any number of conceptions of the divine besides the Christian one. Too often, this lead to accounts of divine providence that—while they articulated a formally non-competitive account of divine and human activity—depicted God and the creature as both "neutral and featureless."[97] In the place of the triune God revealed in Jesus Christ, "God" became "a purely formal concept, denoting a supreme being endowed with absolute, unconditional, and irresistible power."[98] Yet this conception of the supremacy of God could not help but find itself in competition with the autonomy of the creature and the doctrine of *concursus* eventually broke down into a monistic occasionalism on the one hand and a synergistic divinization of the creature on the other.[99]

Barth believes that this entire complex of problems about divine sovereignty and creaturely autonomy can be entirely avoided simply by subordinating a formal account of non-competitive causality to the particular content of revelation.[100] If God is the God revealed in Jesus Christ, then the basis for *concursus* is not an abstract concept of divine power, but the specific concept of divine love revealed in the incarnation of Jesus Christ. In Jesus Christ, the creature sees that God—though absolutely superior to the creature—has graciously and lovingly willed to cooperate with the creature. Therefore, God's decision to give autonomy and freedom to the creature is not an insult to God's nature; it is the most truthful expression of it. Creaturely autonomy arises from the fact that the absolutely superior God who accompanies the creature is the God who from all eternity has elected to express God's unlimited power as self-giving covenant fellowship with humanity. Therefore, divine accompaniment does not suppress creaturely freedom, but confirms it.[101] This is the Christian understanding of divine *concursus*.

Barth's Christocentric formulation of *concursus* does more than just resolve a philosophical contradiction that has plagued the doctrine of providence for centuries. Indeed, even here in his account of some of the most abstract and technical portions of the doctrine of providence, Barth continues to have one eye fixed upon the political ramifications of his dogmatic theology. In the heart of his exposition of *concursus*, Barth explicitly discusses the connection between an insufficiently Christological conception of providence and the ideological appeal of National Socialism. Barth argues that if the concept of God's accompanying presence in world history is not understood as the outworking of the love of a God who is qualitatively distinct from creation, then it will always threaten to unravel into a synergistic account that mixes divine and creaturely elements. In so doing, the doctrine of providence will become a way to theorize the divinization of human political agency.

If the Christological basis and content of the divine accompanying of creation are lost, then the doctrine of *concursus* threatens to become a general theory of the divinization of creation, in which being accompanied by the divine is understood as a way to make the one who is accompanied divine. Barth sets himself against this possibility in the strongest possible terms: "This is a possible point of entry for all the dangerous heresies which have first endangered the knowledge of the divine providence and then Christian knowledge as a whole."[102] It is the temptation to identify God's providence with the power of the creature.[103] Transfixed by this vision of its own power, the creature comes to believe that it is in fact its own power that preserves, accompanies, and rules over the universe.[104] What initially seemed to pass as a Christian doctrine of providence reveals itself in the end as a profound subversion of the doctrine.

Barth's primary concern here is that the Christian church can be tricked into participating and embracing this subversion of its belief. Such was the case, Barth asserts, not only with the providential doctrines of Schiller, Goethe, Fichte, Schelling, and Hegel, but also with the providential rhetoric of National Socialism: "When the building of the National Socialist temple first began, it was commonly believed that at least in the forecourt there would be a Christian, a German-Christian chapel." Barth argues that this seemingly appealing alliance cannot be sustained. Either the church will abandon Jesus Christ or in loyalty to Christ the church will break with this false cult. In the end, "Jesus Christ Himself occupies the position of World-ruler, and side by side with Him there is no room for another."[105]

The last of the three major aspects of the traditional Reformed doctrine of providence is divine *gubernatio* or government of creation. God not only preserves creation at the outset and accompanies creation on its way through time. God also guides creation to its telos. The divine ruling is God's directing, guiding, and leading of creation according to God's final purposes.[106] In keeping with his established pattern, Barth accepts the formal definition of this aspect of the doctrine of providence as it has been formulated in the Reformed tradition, while criticizing the failure of the tradition to specify the Christological content of the doctrine. The "older orthodox theology" too closely identified the divine *gubernatio* with a formal and abstract theory of the cosmic rule of an omnipotent—but anonymous—divine Subject. In describing the God who rules the universe, Christian theologians too often began with their own understandings of rule, and then worked backward to describe the One who rules, such that God was envisioned as little more than "a supreme being furnished with supreme power."[107] Against this error, Barth outlines a concept of divine rule that corresponds to the God revealed in the covenant with Israel and the incarnation of Jesus Christ.

In order to arrive at a *Christian* doctrine of the divine ruling, Barth contends, one must begin from the foundational premise that the *One* who rules is the King of Israel. This is the only possible foundation for the doctrine. The "Subject of the divine world-governance" is the particular one who made a covenant with the twelve tribes of Israel and who fulfilled that covenant in Jesus Christ, the Messiah of Israel and the light to the nations.[108] Divine governance, for Barth, is not "an empty form" or a "general and overriding order and teleology." Instead, to understand divine governance of creation, one must look "at Jesus Christ on the cross; at the One who was not crucified alone, but two thieves with Him."[109] This is the place from which the world is governed.

Here Barth articulates the dogmatic claim upon which he was at that very time basing his judgments about the East-West conflict: world history and salvation history are bound together in Jesus Christ, such that the latter illuminates the former through Him. God's rule in world history is of the exact same character as God's saving activities in salvation history. The hand of God that governs, directs, and guides the universe to its final end is the nail-scarred hand of the crucified Jesus of Nazareth.

Throughout his treatment of the divine ruling, Barth attempts to undermine the ability of any pseudo-Christian ideology of world-governance to disguise itself as the Christian doctrine of providence. Barth claims that because the Subject of the divine world-governance is this particular God, all other schemas of cosmic rule are invalid. No one but God may justifiably claim to rule human creatures.[110] The feigned rule of any other would be "usurped, incompetent, weak; the bungling of an amateur. Open or secret opposition to any such rule would be possible, imminent, and probably successful. Certainly it would be legitimate and necessary."[111] Therefore, Barth asserts, "God laughs at all our attempts to see His rule with the eye of our human reason, let alone at our efforts to take the throne and play the part of world-ruler ourselves. This divine laughter rings out over the folly of all our crude or refined human imperialisms."[112] Barth's doctrine of providence not only refuses ideological colonization but also provides a theological basis for political resistance against those who try to make themselves world-rulers in the place of Jesus Christ.

Barth specifically targets any conception of world-rule that would sacrifice certain subordinate groups for the sake of the whole, contrasting this with government of the one true world-ruler who in fact became one of those who was unjustly sacrificed. This last point takes on an added level of specificity in light of Hitler's attempted extermination of the Jews and the founding of the state of Israel in 1948. Over and against the anti-Semitic and anti-Christic providential vision of National Socialism, Barth makes the endurance of the Jews one of four principal traces of the divine world-governance in world history.[113] Any doctrine of providence that has no place for the Jews has no place for the crucified Jew, Jesus of Nazareth, and, therefore, cannot be a Christian doctrine of providence. By basing the doctrine of divine rule upon Christology, Barth is able to offer a vicious and thoroughgoing critique of the human imperialisms that were birthed out of counterfeit doctrines of providence in the first half of the twentieth century.

Having completed his reconstruction of the three traditional components of the doctrine of providence, Barth closes his doctrine of providence with an account of the creature's relationship to providence. Barth's fourth section represents a shift in perspective from the objective to the subjective: from the divine *Subject* of providence to its creaturely *subject*. Alongside the divine *conservatio*, *concursus*, and *gubernatio*, Barth places the creaturely *participatio*.[114] Given Barth's severe critique of any human pretension to replace Jesus Christ as the one who sits upon the judgment seat of world history, this shift in perspective might seem to run against the grain of his previous account. Once again, the Christological basis of Barth's treatment of the doctrine of providence proves crucial. The human subject of providence—the Christian who is under the universal lordship of God—is the one who *participates* in Christ's kingly office.[115] The Christian, therefore, can never sit *upon* Christ's throne. However, *in Christ*, the Christian really does come *to* that throne. Barth contends that the legitimacy of the entire doctrine of providence hangs upon this fine distinction.

Who is the human subject that has actual knowledge of the ways of God in world history? Barth contends that it is only the Christian that can rightly confess a belief in providence.[116] On its surface, this assertion seems to run contrary to the central impulse of the previous aspects of Barth's account of providence, as well as to the central themes of his occasional writings from this same time period. Not surprisingly, Barth heavily qualifies this claim about the Christian subject in his subsequent exposition.

The Christian subject who has real knowledge of divine providence can only *receive* this knowledge as she or he participates in Christ's providential lordship. He or she can do nothing to merit it. She has no capacities, potencies, or potentialities that prepare her to receive this knowledge or make the reception of this knowledge fitting for her. Nothing sets the Christian apart from the rest of humanity that could serve as a basis for this knowledge. The reason that the Christian has genuine knowledge of providence is not that she has been elevated even the slightest bit from creaturely existence toward divine existence. In fact, Barth argues, it is the opposite. The one advantage that the Christian has over all other creatures is that only the Christian truly affirms the fact that "he has no advantage at all."[117] The Christian is no closer to the divine center of world history than any other creature. The difference is that the Christian *sees* that center in Jesus Christ.[118]

The Christian has no inherent claim or ability to participate in divine providence, and doing so brings no merit to the creature.[119] Locating Christian knowledge of divine providence as an extension of the *participatio Christi* enables Barth to continue to steadfastly reject the doctrine of providence's tendency to theorize the divinization of the creature, while still affirming a genuine knowledge of providence on the part of the creature. It is not as if participation in Christ—which Barth embraces—and the divinization of the creature—which Barth condemns—are simply two different doors to the same room of divine knowledge. The nature and character of the knowledge that the creature receives through participation in Christ is decisively shaped by this very particular way in which it is received.

The knowledge that the creature very genuinely receives through participation in Christ is not *divine* providential knowledge, but *human* knowledge of divine providence. Thus, in practice, Barth asserts, the Christian with knowledge of providence still encounters reality as the limited and finite creature that she or he is. Creaturely knowledge of divine providence offers no escape from the conditions of creaturely existence. In fact, it is quite the opposite. Creaturely knowledge of divine providence enables the creature to truly embrace its creatureliness: "He has no master-key to all the mysteries of the great process of existence as they crowd in upon him." Instead, "He will be the one man who knows that there is no value in any of the master-keys which man has thought to discover and possess."[120] Creaturely knowledge of divine providence does not provide the creature with a master key to world history, but rather frees the creature from the need for one.[121]

Knowledge of divine providence comes through dynamic participation in Christ's rule.[122] A participation which is marked by faith, obedience, and prayer. In faith, the Christian is led by the Holy Spirit from Jesus Christ to the world—from the place where God is revealed to the place where God is still hidden—seeing God's activity in the latter by the light cast by the former.[123] In obedience, the Christian depends upon the Holy Spirit to empower her to cooperate with the divine work in creation. In prayer the Christian participates in the material reality of Christ's rule through intercession and petition.[124]

While the creature has no claim upon a share of God's lordship, God in Jesus Christ has freely and lovingly given that share to the creature. God's sovereignty is such that it encompasses the possibility—and actuality—of creaturely participation in God's preservation, accompaniment, and governance of creation.[125] By identifying Jesus Christ as the content and purpose of divine sovereignty, Barth is able to offer an account of human participation in divine providence that does not encourage or tempt the creature to seek to be like God, but rather enables it to fully embrace being a creature. The "radical correction" of the doctrine of providence that Barth carries out in §48 and §49 of *Church Dogmatics* III/3 is simply a reconstruction of the doctrine with Jesus Christ at its center as the divine Subject of providence and the revelation of the character and purpose of God's providential rule over the cosmos. For Barth, the intersection of world history and divine history is not a possibility to be theorized or a potentiality to be actualized. It has a name: Jesus Christ.

CONCLUSION

In *Church Dogmatics* III/3, Karl Barth critiques a problematic construction of the doctrine of providence that envisions European humanity as the quasi-divine Subject of world history, a vision of intellectual and theological colonialism in which the European subject attempts to "play the part of world-ruler."[126] Barth suggests that this ideological colonization and subversion of the doctrine of providence enabled the church in Germany to be so easily coopted by National Socialism. Barth sets himself against this providential European project—the very same project that Hegel had so thoroughly embraced.

Where for Hegel divine providence is an abstract, teleological process of the progressive incarnation of the divine in world history that sacralizes European humanity, for Barth providence is the concrete and particular rule of the incarnate one, Jesus Christ, beside whom there can be no other divine Subject of history. Where Hegel can say, "Because the essential being of God is revealed through the Christian religion, the key to world history is also given to us," Barth counters with the assertion that the creature "has no master-key to all the mysteries of the great process of existence. . . . On the contrary, he will be the one man who knows that there is no value in any of the master-keys which man has thought to discover and possess."[127] By grounding his conception of the incarnation exclusively in the Jewish humanity of Jesus Christ, Barth is able to draw conclusions about the relationship between divine providence, world history, and European humanity that are radically opposed to Hegel's vision of European man as incarnation and eschaton. While Hegel utilizes the doctrine of providence as a lens through which to envision European humanity as the paradigmatic site of the incarnation of the divine within world history, Barth's Christocentric conception of providence attempts to foreclose upon the possibility that the doctrine may be used by European humanity as a discursive technology of self-sacralization. Twenty years later, James Cone would begin his own theological project, which would not rest content with simply critiquing the colonial and racial captivity of European providential visions, but would proceed to offer a constructive interpretation of God's providential activity in the world as a divine work of liberation.

NOTES

1. *LPWH*, 463–464.
2. The following account of postwar Hungary is particularly indebted to Deborah S. Cornelius's *Hungary in World War II: Caught in the Cauldron* (New York: Fordham University Press, 2011) and Peter Kenez's *Hungary from the Nazis to the Soviets: The Establishment of the Communist Regime in Hungary, 1944-1948* (Cambridge University Press, 2006).
3. Cornelius, *Hungary in World War II*, 370.
4. Ibid., 373.
5. Ibid., 384, 402. At its highest, the daily inflation rate was 158,486 percent.
6. Ibid., 398.
7. Ibid., 399, 412.
8. Ibid., 414–417.
9. Eberhard Busch, *Karl Barth: His Life from Letters and Autobiographical Texts*, trans. John Bowden (Eugene, OR: Wipf & Stock Publishers, 1975), 354.
10. Ibid., 354.
11. Barth's efforts place him within a wider stream of European intellectual reflection on the meaning and consequences of the catastrophic events of the first half of the twentieth century for European civilization. For more on this wider intellectual current within which Barth was moving, see Anson Rabinach, *In the Shadow of Catastrophe: German Intellectuals between Apocalypse and Enlightenment* (Berkeley: University of California Press, 1997); A. Dirk Moses, *German Intellectuals and the Nazi Past* (Cambridge: Cambridge University Press, 2007).
12. Busch, *Karl Barth*, 418–421. This intertextual approach to interpreting the *Church Dogmatics* reflects Barth's own understanding of his theological method: "As far as I can recall there was no stage in my theological career when I had more than the very next step forward in mind and planned for it. . . . I used what I thought I had learned and understood so far to cope with this or that situation, with some complex of biblical or historical or doctrinal questions, often with some subject presented to me from outside, often in fact by a topical subject, e.g. a political issue. It was always something new that got hold of me, rather than the other way round. . . . My thinking, writing, and speaking developed from reacting to people, events, and circumstances with which I was involved . . . That is what working on the *Church Dogmatics* was like for twenty-five years." For a similar methodological approach, see Timothy Gorringe, *Karl Barth: Against Hegemony* (Oxford: Oxford University Press, 1999).

13. Karl Barth, *Church Dogmatics*, ed. and trans. G. W. Bromiley and T. F. Torrance, 14 vols (Edinburgh: T&T Clark, 1956–75), III/3, xii (hereafter cited as *CD* III/3).

14. Ibid., 164.

15. After the World Council of Churches event, Barth found himself embroiled in a second highly publicized controversy with another famous Christian intellectual. This time it was the American theologian Reinhold Niebuhr who publicly lambasted Barth for his position on contemporary sociopolitical issues. However, Niebuhr's attack on Barth so badly misconstrues the logic of Barth's position that the resulting correspondence adds little real substance to the present investigation. For an overview of the Barth-Niebuhr correspondence, see Gary Dorrien, *The Barthian Revolt in Modern Theology: Theology without Weapons* (Louisville: Westminster John Knox Press, 2000), 134–139.

16. Busch, *Karl Barth*, 333, 337, 341.

17. Karl Barth, "The Christian Message in Europe Today," in *Against the Stream: Shorter Post-war Writings 1946-1952* (New York: Philosophical Library, 1954), 167.

18. Ibid., 168.

19. Ibid., 175.

20. Ibid., 176.

21. Ibid., 177.

22. Ibid., 175. Emphasis added.

23. Karl Barth, "Modern Youth: Its Inheritance and Its Responsibility," in *Against the Stream: Shorter Post-war Writings 1946-1952* (New York: Philosophical Library, 1954), 56, 57.

24. Ibid., 57.

25. Karl Barth, "The Christian Community in the Midst of Political Change," in *Against the Stream: Shorter Post-war Writings 1946-1952* (New York: Philosophical Library, 1954), 79.

26. Ibid., 86.

27. Ibid., 91, 93.

28. Karl Barth to Alphons Koechlin, September 20, 1948, cited in Busch, *Karl Barth*, 355.

29. Emil Brunner, "An Open Letter to Karl Barth," in *Against the Stream: Shorter Post-war Writings 1946-1952* (New York: Philosophical Library, 1954), 106–113. For background on the emergence and uses of totalitarianism theory—which sheds much light on Brunner's intention in strategically attacking Barth precisely on the grounds of a failure to reject totalitarianism—see James Chappel, "The Catholic Origins of Totalitarianism Theory in Interwar Europe," *Modern Intellectual History* 8, no. 3 (2011): 561–590.

30. Karl Barth, "Karl Barth's Reply," in *Against the Stream: Shorter Post-war Writings 1946-1952* (New York: Philosophical Library, 1954), 113.

31. Ibid., 115. Emphasis in original.

32. Ibid., 116.

33. Ibid., 117.

34. Busch, *Karl Barth*, 357.
35. Karl Barth, "No Christian Marshall Plan," *The Christian Century* 65, no. 49 (1948): 1330, 1330.
36. Ibid., 1330, 1331.
37. Ibid., 1331, 1331. Emphasis in original.
38. Karl Barth, "The Church Between East and West," in *Against the Stream: Shorter Post-war Writings 1946-1952* (New York: Philosophical Library, 1954), 127.
39. Ibid., 127.
40. Ibid., 128.
41. Ibid., 132.
42. Ibid., 134.
43. Ibid., 136.
44. Karl Barth to Josef Hromádka, September 19, 1938, cited in Busch, *Karl Barth*, 289.
45. Barth, "The Church Between East and West," 137.
46. Ibid., 136, 136.
47. Ibid., 139.
48. Ibid., 140.
49. Ibid., 140.
50. Ibid., 141.
51. Ibid., 141.
52. Ibid., 142.
53. Ibid., 145.
54. Christopher C. Green, *Doxological Theology: Karl Barth on Divine Providence, Evil, and the Angels* (London: Bloomsbury T&T Clark, 2011); Kim, *Deus providebit: Calvin, Schleiermacher, and Barth on the Providence of God*; Darren M. Kennedy, *Providence and Personalism: Karl Barth in Conversation with Austin Farrer, John Macmurry, and Vincent Brümmer* (Oxford: Peter Lang, 2011).
55. Christopher C. Green argues that the heart of Barth's "radical correction" is a "reordering of divine providence to follow the doctrine of election." While this is certainly true in part, it does not quite capture the crucial role played by Christ's humanity in Barth's formulation of providence. If Barth writes *CD* III/3 with an eye toward his doctrine of election in *CD* II/2, then his other eye is firmly fixed on his soon to be written account of the incarnation in *CD* IV/1. See Green, *Doxological Theology*, 28–36.
56. See Kathryn Tanner, "Creation and Providence," in *The Cambridge Companion to Karl Barth*, ed. John Webster (Cambridge: Cambridge University Press, 2000), 122: "God's special history with Israel, as it finds its fulfillment in God's becoming human in Jesus Christ, becomes the model for God's history with the world generally."
57. *CD* III/3, 4.
58. Ibid., 4.
59. Ibid., 5.
60. Ibid., 5. Barth gives Thomas credit for attempting to avoid this error by limiting his account of providence in the doctrine of God solely to the eternal *ratio*

ordinandorum within God Godself, while locating his account of the activity of God's providential government within the doctrine of creation. However, for Barth, even this goes too far toward suggesting an "integration" of the creature into the being of God. For Thomas's "split" account of providence, see Thomas Aquinas, *The Summa Theologiae*, trans. Fathers of the English Dominican Province (New York: Benziger Bro., 1948), I.22-24 and I.103-119.

61. *CD* III/3, 6.
62. Ibid., 7.
63. Ibid., 14.
64. Ibid., 16.
65. Ibid., 18.
66. Ibid., 21.
67. Ibid., 26.
68. Ibid., 26.
69. Ibid., 29.
70. Ibid., 31, 31, 31.
71. Ibid., 33.
72. Ibid., 35.
73. Ibid., 36.
74. Ibid., 36.
75. Ibid., 36, 41.
76. Ibid., 43.
77. Ibid., 37.
78. Ibid., 54.
79. Ibid., xii.
80. Ibid., xi. See also Randall C. Zachman, "Response to: 'I See Something You Don't See'" in *For the Sake of the World: Karl Barth and the Future of Ecclesial Theology*, ed. George Hunsinger (Grand Rapids: Eerdmans, 2004), 139.
81. *CD* III/3, 82.
82. Ibid., 58.
83. Ibid., 60.
84. Ibid., 58.
85. To be fair, Calvin did attempt in his own way to hold together God's power with God's justice and love in his concept of providence. He asserts that the doctrine is not a matter of "that absolute will of which the Sophists babble, by an impious and profane distinction separating his justice from his power—but providence, that determinative principle of all things, from which flows nothing but right." See Calvin, *Institutes of the Christian Religion*, 214. See also John T. McNeill, *The History and Character of Calvinism* (London: Oxford University Press, 1967), 212.
86. *CD* III/3, 58.
87. Ibid., 59.
88. Ibid., 59. Cf. Ps. 36:6, Ps. 73:23, Neh. 9:6, Rom. 11:36, 1 Cor. 8:6, Heb. 1:3.
89. Ibid., 63.
90. Ibid., 82.

91. As Darren M. Kennedy notes, for Barth, "'The limitation of human life' actually becomes a sign of providence in Barth's theology," becoming one of the four concrete signs of God's providential activity in world history, alongside Scripture, the history of the church, and the history of Israel. Kennedy, *Providence and Personalism*, 210.

92. *CD* III/3, 111.

93. Ibid., 90, 91.

94. Ibid., 92, 93. Barth divides the doctrine of *concursus* into three parts: *praecurrit, concurrit,* and *sucurrit*. For a helpful account of these distinctions, see Green, *Doxological Theology*, 83–87.

95. *CD* III/3, 96.

96. Ibid., 97.

97. Ibid., 100.

98. Ibid., 113.

99. Ibid., 115–117. For a similar account, see Paul T. Nimmo, *Being in Action: The Theological Shape of Barth's Ethical Vision* (London: T&T Clark, 2007), 118–135.

100. As Bruce McCormack suggests, Barth reorients *concursus* from being "a solution to a question arising in cosmology" to a "reflex of a christologically grounded soteriology with a very definite content." See Bruce L. McCormack, "The Actuality of God: Karl Barth in Conversation with Open Theism," in *Engaging the Doctrine of God: Contemporary Protestant Perspectives*, ed. Bruce L. McCormack (Grand Rapids: Baker, 2008), 230.

101. *CD* III/3, 146. See also 107–109.

102. Ibid., 111.

103. Ibid., 111.

104. Ibid., 111.

105. Ibid., 111, 112.

106. Ibid., 155.

107. Ibid., 176.

108. Ibid., 178.

109. Ibid., 186, 186.

110. Ibid., 157.

111. Ibid., 157.

112. Ibid., 160.

113. Ibid., 210–226.

114. Ibid., 239.

115. For a full account of Barth's understanding of participation in Christ—albeit one that does not treat the manifestation of this theme within *Church Dogmatics* III/3—see Adam Neder, *Participation in Christ: An Entry into Karl Barth's* Church Dogmatics (Louisville: Westminster John Knox Press, 2009).

116. Ibid., 239.

117. Ibid., 240.

118. Ibid., 241.

119. Ibid., 242.

120. Ibid., 242, 242.

121. From this perspective, participation in divine providence gives the Christian no cause for arrogance or a feeling of superiority over his or her fellow creatures *pace* Caroline Schröder's critique of Barth's doctrine in "'I See Something You Don't See': Karl Barth's Doctrine of Providence," in *For the Sake of the World*, 115–135. See also Kennedy, *Providence and Personalism*, 254.

122. *CD* III/3, 244.

123. Ibid., 246–253.

124. Green, *Doxological Theology*, 140. Emphasis in original.

125. Ibid., 285.

126. Ibid., 160.

127. *LPWH*, 145; *CD* III/3, 242.

Chapter 4

James H. Cone
Providence as the Cities Burned

On Wednesday, July 12, 1967, John Smith, an amateur jazz musician and longtime resident of Newark, New Jersey, drove his cab around a parked Newark Police Department squad car.[1] In response, the two white officers inside the car pulled Smith over, severely beat the Black taxicab driver, and placed him under arrest.[2] Word of Smith's beating and arrest began circulating among cab drivers and local residents, and a crowd quickly assembled outside the headquarters of the police precinct where Smith was being held.

Several local civil rights leaders arrived on the scene and—after demanding that the badly beaten Smith be taken to a hospital—attempted to organize those assembled into a protest march. While some members of the crowd prepared to march, others began hurling bottles, bricks, and Molotov cocktails at the police station. The officers inside the precinct emerged from the station swinging their nightsticks, and the violence of the police fractured the assembly into small groups, which grew rapidly as they spread out across Newark's Central Ward.[3] Over the next five days, local and state authorities engaged in a campaign of ruthless violence. The city and state deployed over 6,000 local and state police officers and National Guardsmen throughout the city. State troopers and National Guardsmen indiscriminately fired live ammunition into crowds of Black civilians, killing young and old alike.[4] By the time Governor Richard Hughes declared that the city had been "returned to control" on Monday, July 17, the officers and soldiers had expended 13,326 rounds of ammunition, approximately 1,400 people had been arrested, 1,100 had been injured, and twenty-six had been killed—twenty-four of whom were Black.[5]

Less than a week later, in the early hours of Sunday, July 23, police officers raided an illegal after-hours saloon in one of Detroit's largest Black neighborhoods, arresting eighty-five people.[6] It was the ninth time police had attempted a raid at this location that year. In response, members of the community assembled in the area and some broke into a nearby store. By noon, a crowd of more than 8,000 people had gathered in the area.[7] George Romney, the Republican governor of Michigan, ordered the National Guard to deploy with support from armored tanks.[8] By the end of the day on Monday, July 24, Romney was forced to request federal intervention, and 5,000 soldiers from the 82nd Airborne division of the U.S. Army—some of whom had been previously deployed to Vietnam—were ordered to occupy a city on U.S. soil, joining 2,000 state and local police and 8,000 National Guardsmen who were already on the ground. At its height, the uprising covered more than seven square miles of the city.[9]

As in Newark, the police and National Guard embraced brute, indiscriminate force. Between July 23 and July 27, 43 people were killed, 1,189 were injured, and more than 7,000 had been arrested.[10] In those five days, National Guardsmen fired an estimated 155,576 rounds of ammunition.[11] Nearly 100 of those rounds were fired into a building from a 50-caliber machine gun, killing a 4-year-old girl, Tonya Blanding, because National Guardsmen saw her father strike a match to light a cigarette and mistook it for the muzzle flash of a rifle.[12] Among the forty-three dead were thirty-three Black civilians, one police officer, and one National Guardsmen.[13] With smoke still hanging heavy in the air, Detroit's liberal, white mayor Jerome P. Cavanaugh—who had previously been lauded for establishing the city as "the nation's model in race relations"—offered a frank reassessment of the situation in the Motor City: "We stand amidst the ashes of our hopes."[14]

Seventy miles southwest of Detroit, a young professor at Adrian College watched the cities burn. James Hal Cone had left Philander Smith College in Arkansas to join the faculty at Adrian the previous year and had been struggling to find meaning in his work as a theologian. As Cone recalls, the "apparent irrelevance of theology" had led him to the verge of a "vocational crisis": "I began to develop an intense dislike for theology because it avoided the really hard problems of life with its talk about revelation, God, Jesus, and the Holy Spirit."[15] It was at this very moment, when a frustrated Cone had begun considering a return to graduate school to complete a second PhD in literature, that the events in Newark and Detroit confronted him as genuine acts of theological revelation in their own right. The Black bodies lying in the city streets constituted an *apokalypsis* of Cone's theological world, shaking him out of his "theological complacency" and demanding an immediate response: "With Black people dying in the streets of America, I just could not keep silent."[16] Cone immediately reevaluated his vocational plans: "There was no time for me to return to graduate school. I had to say something now about God and Black people's struggle for freedom."[17] Yet almost before Cone had the chance to say anything, his theological *krisis* moment was violently exacerbated by the assassination of Martin Luther King, Jr. in April

1968.[18] Finally, two months after King's death, Cone sat down and began to write.

Working for fourteen to fifteen hours a day in June 1968, Cone composed the entirety of his first book in less than a month.[19] Upon its publication in March 1969, *Black Theology and Black Power* exploded like a bomb on the playground of theology in the United States.[20] As Dwight N. Hopkins suggests, "It was as if Cone had entered a dark bell tower, stumbled, accidentally pulled a bell rope, and awakened the entire village population."[21] Framed as a theological analysis of Black Power, the book was Cone's first attempt to fundamentally reconceive the nature and task of Christian theology in light of the "struggle of people to be free in an extreme situation of oppression."[22] For Cone, Black Power meant the total emancipation of Black people by any means necessary. It meant Black freedom, dignity, and self-determination.[23] Cone's conclusion in *Black Theology and Black Power* was decisive: "Black Power, even in its most radical expression, is not the antithesis of Christianity, nor is it a heretical idea to be tolerated with painful forbearance. It is, rather, Christ's central message to twentieth-century America."[24]

In *Black Theology and Black Power*, Cone develops his thesis about the relationship between Black Power and Christianity through at least two distinct arguments. First, he defends the conceptual compatibility of Black Power and *Christianity* understood as two sets of ideas. In this regard, Cone asserts that Black Power's message of liberation by whatever means necessary can be reconciled with a Christian conception of love.[25] Second, alongside this argument for conceptual compatibility, Cone articulates an argument about the theological and historical relationship between Black Power and *God* which leads him to an even stronger conclusion: Black Power is more than just theoretically compatible with Christianity; it is a manifestation of divine activity in history. Black Power, Cone asserts, "is God's new way of acting in America."[26] Cone develops an innovative theological interpretation of God's active relationship to the events of the 1960s, from the urban rebellions in Watts, Newark, Detroit and beyond, to the rise of Black Power.[27] After initially articulating it in *Black Theology and Black Power*, Cone reiterates and expands this account of God's action in history in *A Black Theology of Liberation* and *God of the Oppressed*.

Within the context of the present study, this chapter explicates James H. Cone's account of the liberating presence of Jesus Christ in history as a third constructive theological interpretation of the relationship between providence and race in modern Protestant theology, alongside those of G. W. F. Hegel and Karl Barth. As I have previously argued, Hegel transforms the doctrine of providence into an abstract, teleological theory of historical, geographical, and anthropological progress, in which the male, European subject replaces Jesus Christ as the definitive site of the incarnation of the divine in the world.[28] Barth, on the other hand, articulates his account of the doctrine of providence as a Christological critique of the providential imagination underlying Hegel's racialized vision of world history.[29] Cone, for his part, develops an account of the liberating presence of Jesus Christ in history that serves as a providential hermeneutic for interpreting divine activity in a racialized world. According to Cone, Christ is not trapped in the first century, but is at work in the present world through the power of the Holy Spirit. From this perspective, Cone reframes the abstract issue of providential action in terms of a concrete Christological question: "Who is Jesus Christ for us today?"[30] Cone's judgment that Jesus is at work in Black Power rests on the particular content of his Christology. For Cone, Christ's presence in liberation struggles is a direct correlate of Christ's Blackness. Indeed, as Cone's thought develops, his early questions about divine action increasingly resolve into questions about Christology in general and about the Blackness of Jesus in particular.

This chapter charts the points of connection between Cone's Christology and his theology of liberative divine action, arguing that the theological warrant for Cone's judgments about the present activity of God is the Blackness of Jesus Christ. Christ's Blackness—which emerges from a dialectical interpretation of the relationship between Christ's past, present, and future—functions as the hermeneutical lens through which Cone interprets divine action in relationship to contemporary events. This interpretation of Cone's thought foregrounds the centrality of the Holy Spirit in his theology, as it is the Spirit who makes Christ present to humanity between the ascension and the second coming, enabling Cone to affirm the intimate connection between Christ and Black humanity.[31] Cone's account embodies the imperative of 1 John 4: he attempts to "test the spirits" in order to "recognize the Spirit of God" who "acknowledges that Jesus Christ has come in the flesh."[32] To substantiate this interpretation of Cone's thought, I will trace the development of his account of divine action in history across three of his early publications: *Black Theology and Black Power*, *A Black Theology of Liberation*, and *God of the Oppressed*.

BLACK THEOLOGY AND BLACK POWER: PROVIDENCE AS THE LIBERATING PRESENCE OF JESUS CHRIST

In outlining the nature of his emerging theological project in *Black Theology and Black Power*, Cone acknowledges both the risks involved in making judgments about divine action and the inescapable necessity of making those judgments nonetheless. Cone is well aware of the temptation to construct a theological ideology that is nothing more than a religious smokescreen for one's own subjective interests—this is, after all, one of his fundamental criticism of white Christianity. Yet despite this risk, agnosticism about God's action is not an option. While "Jesus did not give us a blueprint for identifying God and his work," Cone concludes, "We must speak of God and his work, if we intend to join him."[33] Cone clearly agrees with Barth—over and against Hegel—that humanity has no "master key" with which to decipher God's action in history.[34] Yet he also believes that the fraught endeavor of discerning and faithfully responding to divine action is an integral part of the Christian life. *Black Theology and Black Power* represents Cone's attempt to navigate this theological and ethical paradox in the context of the specific historical phenomenon of Black Power at the end of the 1960s.[35]

In this short work, Cone develops an account of divine action as the liberating presence of Jesus Christ in history and performs Christologically grounded, theological judgment making about divine action in history. Cone builds this account upon a series of increasingly specific theological claims about divine action. First, Cone claims that God is active in history. Second, he characterizes the nature and shape of this activity as liberating presence. Finally, he articulates this account of liberating presence Christologically, as a property of the continuing work of the resurrected Christ through the Holy Spirit. Like an optometrist who has her patient look through a series of lenses until their vision becomes clear, Cone applies this series of theological lenses to contemporary events until Black Power comes into focus as one particular manifestation of Christ's liberating presence in history.

Cone's first and most basic warrant for his claims about divine action is the Bible. Scripture bears witness to a God who acts in history. Cone appeals to this basic principle repeatedly in *Black Theology and Black Power*. It first comes up in his discussion of the character of God's righteousness: "God's righteousness refers not so much to an abstract quality related to his Being in the realm of thought . . . but to his *activity in human history*, in the historical events of the time and effecting his purpose despite those who oppose it. This is the biblical tradition."[36] In the Old and New Testaments, divine righteousness appears first and foremost as a dynamic, intrahistorical activity, not as a static, metaphysical property. For Cone, the central paradigms of this activity are the liberation and election of Israel and the incarnation of Jesus Christ.[37]

This same line of argument drives Cone's analysis of eschatology. He delineates two different understandings of eschatology that have marked Black Christianity in the United States. The first of these embraces a strong dualism between God and history, manifesting in a belief in otherworldly, "pie in the sky" salvation. However, "this is not the perspective of biblical faith."[38] As Cone makes clear, this conception of eschatology is a distortion of Christian belief, not only because it rendered slaves passive and accepting of their oppression but also because it does not comport with Scripture.

A second conception of eschatology stands in radical antithesis to the impulse to distance God from history. This latter perspective Cone claims as his own and as the stance of Black theology. He rejects any theology that would impose a "cleavage" between God and the world: "Genuine biblical faith relates eschatology to history, that is, to what God has done, is doing, and will do for his people."[39] In no small part, then, the impetus to think about divine action in relationship to Black Power emerges from Cone's reading of the Bible. In the Old and New Testaments, Cone argues, "God is revealed as a God who is involved in history."[40] God is active in history because God reveals Godself to be active in history through Israel and Jesus. From this initial conviction, Cone develops his account of divine activity by further specifying its character and inner theological structure.

Taking Israel and Jesus as paradigmatic representations of God's action in history, Cone moves beyond a formal account of divine activity to a specification of the concrete character of that divine action as "liberating presence."[41] God's revelation of the particular way that God acts is first displayed in the election of Israel, manifested in the exodus and the Sinai covenant.[42] God does not act as an abstract, omnicausal force in the universe. Indeed, without being tied to revelation, divine action is an empty concept. Instead, Cone joins his account of divine action to God's revelation of Godself through the covenant with Israel, so that it acquires the specific material content of liberation.

This pattern of divine action as liberation, initially made visible in the exodus, is reaffirmed and extended in the incarnation. Jesus reveals "the full meaning of God's action in history and man's place within it." It is liberation: "In Christ, God enters human affairs and takes sides with the oppressed."[43] Alongside Israel, the incarnation provides the specific material content for what would otherwise be a wholly formal account of divine action. In Jesus, God revealed Godself to be a God who works for the liberation of the oppressed. At this first level of Cone's Christological argument about the liberating character of divine action, his focus is decidedly historical. The incarnation provides a template for divine action. Jesus functions as an exemplar of divine activity, displaying the characteristic principle of God's action in history: liberation. However, Cone quickly moves to expand the scope of his Christology beyond mere exemplarity.

Up to this point, Cone's account is not decisively different from Hegel's understanding of the nature of divine providence. Indeed, Hegel was also strongly committed to an interpretation of divine action linked to the concept of freedom. If Israel and Jesus only reveal the characteristic *principle* of divine action, then that principle remains liable to replace Jesus as the criterion for judging divine action. However, Cone does not allow liberation to function as a formal principle of divine action independent of the humanity of

Jesus Christ. Rather, as J. Kameron Carter has demonstrated, Cone's analysis reflects a deep commitment to "Being's concreteness which is revealed in Jesus of Nazareth."[44] Indeed, liberation—as Cone articulates it—is in the end not a formal principle, but a particular person.

Within Cone's understanding of divine action, Jesus Christ cannot be confined to the role of historical exemplar. Christology is not simply an earlier chapter in a larger historical narrative of divine action. It is quite the opposite. Ongoing divine action in history is, for Cone, an outworking of Christology. Providence is an extension of Christology. Specifically, divine providence is Christ's human agency operating in creation through the power of the Holy Spirit after the resurrection.

The Christological trajectory upon which Cone plots contemporary divine activity begins with the birth of Christ. In the incarnation, God enters into human life "for the sole purpose of striking off the chains of slavery, thereby freeing man from ungodly principalities and powers."[45] The subsequent life and teachings of Jesus confirm this truth, which Jesus makes evident through his proclamation of the Jubilee year in Luke 4:

The Spirit of the Lord is upon me,
because he has anointed me to preach the good news to the poor.
He has sent me to proclaim release to the captives
and recovering of sight to the blind,
To set at liberty those who are oppressed,
To proclaim the acceptable year of the Lord.[46]

Jesus' ministry inaugurates "an age of liberation," in which, as Luke 7:22 suggests, "the blind receive their sight, the lame walk, the lepers are cleansed, the deaf hear, the dead are raised, the poor have good news brought to them."[47] In the New Testament, Cone finds a Jesus whose life is marked from start to finish by the struggle for liberation. Christ's "whole life was a deliberate offensive against those powers which held man captive."[48] Jesus inaugurates his ministry by entering into conflict with Satan in Luke 4 and continues it for the rest of his ministry, particularly through his exorcisms. From this perspective, liberation is not a formal principle that Christ merely exemplifies. The humanity of Jesus Christ is the concrete embodiment and norm of liberation.

The crucifixion represents the climactic clash between the new way of being human revealed and made possible in Jesus Christ and the power of Satan. The crucifixion was the "decisive battle" in which the "tyranny" of Satan was abolished.[49] This victory over Satan is revealed to humanity in Christ's resurrection.[50] This narration of the birth, life, death, and resurrection of Jesus Christ provides the material content to Cone's concept of liberation.

Cone's narration of the incarnation does not end with the resurrection. Rather, Cone extends his analysis of God becoming flesh in Jesus into the remainder of history prior to Christ's return. After the resurrection, Jesus does not leave human history, any more than Jesus could abandon his human nature. As Cone puts it, "Jesus is not safely confined in the first century. He is our contemporary, proclaiming release to the captives and rebelling against all who silently accept the structures of injustice."[51] Cone inserts an additional stage into the familiar narrative pattern of the incarnation—birth, life, death, resurrection, ascension, final return—by including the resurrected Christ's historical activity between the ascension and his final return as an important facet of Christology.

Cone's attention to pneumatology makes possible his assertion of the contemporaneity of Christ.[52] While Christ is ascended, his power and presence continue through the work of the Spirit. Through Pentecost, the Spirit is given to all those who respond to God's work in Christ. The Holy Spirit "is the power of God at work in the world effecting in the life of his people his intended purposes."[53] Taking seriously the role of the Spirit allows Cone to speak of continuing divine action in history without discarding his Christocentric focus. Divine providence after Christ's ascension does not leave Christ behind. Rather, the Spirit of Christ makes Christ present and continues Christ's work. There is no bifurcation between Cone's Christology and his theory of divine action in history after the ascension. Divine action post-ascension is itself a property of Christology when the Holy Spirit is taken seriously. In short, Cone's doctrine of providence is a doctrine of the *pneumatological contemporaneity of Christ*. Therefore, to understand how Cone comes to judgment about the relationship between God and Black Power, it is necessary to examine the specific content of his Christology rather than a general theory of divine action calibrated around a formal principle of liberation.

Cone's verdict that Black Power is synonymous with the action of God derives from a very particular judgment about the identity of Jesus Christ. Rejecting the possibility of articulating contemporary divine action as independent from—or a historical supersession of—the incarnation, Cone identifies Jesus Christ as the inner, material content of divine providence. For Cone, God's liberating presence is not a formal concept, abstract theory, or teleological scheme. God's liberating presence is Jesus Christ, crucified and resurrected, acting in creation through the power of the Holy Spirit. Given this Christological determination of divine providence, questions about divine activity become questions about Christology: one's understanding of Jesus Christ significantly shapes how and where one sees God active today.

This Christological reframing of divine action raises new questions for Cone. As he learned from Malcolm X, it all depends on which Jesus you are talking about: "Brothers and sisters, the white man has brainwashed us black people to fasten our gaze upon a blond-haired, blue-eyed Jesus! We're worshipping a Jesus that doesn't even *look* like us! Oh, yes! . . . Now just think of this. The blond-haired, blue-eyed white man has taught you and me to worship a *white* Jesus, and to shout and sing and pray to this God that's *his* God, the white man's God."[54] Given the logic of his position, Cone's account of divine providence—and, therefore, also his judgment that Black Power is a site of divine activity—rests upon the specific content of his Christology. In *Black Theology and Black Power*, Cone is only able to sketch the outline of his thought at this specific point. Yet even at this early point, the main contours of Cone's position are clear: if Jesus Christ is the inner, material content of God's liberating presence, then the Blackness of Jesus Christ constitutes the specific mode of Christ's presence.

Cone's initial exploration of the Blackness of Christ in *Black Theology and Black Power* is brief and therefore ambiguous. Rejecting depictions of Jesus as either white or raceless, Cone asserts that *"Christ is black baby."*[55] In this first account of Jesus' Blackness, the warrant that Cone presents for his claim seems to invoke, what J. Kameron Carter has identified as, "an analogy of existential situation and condition between Jesus and us," rather than a more particularistic and concrete account of Christ's continued presence to humanity after the ascension through the power of the Holy Spirit.[56] In his early treatment of these issues, Cone wavers between identifying the Blackness of Christ as a symbolic and analogical postulation or as a concrete and pneumatological reality.

At this early stage, the relationship between Christ's Jewishness and Christ's Blackness remains particularly underdeveloped: "God's word in Christ not only fulfills his purposes for man through his elected people, but also inaugurates a new age in which all oppressed people become his people."[57] The relationship between the elected people of Israel and the identification of the oppressed as God's people remains vague. Is this a supersession of the particular covenant with Israel by a universal election of the oppressed? Or is it a "theology of the nations" in which Israel's election includes the engrafting of others into Israel's covenant promises?[58] Cone would delay the resolution of these interpretive ambiguities until his more thorough accounting of these matters in *A Black Theology of Liberation* and *God of the Oppressed*.

While the material content of his Christology remains underdeveloped in *Black Theology and Black Power*, the basic theological framework through which Cone attempts to interpret God's relationship to Black Power is clear. The hermeneutic of providence that Cone develops in order to assess theologically the significance of Black Power rests upon his understanding of the contemporaneity of Christ with the present age. For Cone, judgments about divine action should not unfold from the application of an abstract theory.

Rather, they are particular, contingent attempts to discern the activity of Jesus Christ in the present through the Holy Spirit, which are themselves made possible by that Spirit.

Cone does not seek to ontologically bind the movement of God in history to Black Power. Jesus Christ remains the criterion for judging divine action in such a way that Cone's verdict about Black Power can only ever be provisional. Black Power has no independent claim to divine backing or approval. Rather, Black Power participates in God's action as long as it responds to and addresses the cries of the oppressed. Only then is it "the work of God's Spirit."[59] Indeed, Cone goes so far as to use the language of needing to "wait and see" with Black Power.[60] In *Black Theology and Black Power*, Black Power does not take over the mantle of divinity from Jesus Christ. Rather, it is only as Black Power aligns with Jesus Christ that it can be called the work of God.[61]

A BLACK THEOLOGY OF LIBERATION: THE PAST AND PRESENT OF CHRIST'S LIBERATING PRESENCE

Continuing on the trajectory set by *Black Theology and Black Power*, Cone published *A Black Theology of Liberation* only a year after the former work. While maintaining his conviction that all theology is contextual, addressed to specific situations at specific moments in time, Cone felt the need to extend and deepen the analysis of Christian doctrine that he had sketched out in his first book. As Gayraud Wilmore argues, the two books "are actually companion pieces. In the language of the boxing ring, they belong together like the old 'one-two,' a left hook followed by a quick right cross."[62] *A Black Theology of Liberation* engaged in a more sustained and systematic exploration of the doctrine of providence in response to the same question that drove Cone's analysis in *Black Theology and Black Power*: "What has the gospel of Jesus Christ to do with the black struggle for justice in the United States?"[63]

Cone is rightly hesitant about the prospect of engaging the doctrine of providence: "It is difficult to talk about divine providence when men and women are dying and children are tortured."[64] He frames his own account of the doctrine as a critique of traditional invocations of the doctrine in the mode of theodicy. Cone writes, "To suggest that black suffering is consistent with the knowledge and will of God and that in the end everything will happen for the good of those who love God is unacceptable to blacks."[65] Providence, for Cone, is not a theoretical explanation about the future, which reassures Christians that everything happens for a reason or will work out for the best in the end. Rather, providence names the present reality of Jesus Christ's ongoing work of liberation. The content of God's will is on display in the death and resurrection of Jesus: God wills—and is acting to achieve—liberation for the oppressed. For Cone, "Divine providence is seeing divine reality in the present reality of black liberation—no more, no less."[66] Belief in providence requires the risky work of practical discernment and judgment that attempts to interpret Christ's ongoing liberative work in history.

In *A Black Theology of Liberation*, Cone underlines the necessity of undertaking the risky work of coming to providential judgments about God's relationship to contemporary events. Black theology "tries to discern the activity of the Holy One in achieving the purpose of the liberation of humankind." However, without a divine blueprint or a "perfect guide," those who would discern and respond to God's work find themselves having to "make decisions without a guaranteed ethical guide. This is the risk of faith."[67] As Cone understands the task, discerning the present work of God is a highly contingent and provisional—but nevertheless necessary—activity. He develops a Christological and pneumatological interpretation of his claim that the struggle for Black liberation is God's action in history, expanding his previous account of the liberating presence of Jesus Christ in history. In a clarification of the ambiguities of his position in *Black Theology and Black Power*, Cone offers a more detailed account of the Blackness of Jesus as the defining character of Jesus Christ in the present, and, therefore, as a key criterion for judging Christ's ongoing work in contemporary events. His account of the Blackness of Jesus rests upon a concrete, pneumatological connection between the first-century Jewishness and twentieth-century Blackness of Jesus Christ.

In the first several chapters of the book, Cone reconceives the nature of Christian theology in such a way to bring the question of divine action to the center. Cone asserts that theology's "sole reason for existence is to put into ordered speech the meaning of *God's activity in the world*."[68] Theology reflects on what God is doing in the world, "so that those who labor under enslaving powers will see that the forces of liberation are the very activity of God."[69] The paradigms of God's activity in history—which theology reflects upon in order to shed light on God's activity in the present—remain Israel and Jesus. Judgments about liberating divine action in the present are, therefore, specifically Christological. Indeed, Cone uses the language of "Jesus-event" to name instances of divine action after the resurrection.[70]

In *A Black Theology of Liberation*, Cone continues to connect this Christocentric understanding of divine action with his pneumatology. The Holy Spirit plays an integral role in Cone's conception of the nature of Christ's ongoing historical work: "The God who was revealed in the life of oppressed Israel and who came to us in the incarnate Christ and is present today as the Holy Spirit has made a decision about the black condition."[71] The Spirit stands at the center of his understanding of Christ's action in history.

The central conceptuality through which Cone understands God's action in history is liberating presence, and it is the Spirit who is, for Cone, God *present* to humanity after Christ's resurrection.[72] The union between Jesus Christ and Black humanity is, therefore, not a symbolic, analogical union based upon similarity of existential situation, but quite literally a *Spiritual* one, based upon the actual, concrete presence of Jesus Christ in history through the Holy Spirit.

It is this pneumatological construal of divine action that allows Cone to hold together his Christocentrism with his commitment to making judgments about divine action in the present. The Spirit makes possible a non-competitive account of the divine agency of Christ and the human agency of the Black community engaged in the struggle for liberation: "Though black theology affirms the black condition as the primary datum of reality to be reckoned with, this does not mean that it denies the absolute revelation of God in Jesus Christ. Rather it affirms it. Unlike white theology, which tends to make the Jesus-event an abstract, unembodied idea, black theology believes that the black community itself is precisely where Jesus Christ is at work."[73] The struggle for liberation from oppression does not displace Israel and Jesus Christ as the center of God's action in history. Rather, it is an extension of the concrete, particular work of God revealed and determined paradigmatically in Israel and Jesus. Cone's Black theology does not employ procedures of abstraction, sublation, or displacement in order to align God's providential action in history with Black humanity. Rather, it asks how Jesus Christ, the crucified and resurrected Jewish human being, continues to be present in history through the activity of the Spirit.

In short, Cone articulates a non-supersessionist and Christocentric conception of providence that is still able to support constructive judgments about God's continuing activity in history through the Holy Spirit. As Cone asserts, identifying the Black struggle for freedom as a manifestation of divine activity arises from "the conviction that the transcendent God who became immanent in Israelite history and incarnate in the man Jesus is also involved in Black history."[74] For Cone, the central criterion for judging God's action in history remains Jesus Christ. Yet this assertion does not close down the possibility of discerning continuing divine action after Christ's resurrection because—as Cone is fond of repeating—Jesus Christ is not confined to the first century, but continues to be present through the Holy Spirit. Given this framework, judgments about divine providence are a function of the relationship between Jesus' past and Jesus' present, which—as Cone articulates it—centers on the question of Jesus' Blackness.

Discerning God's action in history is risky business, and Cone is not afraid to name it as such. Consequently, *A Black Theology of Liberation* gives a careful accounting of how such a fraught task is to be undertaken.[75] For Cone, this is ultimately a question about revelation and, more specifically, a question about the "contemporary significance" of God's revelation of Godself in Jesus.[76] Cone writes, "God has been fully revealed in the man Jesus so that the norm of all existence is determined exclusively by him. He is *the* revelation of God."[77] The validity of claims about God's activity in the present, then, must be evaluated in light of God's revelation of Godself in Jesus.

Having seen the way in which white Christians have ideologically constructed a white Jesus who simply mirrors their own values and experiences, Cone is keen to avoid a repetition of their "chief error."[78] To do this, Cone turns to the concrete humanity of Jesus: "The historical Jesus must be taken seriously if we intend to avoid making Jesus into our own image."[79] While Cone articulates this point using the idiom of historical Jesus scholarship, it is not clear that his conclusion is integrally tied to that particular methodology. Rather, Cone is chiefly concerned to prevent the ideological construction of a Jesus that simply reflects one's own interests and perspectives back to oneself. Whether historical-critical reconstructions of the life of Jesus of Nazareth in fact prevent such constructions is certainly open to debate. Cone himself notes Albert Schweitzer's famous conclusion that, at least empirically speaking, quests for the historical Jesus have regularly resulted in precisely the kind of ideological construction that Cone wishes to avoid.[80]

In point of fact, Cone quickly leaves behind the language of the historical Jesus and speaks alternatively of an encounter with the revelation of Scripture as preventing visions of a Jesus made in one's own image. Black theology's Black Jesus is not simply the inverse of the white Jesus of white theology, as if these were two ideological articulations of Jesus reflecting their particular communities' existential situations.[81] Instead, Cone's judgment about where and how Christ is present today flows from the incarnation of the Word of God as a Jewish human being in first-century Palestine: "We want to know who Jesus *was* because we believe that that is the only way to assess who he *is*."[82]

The same Jesus who was born, who was baptized and tempted in the wilderness, who conducted a public ministry for three years, and who was crucified, and resurrected, all in the first century, is now present in the twentieth century through the Holy Spirit. This provides the basis for Cone's claim that Jesus is Black. Jesus' birth reflects God's concern to align Godself with the "lonely and downtrodden." The baptism and temptation reveal "Jesus' identification with the oppressed." In his ministry, Jesus taught and enacted the coming of the Kingdom of God, which is "the rule of God breaking in like a ray of light, usurping the powers that enslave human lives." His death is "the revelation of the freedom of God, taking upon himself the totality of human oppression." His resurrection discloses that "God is not defeated by oppression but transforms it into the possibility of freedom."[83] Finally, in His continued presence to creation through the Holy Spirit, this same Jesus is at work in the world *in this same way* in between His ascension and second coming.

For Cone, this warrants the claim that Jesus is Black: "The definition of Jesus as black is crucial for Christology if we truly believe in his continued presence today. . . . The life, death, and resurrection of Jesus reveal that he is the man for others, disclosing to them what is necessary for their liberation from oppression. If this is true, then Jesus Christ must be black."[84] To say that Jesus is Black is not to trade in abstract, racial essentialisms; it is a particular, contingent judgment about the concrete way in which Jesus Christ is present in the United States in the twentieth century.

Moving beyond the ambiguities of *Black Theology and Black Power*, Cone makes clear that his assertion of the Blackness of Christ is an attempt to make a judgment about the concrete character of Christ's presence in a "specific time and place."[85] Such a judgment ought not to be interpreted as an effort to say "the final word about the gospel," but as a contingent and provisional act of discerning the Spirit who makes Christ present in creation and enables creation to participate in the already accomplished work of Christ.[86] Cone's verdict about the Blackness of Christ does not empty Christ of His particularity, turning Jesus into a cipher for reading an abstract concept of liberation back into God's relationship to creation. Rather, it is an extension of Christ's particularity, given the fact of creaturely participation in Christ through the Holy Spirit. While this claim is already well underway to being fully developed in *A Black Theology of Liberation*, Cone would offer the definitive articulation of the pneumatological contemporaneity of Christ five years later in *God of the Oppressed*.

GOD OF THE OPPRESSED: JESUS CHRIST'S LIBERATING PRESENCE FOR US TODAY

In *God of the Oppressed*, Cone formulated his "most developed" theological position, deepening and building on the work of his first two books.[87] Having had time to consider the responses of both Black and white theologians to *Black Theology and Black Power* and *A Black Theology of Liberation*, Cone gave special attention to the questions and critiques generated by these earlier publications, honing and expanding his previous arguments about the relationship between Christology, revelation, ideology, and contemporary divine presence. Cone noted that this relationship had been the site of a shared criticism by both Black and white theologians. White theologians accused Cone of subordinating revelation to Black experience and creating a Jesus in his own image, while Black theologians like Gayraud Wilmore had argued that Cone was merely "Blackenizing" white Christian theology with his continued emphasis on the centrality of Jesus Christ.[88] Thus, from both ends of the theological spectrum, Cone was being pressed to restate and expand his Christology in light of questions about the relationship between revelation and ideology. In particular, Cone's commitment to affirming and discerning the ongoing presence of Christ in history required further explication.

Jesus, according to Cone, should not be understood as an abstract theological idea, but rather in specific relationship to Christ's "liberating presence in the lives of the poor in their fight for dignity and worth."[89] Because Jesus is not trapped in the first century, but is—through the Spirit—doing the work of liberation in the present, Cone argues, one cannot know Jesus "independent of the history and culture of the oppressed."[90] Given this close relationship between finite and fallen human experience and God's revelation of Godself in Jesus Christ, concerns about the ideological use of theology to lend divine authority to human interests are warranted. Cone wants to prevent Black theology from simply "identifying God's will with anything black people should decide to do at any given historical moment."[91] To address this potential problem, Cone turns to revelation. Black theology is not simply "the function of the subjective interest of an individual or group."[92] Rather, as Christian theology, it is rooted in divine revelation.[93] It is the task of the theologian to embrace the "burden and risk" of speaking meaningfully about God's presence in history in a way that is faithful to the reality of God's revelation of Godself in Jesus Christ.[94] For Cone, this entails locating the present as a moment within the primary reality of Jesus Christ by asking "Who is Jesus Christ for Us Today?" Cone maps this Christological framework as a dialectical encounter between Jesus' past, present, and future, out of which the Blackness of Jesus emerges as a contingent judgment about the way in which the Spirit is making Christ present in Cone's contemporary context.

God's paradigmatic action in history—the incarnation of Jesus Christ—provides the criterion by which all further attempts to discern God's historical work must be evaluated: "There is no knowledge of Jesus Christ today that contradicts who he was yesterday, i.e., his historical appearance in first-century Palestine."[95] Jesus' past constitutes a check against ideological subjectivism. Christ's identity has already been revealed and determined in the incarnation. It, therefore, is not open to being reconstrued according to one's political interests.[96]

More specifically, Cone concretely links Jesus' past to Jesus' humanity. Cone's Christology beings "with an affirmation of who Jesus was in his true humanity in history, using that point as the clue to who Jesus is for us today."[97] Docetic Christologies that downplay the significance of Jesus' human nature open the door to the ideological subjectivism that Cone sees running rampant in white Christianity, where white pastors and theologians have redefined Jesus according to "white people's political and economic interests."[98] The referent of Christology is the particular human being Jesus of Nazareth. By drawing this connection, Cone seeks to prevent Christology from functioning as a Feuerbachian projection of one's own experience and social context.

Within this emphasis on the human nature of Jesus of Nazareth, Cone foregrounds Jesus' Jewish identity as the paradigmatic characteristic of Christ's humanity. While Jesus' Jewishness had not been a point of great significance in *Black Theology and Black Power* or *A Black Theology of Liberation*, in *God of the Oppressed* it moves to the center of Cone's account of the incarnation: "*Jesus was a Jew!* The particularity of Jesus' person as disclosed in his Jewishness is indispensable for Christological analysis."[99] Cone sees Jesus' Jewishness as having two functions. First, it reaffirms the concreteness of Christ's incarnation in one particular human being as a central aspect of Christian faith. Second, it "connects God's salvation drama in Jesus with the Exodus-Sinai event," providing the point of continuity between God's two great acts of self-revelation: the covenant with Israel and the incarnation.[100] In both of these dimensions, Jesus' Jewishness indelibly imprints divine action in history with the specific character of God's liberating, covenantal presence. In the Jewish human being Jesus of Nazareth, God made Godself humanly present "with the poor and the wretched."[101] This provides the basis for all future judgments about divine action.

Because Scripture speaks of Christ's continued presence in history after the resurrection through the Holy Spirit, Cone argues that it is not just permissible—but in fact necessary—for Christian theologians to speak of Christ's activity in the present. Jesus is not only a figure from the past who was executed by the Roman authorities. Instead, "The Crucified One is also the Risen Lord." Therefore, Cone concludes, "While the *wasness* of Jesus is Christology's point of departure . . . the *isness* of Jesus relates his past history to his present involvement in our struggle."[102] To move from Jesus' past to Jesus' present is not to transition from a historical and theological Christology to a subjective and existential one because Jesus' presence in creation did not terminate at the ascension.

Cone rejects the agnosticism of Pannenberg on this issue, which defers the experience of Christ's presence to the eschaton and identifies the *saeculum* as marked by Christ's absence. Here Cone explicitly draws out the pneumatological framework that underlies his entire position, appealing to the outpouring of the Holy Spirit in Acts 1-2 and to the witness of Black church traditions.[103] Through the Spirit, the resurrected Christ continues to be present in history. Given this fact, a full account of Jesus' identity will include an interpretation of Christ's presence in contemporary events through the Spirit.[104]

The Spirit provides the continuity between who Jesus was and who Jesus is. For Cone, Jesus' past activity and Jesus' present activity stand in a dialectical relationship. On the one hand, Jesus' past activity is determinative of Jesus' present activity. Jesus does not act differently today than He did in the incarnation. On the other hand, Jesus' past activity alone does not capture the fullness of who Jesus is after the resurrection and ascension through the Holy Spirit: Jesus is also present in "our contemporary existence."[105] Rather than framing divine action in the present as a supersession or sublimation of Christ's incarnation within a general theory of divine providence, Cone identifies it as an integral aspect of Christology itself by underlining the role of the Holy Spirit in making Christ present to humanity between the ascension and the second coming.

Jesus is more than just his past and his present. The dialectical encounter between Jesus' *wasness* and Jesus' *isness* must be further expanded to include a relationship to who Jesus will be: the one who will return again to fulfill and complete the work of liberation that is already ongoing now.[106] Cone notes that there are obvious parallels between this emphasis on the eschatological dimension of Christology and the theology of hope being developed contemporaneously by Jürgen Moltmann and others. However, where the Euro-American theology of hope emerged relatively recently through a dialogue with Marxism, Cone contends, Black theology draws on a much older source: "Black people's encounter with the crucified and risen Lord in the context of American slavery."[107] This second tradition of hope theology was generated by a collision between Jesus' present and Jesus' future under the conditions of slavery. Cone writes, "Their hope sprang from the *actual presence* of Jesus breaking into their broken existence, and bestowing upon them a foretaste of God's promised freedom."[108] The presence of Jesus Christ in contemporary events is shot through with the future that Christ is bringing at the end of time.

Jesus' present, therefore, stands in a two-way dialectical relationship with Jesus' past and Jesus' future. Only by locating it in relation to these two other Christological temporalities can one accurately calibrate one's judgment about where and how Christ is present in contemporary events: "We can truly know Jesus' past and its soteriological significance only if his past is seen in dialectical relation to his present presence and his future coming."[109] Jesus' past and present are incomplete without Jesus' future. Discerning Christ's presence in the contemporary moment means looking both backward and forward. Christ's present action cannot be different than Christ's past action, but it must also be in conformity with Christ's future action in which He will bring an end to the suffering of the oppressed.

Concretely, Cone's emphasis on the relationship between Jesus' present and Jesus' future further focuses Christ's present action around struggles against oppression: "Who Jesus Christ is for us today is connected with the divine future as disclosed in the liberation fight of the poor." Therefore, Cone argues, "There can be no talk about hope in the Christian sense unless it is talk about the freedom of black, red, and brown people."[110] Jesus' presence through the Holy Spirit stands between the resurrection and the ascension, on the one hand, and the second coming, on the other, and it receives its character from both. In the Spirit, Jesus Christ is present today as crucified Jew, resurrected and ascended Lord, and coming Liberator. This is the Christological framework within which Christ's present action must be discerned.

In light of this dialectical relationship between Jesus' past, present, and future, Cone arrives at a final judgment about the nature and shape of Christ's presence in the first half of the nineteen-seventies: Jesus is Black. Jesus' Blackness functions as the hermeneutical lens through which to make concrete judgments about Jesus' ongoing activity in history. Within the hermeneutical framework that Cone develops for discerning divine action in history, the contemporary Blackness of Jesus sits at the center, as the point of convergence between Jesus' past, present, and future.[111]

Cone is at pains to make clear that his verdict about the Blackness of Jesus represents a complex, theological judgment, rather than an "an ideological distortion of the New Testament for political purposes."[112] Cone develops an account of the Blackness of Jesus as a specific, contingent judgment about the way in which Jesus' past and future imbue Jesus' present with a certain content and character in the United State in the twentieth century.

Cone's refusal to ground Christ's Blackness in an ideological reconstruction of Jesus in Black humanity's own image becomes even more apparent when one compares Cone's account to other accounts of the Blackness of Christ that emerged from traditions of Black Nationalism, such as Albert Cleage's account of Jesus as the Black messiah. Cone self-consciously formulated his own Christology as a corrective to Cleage, arguing that Cleage's theology reduces "the Christian gospel to a *literal* identification with the ideology of black power."[113] While Cone concludes that, in general, he has much in common with Cleage, he differs from him precisely in his rejection of the understanding of Christ's Blackness that Cleage embraced.[114]

The central issue that Cone explores in order to formulate his alternative theological conception of the Blackness of Jesus is the relationship between Jesus' Jewishness and Jesus' Blackness. Jesus' Blackness is anchored in the concrete particularity of Jesus' Jewish flesh. It is not a result of a supersession of, or abstraction from, that flesh: "I begin by asserting once more that *Jesus was a Jew*. It is on the basis of the soteriological meaning of the particularity of his Jewishness that theology must affirm the Christological significance of Jesus' present blackness. He *is* black because he *was* a Jew."[115] Jesus' Blackness does not supersede Jesus' Jewishness. Rather, Cone conceptualizes Jesus' Blackness with the framework of a theology of the nations, which envisions non-Jewish humanity's union with Christ as a gracious opening of Israel's covenant.

The cross and resurrection open up Jesus' Jewishness to include Jesus' Blackness. Cone explicitly invokes the theology of the nations rooted in Isaiah 42 to conceptualize this relation: "Without negating the divine election of Israel, the cross and resurrection are Yahweh's fulfillment of his original intention for Israel to be 'a light to the nations, to open the eyes that are blind, to bring out the prisoners from the dungeon, from the prison those who sit in darkness.'"[116] The cross and resurrection for Cone do not invalidate the particularity of Jesus' Jewishness—nor the election of Israel which that flesh embodies. Rather, they show that Jesus' Jewishness and Israel's election are not self-referential and self-limiting, but includes those "who once were far off," as Paul writes in Ephesians 2. The resurrection opens up Israel's covenant promise to all, without thereby superseding the priority or uniqueness of Israel.[117] As Timothy McGee suggests, "The resurrection of Christ does not offer a universal or generic mode of ungrounded creaturely life but a particular one, one arising within and as the movement between two particularities, the joining or setting side-by-side the divine life in Jesus Christ and Black movements for survival and freedom."[118] It is within this covenantal understanding of Jesus' Jewish flesh, with its concomitant theology of the nations, that Cone locates Jesus' Blackness.

Just as Israel's election cannot be superseded by, but ultimately includes the Gentiles, so Jesus Jewishness' cannot be superseded by, but ultimately includes Jesus' Blackness. Cone writes, "It is in the light of the cross and the resurrection of Jesus in relation to his Jewishness that Black Theology asserts that 'Jesus is black.'"[119] To call Jesus Black is to make a contingent judgment about how Jesus' Jewish flesh is active in creation today through the power of the Holy Spirit: "Christ is black, therefore, not because of some cultural or psychological need of black people, but because and only because Christ *really* enters into our world where the poor, the despised, and the black are, disclosing that he is with them, enduring their humiliation and pain and transforming oppressed slaves into liberated servants."[120] The Jewishness of Jesus provides the fundamental warrant for the claim that Christ is Black in the United States in the twentieth century. The *particularity* of Jesus' Jewish humanity—which is determinative of the character of Jesus' bodily presence in history both prior to the ascension and after the second coming—necessitates contextual judgments about the *particular* ways that Jesus continues to be present through the Spirit in the time between those two events.[121]

Given this analysis, the Blackness of Christ functions in Cone's thought as the hermeneutical lens through which Christ's present action through the Holy Spirit can be faithfully discerned. Emerging from the dialectical relationship between Jesus' past, present, and future, Jesus' Blackness is not an ideological reconstruction of Christ in light of Cone's subjective interests. It is rather a statement about how and where the Holy Spirit is making Christ concretely present in history at one particular moment between the ascension and the second coming. When Cone claims that Jesus *was* a Jew, but that Jesus *is* Black, this does not reflect a latent supersessionism in Cone's thought, in which Blackness replaces Jewishness as the fundamental characteristic of Christ's humanity. Rather, it is a statement about the way in which the Holy Spirit continues to unite humanity with Jesus Christ after the ascension. Through the Holy Spirit Jesus' present Blackness participates in, rather than supersedes, Jesus' Jewishness.

CONCLUSION

In *Black Theology and Black Power*, *A Black Theology of Liberation*, and *God of the Oppressed*, the same basic premise underlies Cone's efforts to conceptualize the nature and shape of contemporary divine action. This is his conviction that, though he sees the inherent danger involved in trying to speak meaningfully about God's action in the present, he is compelled to do so by the fact of Christ's resurrection and continued presence in history through the Holy Spirit. Cone's perspective is not triumphalist. As Vincent Lloyd suggests, he never fails to emphasize "the precarious nature of this analysis and action."[122] But while speaking of God's activity is a risk and a burden, it is nevertheless a necessity. Given the seriousness with which Cone takes his task, as well as his recognition that it is fraught with the dangers of idolatry and self-deception, it is little wonder that he returns to refine his account of divine action again and again in his early writings. Having explored each of them in turn, it is now possible to offer an assessment of the overall shape and trajectory of Cone's doctrine of providence as he developed it in the midst of Black Power's heyday between 1968 and 1975.

Cone understands providence as the pneumatological contemporaneity of Christ with the present age. He inscribes providence within the narrative arc of the liberation and election of Israel and Christ's incarnation. Importantly, Cone argues that the story of Jesus' birth, life, death, resurrection, ascension, and second coming *includes* Jesus' presence in the present time prior to His final return. In this way, providence becomes an aspect of Christology. For Cone, the crucial actor who makes this possible is the Holy Spirit. The Spirit continues to make Christ present in history after the ascension. In this way, providence, for Cone, is not a general theory of divine action, but a very specific commitment to Jesus Christ's ongoing agency in creation. Jesus is not trapped in the first century, but is present through the Holy Spirit. This understanding of providence necessarily leads to the question of discernment: where and how is Christ present through the Spirit today?

Because divine providence is a function of Christology, as Jesus remains the central criterion for judging God's ongoing action in history, Jesus' identity operates as the lens through which to conceptualize contemporary divine action. The shape of God's ongoing action in history emerges from the dialectical relationship between Christ's past, present, and future. The Spirit plays a crucial role once again, providing the continuity between who Jesus was, who Jesus is, and who Jesus will be. Through the Spirit, Christ continues to be present as the crucified, resurrected, and ascended Jewish human being. Indeed, Jesus' particular identity as a Jewish human being in first-century Palestine definitively shapes the particular ways that Christ continues to be present through the Spirit. For Cone, the particularity of Christ's Jewish human flesh does not close down the possibility that other flesh might participate in it. It is in this regard, in terms of the concrete, pneumatological participation of humanity in Christ's ongoing presence in history between the ascension and the second coming, that Cone argues that Jesus is Black.

The Blackness of Jesus represents the point at which the dialectical relations of Jesus' past, present, and future converge in Cone's historical moment in the United States. Christ's Blackness names the specific content of Christ's present as it is determined by its dialectical relationships with Christ's past and Christ's future. The particularity of Christ's incarnation in Jewish flesh determines the particular mode of Christ's presence through the Holy Spirit in the present. This Jesus, in whose flesh God's liberating covenant with Israel was opened up to include the nations, in whose birth God identified Godself with the downtrodden, whose ministry proclaimed the coming of the Kingdom of God, who in his death and resurrection defeated the demonic powers of oppression, slavery, and death, and whose second coming will bring final and complete liberation for the oppressed—this same Jesus is doing this same work in the present through the Holy Spirit. In Cone's particular context, Blackness represents humanity at its most attuned to this work, at its most receptive to the Spirit, and, therefore, participating most fully in Jesus' presence. Thus, far from an ideological distortion of Christology, the Blackness of Christ names the lens through which one can most truthfully see Jesus Christ's presence in history.

The paradigmatic instances of Christ's providential presence through the Spirit in Cone's early writings are the uprisings in Watts, Newark, Detroit, and beyond. Cone concludes, "Black rebellion is a manifestation of God himself actively involved in the present-day affairs of men for the purpose of liberating a people."[123] Christ is not just active in an abstract "struggle." Christ is present in and with Black people in Newark and Detroit in the affirmation of their own humanity and in their suffering and death at the hands of the American police and military apparatus. As Cone is quick to point out, the violence generated by the urban rebellions has more to do with white society's response to Black self-affirmation than anything else. The urban rebellions are an attempt by Black people simply to say, "Yes to truth and No to untruth even in death. The question, then, is not whether Black people are prepared to die—the riots testify to that—but whether whites are prepared to kill them. Unfortunately, it seems that that answer has been given through the riots as well."[124]

For Cone, Christ was present in Newark on July 12, 1967. Christ was present in Detroit on July 23, 1967. Therefore, Black and white Christians are confronted with the necessity of how they will respond to Christ's work. "The white church," Cone argues, "is placed in question because of its contribution to a structure which produces riots." To join with Christ, the white church is called to "fight against the conditions which cause [the riots]." This is not a matter of strongly worded resolutions, but of "involvement in the affairs of people who suffer."[125] Similarly, Cone warns the Black church not to "admonish its people to be 'nice'" or "condemn the rioters." Rather, he charges the Black church to "make an unqualified identification with the 'looters' and 'rioters.'"[126] When Christ is present in history, Christians are called to respond. Neither the white nor the Black church embodies the presence of Christ by default. Rather, human communities—ecclesial or otherwise—only embody the presence of Christ as those communities move into action to be where Christ is and do what Christ is doing through the Spirit. For Cone, "The existence of *the* Church is grounded exclusively in Christ."[127] For the church to be the church, it must be converted to Christ by radically reorienting itself and joining Christ in his work: "'Where Christ is, there is the Church.' Christ is to be found, as always, where men are enslaved and trampled underfoot; Christ is found suffering with the suffering; Christ is in the ghetto—there also is his Church."[128]

NOTES

1. Kevin Mumford, *Newark: A History of Race, Rights, and Riots in America* (New York: New York University Press, 2007), 128. For other historical analyses upon which the present account of the 1967 Newark and Detroit uprisings draws, see Sidney Fine, *Violence in the Model City: The Cavanagh Administration, Race Relations, and the Detroit Riots of 1967* (Ann Arbor, MI: The University of Michigan Press, 1989); Max Arthur Herman, *Fighting in the Streets: Ethnic Succession and Urban Unrest in Twentieth-Century America* (New York: Peter Lang, 2005); Max Arthur Herman,

Summer of Rage: An Oral History of the 1967 Newark and Detroit Riots (New York: Peter Lang, 2013); Peniel E. Joseph, *Waiting 'Til the Midnight Hour: A Narrative History of Black Power in America* (New York: Henry Holt and Co., 2006); Malcolm McLaughlin, *The Long, Hot Summer of 1967: Urban Rebellion in America* (New York: Palgrave Macmillan, 2014); Thomas J. Sugrue, *The Origins of the Urban Crisis: Race and Inequality in Postwar Detroit* (Princeton: Princeton University Press, 1996).

2. A variety of proposals for the capitalization of racial terminology such as "Black" and "white" have recently been proposed. In the present work, I follow Jennifer Harvey in capitalizing "Black" but not "white." This reflects the fact that while Black people have intentionally forged a constructive and liberating form of racial identity, white people as a collective group have not developed their racial identity in any way other than through violence and oppression. However, in recognition that the question of capitalization is far from settled, I have preserved the capitalization practices of other authors when quoting their work. See Jennifer Harvey, *Raising White Kids: Bringing Up Children in Racially Unjust America* (Nashville: Abingdon Press, 2017), 7. For a full discussion of the lack of parallelism between Black and white, see Jennifer Harvey, *Dear White Christians: For Those Still Longing for Racial Reconciliation*, 2nd ed. (Grand Rapids: Wm. B. Eerdmans Publishing Co., 2020), 41–62.

3. Herman, *Summer of Rage*, 9–13.

4. Ibid., 143. Out of 6,000 law enforcement and military personnel deployed in the city, the only one to die was shot by three men who had witnessed the police open fire on a crowd, killing a seventy-year-old man and injuring a little girl. See also, Joseph, *Waiting 'Til the Midnight Hour*, 184.

5. Mumford, *Newark*, 125, 147–148.

6. Sugrue, *Origins of the Urban Crisis*, 257.

7. Fine, *Violence in the Model City*, 156, 166.

8. Joseph, *Waiting 'Til the Midnight Hour*, 185.

9. In her essay "The (Black) Jesus of Detroit: Reflections on black power and the (white) American Christ," in *Christology and Whiteness: What Would Jesus Do?*, ed. George Yancy (New York: Routledge, 2012), M. Shawn Copeland relates a fascinating episode that occurred in the midst of the violence: "A little-known, yet highly symbolic, incident during those days involved a statue of the Sacred Heart of Jesus on the grounds of the major seminary of the Roman Catholic Archdiocese.... On the second day of the disturbance, an African American housepainter reportedly applied black paint to the hands, feet, and face of the statue of the Sacred Heart of Jesus. At least twice, the color was removed, but black paint prevailed and, over the past four decades, the seminary has kept it fresh" (180).

10. Herman, *Summer of Rage*, 18, 200.

11. Ibid., 203. The soldiers of the 82nd Airborne division arrived late in the conflict and did not engage citizens with the same degree of violence as the police and National Guard.

12. McLaughlin, *The Long, Hot Summer of 1967*, 115.

13. Fine, *Violence in the Model City*, 299.

14. Ibid., 453, 301.

15. James Cone, *My Soul Looks Back* (Nashville: Abingdon, 1982), 43.

16. James Cone, *The Cross and the Lynching Tree* (Maryknoll, NY: Orbis Books, 2012), xvi; James Cone, *Risks of Faith: The Emergence of a Black Theology of Liberation, 1968-1998* (Boston: Beacon Press, 1999), xxii. See also Cornel West, "Black Theology and Human Identity," in *Black Faith and Public Talk: Critical Essays on James H. Cone's* Black Theology and Black Power, ed. Dwight N. Hopkins (Maryknoll, NY: Orbis Books, 1999), 12: "We can imagine the young James Hal Cone saying, 'I'm overwhelmed by this. What do I have to say? I either write this book or I'll go crazy.' That is the kind of theology I like. Outcry."

17. Cone, *My Soul Looks Back*, 43.

18. Ibid., 44. Cone did compose one essay, entitled "Christianity and Black Power," in between the events of Newark and Detroit in July 1967 and the assassination of King in April 1968. See James Cone, "Christianity and Black Power," in *Risks of Faith: The Emergence of a Black Theology of Liberation, 1968-1998* (Boston: Beacon Press, 1999), 3–12.

19. Cone, *My Soul Looks Back*, 52.

20. This phrase was, of course, first used to describe Karl Barth's *Epistle to the Romans*. See Dorrien, *Barthian Revolt in Modern Theology*, 45. Cone himself has noted the similarities between the two works in *Risks of Faith*: "In writing *Black Theology and Black Power*, I suddenly understood what Karl Barth must have felt when he first rejected the liberal theology of his professors in Germany. . . . Although separated by nearly fifty years and dealing with completely different theological situations and issues, I felt a spiritual kinship with Barth" (xxiii). See also Dwight N. Hopkins, "Black Theology on Theological Education, in *Black Faith and Public Talk: Critical Essays on James H. Cone's* Black Theology and Black Power, ed. Dwight N. Hopkins (Maryknoll, NY: Orbis Books, 1999), 41: "Cone's *Black Theology and Black Power* dropped a bombshell that shook the intellectual stools of the academy then; even today we still feel the reverberations."

21. Dwight N. Hopkins, "Introduction," in *Black Faith and Public Talk: Critical Essays on James H. Cone's* Black Theology and Black Power, ed. Dwight N. Hopkins (Maryknoll, NY: Orbis Books, 1999), 4.

22. James Cone, *Speaking the Truth: Ecumenism, Liberation, and Black Theology* (Grand Rapids: Wm. B. Eerdmans Publishing Co., 1986), 39.

23. BTBP, 6. Emphasis in original. While not limiting the term to any one figure's conception of it, Cone does repeatedly turn to Stokely Carmichael as a key progenitor of the concept. See Stokely Carmichael and Charles V. Hamilton, *Black Power: The Politics of Liberation in America* (New York: Random House, 1967).

24. BTBP, 1. Cone's definition of Black Power reflects the same entanglement with patriarchy with which Black Power groups like the Black Panther Party for Self-Defense were struggling at that very moment. Like the early Panthers, Cone struggled to avoid framing Black Power as a reclamation of black masculinity. However, Black Power itself was a complex movement that expressed itself in a variety of political, cultural, and economic modes and contained diverse attitudes toward religion, gender, racial separatism, and violence. For recent historiography of Black Power that underlines this point, see Rhonda Y. Williams, "Black Women, Urban Politics,

and Engendering Black Power," in *The Black Power Movement*, ed. Peniel E. Joseph (New York: Routledge, 2006), 79–104; Kimberly Springer, "Black Feminists Respond to Black Power Masculinism," in *The Black Power Movement*, ed. Peniel E. Joseph (New York: Routledge, 2006), 105–118; Kathleen Cleaver, "Women, Power, and Revolution," in *Liberation, Imagination, and the Black Panther Party*, ed. Kathleen Cleaver and George Katsiaficas (New York: Routledge, 2001), 123–127; Tracye Matthews, "'No One Ever Asks, What a Man's Place in the Revolution Is': Gender and the Politics of the Black Panther Party 1966-1971," in *The Black Panther Party [Reconsidered]*, ed. Charles E. Jones (Baltimore: Black Classic Press, 1998), 267–304; Bettye Collier-Thomas and V. P. Franklin, ed.'s, *Sisters in the Struggle: African American Women in the Civil Rights-Black Power Movement* (New York: New York University Press, 2001); Christina Greene, *Our Separate Ways: Women and the Black Freedom Movement in Durham, North Carolina* (Chapel Hill, NC: The University of North Carolina Press, 2005).

25. Ibid., 47–56. This first argument about conceptual compatibility quickly became the center of a debate about Christianity, reconciliation, and violence between Cone, J. Deotis Roberts, and Major Jones. See J. Deotis Roberts, *Liberation and Reconciliation: A Black Theology* (Philadelphia: Westminster Press, 1971); Major Jones *Black Awareness: A Theology of Hope* (Nashville: Abingdon Press, 1971).

26. *BTBP*, 61.

27. Between 1964 and 1969 there were more than 300 uprisings in 257 cities. See West, "Black Theology and Human Identity," 12.

28. Cone should not be read as simply inverting Hegel's providential vision, producing an "equal and opposite" doctrine that merely provides ideological cover for Black liberation instead of European conquest. See, for example, Victor Anderson, *Beyond Ontological Blackness: An Essay on African American Religious and Cultural Criticism* (New York: Continuum Publishing Co., 1995), 86: "If white theology was viewed as an ideology of oppression, then black theology would become the ideology of liberation." I do not discount Anderson's important criticisms of Cone's work, but rather I seek to show that Cone could speak paradoxically and in multiple registers, which complicates efforts to make any cumulative judgment about the nature of his project. My interpretive approach to Cone is therefore formally similar to that developed by Vincent Lloyd in "Paradox and Tradition in Black Theology," *Black Theology* 9, no. 3 (2011): 265–286.

29. While there are definite affinities between the theological proposals of Cone and Barth—inasmuch as both engage in Christological reflection in order to critique any attempt to link divine providence to the movement of white peoples and their civilizations—Cone foregrounds a constructive alternative that differentiates him from Barth. Where Barth's primary theme is that the project of Western civilization cannot be identified with the movement of God in history, Cone goes beyond this, identifying the struggle for black liberation as a positive manifestation of Christ's ongoing action in history. The extent to which Barth would or would not approve of Cone's constructive conclusion lies beyond the scope of this work. However, I do not believe that Barth would completely recoil from Cone's identification of Black Power with the movement of God in history. The early Barth of the *Romans* commentary and the "infinite

qualitative distinction between God and man" certainly would not have approved. However, as Christology moved increasingly to the center of Barth's thought, he was more and more able to speak constructively about the positive relationship between God and humanity. By the late nineteen-forties, while Barth continued to beat the drum against baptizing any political system or movement as divinely sanctioned, he was increasingly speaking positively of a Christological politics focused on the lives of the ordinary human beings for whom Christ died. This seems to be a significant step in the direction that Cone takes. It certainly is a long way from a one-sided commitment to the "infinite qualitative distinction." For a full exploration of these issues, see Beverly Eileen Mitchell, "Karl Barth and James Cone: The Question of Liberative Faith and Ideology" (PhD diss., Boston College, 1999), ProQuest (9930882).

30. James Cone, *God of the Oppressed* (Maryknoll, NY: Orbis Books, 1975), 99 (hereafter cited as *GO*).

31. Cone's pneumatology—and his understanding of the Trinity in general—have not received the attention they merit from interpreters of Cone's thought, who have generally focused their analyses on his Christology. Isolating Christology from the wider Trinitarian framework present in Cone's work leads to a variety of misinterpretations of the former. In particular, leaving out the work of the Spirit makes it difficult to explicate accurately Cone's claims about the relationship between Christ and Black humanity. For a related account of these issues, see Timothy McGee, "God's Life In and As Opening: James Cone, Divine Self-Determination, and the Trinitarian Politics of Sovereignty," *Modern Theology* 32, no. 1 (2016): 100–117.

32. 1 John 4:1-3 (New Revised Standard Version).

33. *BTBP*, 49.

34. *LPWH*, 145; *CD* III/3, 242.

35. This is yet a further dimension of the paradoxical nature of Cone's thought explored in Lloyd, "Paradox and Tradition in Black Theology," 269–282.

36. *BTBP*, 44.

37. Ibid., 44–45.

38. Ibid., 123. Emphasis added. In *Black Theology and Black Power*, Cone is particularly critical of the otherworldliness of the Spirituals: "Even a casual look at the black Spirituals shows their otherworldly character" (121). Over the next several years, Cone realized that his look at the Spirituals had been too casual indeed, and he reevaluated this criticism after a more careful investigation in *The Spirituals and the Blues* (Maryknoll, NY: Orbis Books, 1972).

39. *BTBP*, 126.

40. Ibid., 134.

41. James Cone, *A Black Theology of Liberation* (Maryknoll, NY: Orbis Books, 1986), xvii (hereafter cited as *BTL*). Cone's invocation of divine presence—and his emphasis on the Holy Spirit—suggests some interesting points of connection with more contemporary works on pneumatology and providence, such as Gordon Fee's *God's Empowering Presence: The Holy Spirit in the Letters of Paul* (Grand Rapids: Baker Academic, 2009) and Wright's *Providence Made Flesh*. These connections will be explored in the final chapter of this study.

42. *BTBP*, 44.

43. Ibid., 36, 36.
44. Carter, *Race: A Theological Account*, 158. "A concrete conceptualization of Being stands over against abstract conceptualizations of Being, along with their attendant racial politics."
45. *BTBP*, 35.
46. Luke 4:18-19.
47. *BTBP*, 36.
48. Ibid., 40.
49. Ibid., 40.
50. Ibid., 40.
51. Ibid., 38.
52. For an account that helpfully situates Cone's pneumatology within traditions of Black religious belief and practice in the United States, see Garth Baker-Fletcher, "Black theology and the Holy Spirit," in *The Cambridge Companion to Black Theology*, ed. Dwight N. Hopkins and Edward P. Antonio (Cambridge: Cambridge University Press, 2012), 111–125.
53. *BTBP*, 57.
54. Malcolm X and Alex Haley, *The Autobiography of Malcolm X* (New York: Grove Press, 1965), 253. Quoted in Cone, *Black Theology and Black Power*, viii.
55. *BTBP*, 68. Emphasis in original.
56. Carter, *Race: A Theological* Account, 171.
57. *BTBP*, 69.
58. Carter, *Race: A Theological Account*, 158. For a critical engagement with Carter on these issues, see Victor Anderson, "The Mimesis of Salvation and Dissimilitude in the Scandalous Gospel of Jesus," in *Christology and Whiteness: What Would Jesus Do?*, ed. George Yancy (New York: Routledge, 2012), 196–211.
59. *BTBP*, 60. Emphasis added.
60. Ibid., 80.
61. Ibid., 60.
62. Gayraud S. Wilmore, "Black Theology at the Turn of the Century: Some Unmet Needs and Challenges," in *Black Faith and Public Talk: Critical Essays on James H. Cone's* Black Theology and Black Power, ed. Dwight N. Hopkins (Maryknoll, NY: Orbis Books, 1999), 232.
63. *BTL*, ix.
64. Ibid., 83.
65. Ibid., 17–18.
66. Ibid., 86.
67. Ibid., 7, 7. Emphasis in original.
68. Ibid., 1. Emphasis added.
69. Ibid., 3.
70. Ibid., 5.
71. Ibid., 12–13. Emphasis in original.
72. Cone makes several programmatic statements in which he identifies divine presence as a key conceptuality through which he conceives of God's action in history. See *BTBP*, vii; *BTL*, xvii; Cone, *The Cross and the Lynching Tree*, 2.

73. *BTL*, 5.
74. Ibid., 15.
75. Ibid., 42.
76. Ibid., 47.
77. Ibid., 54. Emphasis in original.
78. Ibid., 119.
79. Ibid., 119.
80. Ibid., 117.
81. For a thoughtful critique of the limitations of deploying Christology as a resource for resisting white supremacy that attends precisely to this issue, see Anthony B. Pinn, "Looking Like Me? Jesus images, Christology, and the limitations of theological blackness," in *Christology and Whiteness: What Would Jesus Do?*, ed. George Yancy (New York: Routledge, 2012), 169–179.
82. *BTL*, 118. Emphasis in original.
83. Ibid., 121, 121, 124, 124–125, 125.
84. Ibid., 127.
85. Ibid., 153.
86. Ibid., 154.
87. *GO*, ix.
88. Ibid., 33 n. 38. See Gayraud Wilmore, *Black Religion and Black Radicalism*, 296.
89. Ibid., xiii.
90. Ibid., 33.
91. Ibid., 77.
92. Ibid., 83.
93. Ibid., 87.
94. Ibid., 89.
95. Ibid., 106.
96. Ibid., 106.
97. Ibid., 108.
98. Ibid., 109.
99. Ibid., 109. Emphasis in original.
100. Ibid., 109.
101. Ibid., 110.
102. Ibid., 110, 110.
103. Ibid., 111. See Wolfhart Pannenberg, *Jesus, God and Man*, trans. Lewis L. Wilkins and Duane A. Priebe (Philadelphia: Westminster Press, 1968), 28.
104. *GO*, 112.
105. Ibid., 115.
106. Ibid., 116.
107. Ibid., 117.
108. Ibid., 117.
109. Ibid., 120. Christology "from below," is therefore only one aspect of Cone's understanding. It is, therefore, not quite the case—as Harry H. Singleton III argues—that Cone endorses a Christology "from below" in opposition to a Christology "from

above." Rather, Cone challenges the fundamental logic of these distinctions. See Harry H. Singleton III, *Black Theology and Ideology: Deideological Dimensions in the Theology of James H. Cone* (Collegeville, MN: The Liturgical Press, 2002), 78.

110. *GO*, 118, 117.

111. For a related defense of Cone's use of Blackness as an anti-ideological hermeneutic, see Singleton, *Black Theology and Ideology*, 68–91.

112. *GO*, 122–123. Rufus Burrow, Jr. makes an important argument that though Cone addressed certain criticisms of his work by white theologians, this did not imply that his chief concern was to win over his white audience. See Rufus Burrow, Jr., *James H. Cone and Black Liberation Theology* (London: McFarland & Company, Inc., 1994), 57–77.

113. James Cone, *For My People: Black Theology and the Black Church* (Maryknoll, NY: Orbis Books, 1984), 36. Emphasis in original.

114. Ibid., 225 n. 6. For an extended account of Cleage's theology, see Cardinal Aswad Walker, "Princes Shall Come Out of Egypt: A Theological Comparison of Marcus Garvey and Reverend Albert B. Cleage Jr.," *Journal of Black Studies* 39, no. 2 (2008): 194–251.

115. *GO*, 123. Emphasis in original.

116. Ibid., 124. This passage provides a paradigmatic example of J. Kameron Carter's claim that "black theology, understood from this vantage, gestures towards a theology of the nations, one that emanates from and is consonant with a Christian theology of Israel." See Carter, *Race: A Theological Account*, 158.

117. *GO*, 124.

118. Timothy McGee, "Against (White) Redemption: James Cone and the Christological Disruption of Racial Discourse and White Solidarity," *Political Theology* (2017): 1–18.

119. *GO*, 124.

120. Ibid., 124. Emphasis in original.

121. Carter, *Race: A Theological Account*, 166: "For Cone, the Jewishness of Jesus is tacitly invoked as a means of moving away from imaging others in abstract terms and toward viewing and engaging them concretely."

122. Lloyd, "Paradox and Tradition in Black Theology," 277. Lloyd rightly draws out the importance of the messiness, contingency, finitude, and humility which mark Cone's discussion of divine action through Cone's embrace of paradox in his early theological writings.

123. *BTBP*, 38.

124. Ibid., 30.

125. Ibid., 79, 80, 80.

126. Ibid., 113, 113.

127. Ibid., 112.

128. Ibid., 66.

Chapter 5

Liberating Providence
The Spirit, Christ's Presence, and Creaturely Participation

This study has engaged the fraught theological issue of how Christians read the world in relationship to God's activity in it. More specifically, it has sought to identify and examine the particular way in which modern Christian attempts at such theological readings of the world have both resourced and contested racial visions of global humanity. The three previous chapters of this study have each explicated an influential account of providence in the history of modern Protestant theology, demonstrating how Christian theological reflection on the topic of providence lies near the center of the racial and political architecture of modernity.

Hegel, Barth, and Cone all connect their accounts of providence to the question of modern, racialized humanity. For Hegel, it is the question of spirit's relationship to the culmination of European modernity and the global imperial conquests of European humanity in the first half of the nineteenth century. Alternatively, Barth investigates God's preservation, accompaniment, and government of creation in relationship to the ideological captivity of Christian theological discourse to Nazism and the emerging East-West conflict in the years immediately preceding 1950. Lastly, an exposition of Christ's work in the urban rebellions and the Black liberation struggles of the 1960s and 1970s drives Cone's account of divine action throughout his early writings. In each case, a different conception of the doctrine of providence shapes its author's theological interpretation of contemporary events, particularly as these events connect to fundamental questions about modernity, Western civilization, and racial humanity.

Up until this point in the present study, I have largely considered each of these cases in isolation from each other in order to avoid the temptation to shoehorn three diverse case studies into an overly tidy genealogy. Yet respect for the integrity and individuality of these three portraits need not be antithetical to the desire to make connections between them. Indeed, the authors themselves explicitly make these connections: Barth identifies Hegel as a key interlocutor at several points in *Church Dogmatics* III/3, while Cone has a running engagement with Barth throughout his early works. In this specific case, then, respect for the individual texts necessitates an analysis of the broader narrative that results from placing them in conversation with one another. The present chapter identifies the narrative trajectories that emerge organically from a critical comparison of these three accounts and extends those trajectories to formulate a constructive account of providence that follows the lead of Barth and Cone in order to respond to the way that race continues to shape Christian attempts to discern what God is doing in the world today.

In the first part of the present chapter, I conduct a comparative analysis of the accounts of divine providence developed by Hegel, Barth, and Cone, identifying both the positive conclusions and the unresolved problems that emerge from reading the three figures as part of a single developing trajectory of thought. On the basis of this comparison, I argue that the developing trajectory of thought in Hegel, Barth, and Cone proves instructive for present-day reflection on the doctrine of providence, both in terms of that trajectory's positive conclusions and its unresolved problems. Positively, I suggest three themes that emerge from this comparative analysis which should guide contemporary accounts of divine providence: the *centrality of the incarnation* of Jesus Christ for conceptualizing God's providential action, the *creatureliness* of human beings, and *the work of the Holy Spirit* in making Jesus Christ present to creation between ascension and eschaton. Negatively, I identify two issues that remain unresolved by the line of thought developed from Hegel, through Barth, to Cone: the *persistent masculinity* of divine providence and the struggle against *a reductive pneumatology* in which the work of the Spirit is either problematically independent from or simply reducible to the work of the Son.

In the second half of the chapter, I formulate a constructive account of providence which builds on the positive conclusions drawn from the analysis of Hegel, Barth, and Cone, while addressing the problems that they leave unresolved. I develop an account of divine providence as the work of the Holy Spirit in making Jesus Christ present to creation between ascension and eschaton and enabling human creaturely participation in Christ's presence in this time between the times. More succinctly, I argue for a pneumatological conception of providence in terms of Christological *presence* and anthropological *participation*.

By understanding providence in terms of presence and participation, I am able to make sense of a number of traditional challenges of the doctrine of providence while also weaving together the three central themes identified as key lessons in the analysis of Hegel, Barth, and Cone: Christocentricity, creatureliness, and pneumatology. Extending Cone's argument, I suggest that understanding providence in terms of the theological trope of *presence* holds Christ and the Spirit together in a non-competitive relationship that does justice to the particularity of each without problematically separating them from one another. Furthermore, providence as presence comports with and clarifies the traditional distinction between God's general and special providence. Similarly, I argue that conceptualizing providence in terms of *participation* makes it possible to speak of humanity's genuine relationship to Christ's presence in a way that fully embraces human creatureliness, neither denigrating the human subject in the face of God's providence nor exalting the human subject as itself divine. Providence as participation, therefore, helps to resolve a traditional point of difficulty in the doctrine of providence: the relationship between divine action and human agency.

In addition to extending the Christological, creaturely, and pneumatological trajectories elaborated in my analysis of Hegel, Barth, and Cone, providence as presence and participation also addresses the two problems left unresolved by the developing conversation about providence that I have traced across the work of these three figures. Following the lead of womanist theologians Delores S. Williams and M. Shawn Copeland and drawing on conversations in contemporary pneumatology, I demonstrate that a pneumatological account of providence centered on the themes of Christ's presence and human participation through the Spirit is able to avoid two problems which the accounts of Hegel, Barth, and Cone fail to resolve: first, consistently masculine characterizations of God's providential action in the world and, second, a tendency to locate the Spirit and Christ in a competitive relation in which the Spirit's activity in creation is either problematically independent of or wholly reducible to the activity of Christ.

To this end, I examine the Spirit's relationship to *bodies*, *community*, and *time*, filling out the formal framework of providence as presence and participation with a specific material content. I argue that paying attention to the Spirit's particular relationship to bodies, community, and time provides an alternative to persistently masculine characterizations of God's providential activity that simultaneously does justice to the uniqueness of the Holy Spirit's activity in creation in a way that does not render that activity problematically independent of God's revelation of Godself in Jesus Christ.

Most basically, the account of providence developed in this chapter builds upon Barth's account of creaturely participation in providence and Cone's account of Christ's presence through the Spirit to articulate a vision of divine providence that can identify Jesus Christ at work through the Spirit in ordinary, overlooked, and oppressed human creatures who are daily engaged in quotidian struggles to survive and carve out a flourishing life for themselves, their families, their neighborhoods, and their world.

140   Chapter 5

NARRATIVE TRAJECTORIES: HEGEL, BARTH, AND CONE

In the three central chapters of the present study, I have made a point to examine the doctrines of providence articulated by Hegel, Barth, and Cone with reference to the particular contexts in which they were composed. I have argued in each case that the author in question explicitly addressed their explorations of the doctrine of providence to these contemporary circumstances, as a way to make sense theologically of what was going on in their world. However, this emphasis on locating theological texts in their historical and sociopolitical contexts need not prevent a fruitful comparative analysis of the three cases. Indeed, for all three authors, engagement with alternative conceptions of the doctrine of providence was one of the primary modes in which they formulated their own understandings of the doctrine: Hegel differentiates himself from prior Christian accounts of providence that maintain the conviction that the specifics of God's providential plans are "hidden from our eyes"; Barth argues that his account rules out the possibility of believing "as Hegel did, in a self-development of the absolute spirit to be realized in history and more or less attained in 1830"; Cone maintains that Jesus Christ is not confined in the first century in response to "Barth's early emphasis on 'the infinite qualitative distinction between God and man.'"[1] All three authors provide ample precedent for reading their accounts as part of a developing trajectory of modern Protestant thought about how the doctrine of providence ought to shape Christian attempts to discern God's relationship to particular historical moments and events.

G. W. F. Hegel, Karl Barth, and James Cone offer their readers three different formulations of the doctrine of divine providence, each of which is linked to a corresponding judgment about God's relationship to racial humanity in the historical events of their respective times. In Hegel's *Lectures on the Philosophy of World History*, we find providence constructed as an abstract teleology of divine incarnation, articulated in terms of historical, geographical, and anthropological progress and calibrated to a vision of Western European humanity as the paradigmatic site of the revelation, incarnation, and eschatological consummation of divine life in history. Hegel deploys this providential framework to rationalize the global imperial and colonial endeavors of European civilization, the genocide of the indigenes of the Americas, and the continued practice of human slavery in Africa.

In *Church Dogmatics* III/3, Karl Barth elaborates a Christological delimitation of the doctrine of providence in which God's relationship to world history in general can only be understood in terms of God's special relationship to world history in the covenant with Israel and the incarnation of

Jesus Christ. Providence names the concrete and particular rule of the God revealed in Jesus Christ. Barth adopts this understanding of providence as the basis for a critique of any providential ideology that would seek to identify God's historical action with a human subject other than Jesus Christ. In the context of the emerging East-West conflict, this understanding of providence led to Barth's strident critiques of the ideological colonization of Christian proclamation and witness by the Western capitalist order in its global struggle against Soviet communism. Barth was unrelenting on this point: Western humanity could not claim that God was on their side in the Cold War.

Across his early writings, James Cone refines an account of divine providence as the liberating presence of Jesus Christ in history through the Holy Spirit. Arguing that the Blackness of Christ represents a contextual judgment about the specific shape of divine providence in his particular moment in the United States in the late 1960s and early 1970s, Cone argued that Jesus Christ was active in and identified with Black people's struggle for liberation in the Black Power movement in general and urban rebellions in particular. For Cone, it is not only the case that Christians should resist any efforts to align divine providence with European humanity or Western civilization (Barth's contention), but also that God's providence is manifested in Black liberation struggles *against* the oppression that has grown out of these providential visions of white supremacy.

Having reviewed these three visions of divine providence and the judgments about racialized humanity that they legitimize, it is now possible to explore the points of continuity and discontinuity between them in more detail. In what follows, I analyze these three engagements with providence by examining three points of comparison: the relationship between providence and Christology, the relationship between providence and humanity, and the relationship between providence and pneumatology.

When it comes to the relationship between Christology and providence, there is a decisive difference between Hegel on the one hand and Barth and Cone on the other. For Hegel, the doctrine of providence *replaces* Christology as the locus of the doctrine of the incarnation: the person and work of Jesus Christ are subsumed as a single moment within a process of divine incarnation that extends across the entire arc of human history.[2] Within Hegel's construal of providence, the culmination of the incarnation of the divine in history is not Jesus Christ, but modern European humanity. Not only does Hegel's doctrine of providence float free of any Christological moorings, it in fact represents a profound subversion of Christology itself, all but severing the doctrine of the incarnation from Jesus Christ.

In stark contrast, Barth founds his doctrine of providence upon a complete and total rejection of any relativization of the significance of Jesus Christ. For

Barth, it is only in God's action in Jesus Christ that one can learn anything about God's action more generally. The form and content of the doctrine of providence are exhaustively determined by the fact that the divine Subject of the doctrine is the triune God revealed in Jesus Christ. The place at which God's action intersects with history is first and foremost in the person of Jesus. Any attempt to speak of God's action in history outside of this one particular event—and the covenant with Israel which it recapitulates—must be judged by its conformity to that one event: "The doctrine of providence presupposes that this special history is exalted above all other history. It can and will understand all other occurrence only in its relation to this special occurrence."[3] In short, God never acts differently than God has acted in the covenant with Israel and the incarnation of Jesus Christ.

Cone proceeds even farther than Barth in subordinating providence to Christology. He does not even treat providence as an independent doctrine, but rather locates God's action in the *saeculum* as a concrete aspect of the incarnation of Jesus Christ itself. For Cone, the incarnation of Jesus includes not only Jesus' birth, life, death, resurrection, ascension, and second coming but also Jesus' activity in history through the Spirit between ascension and second coming. There can be no general questions about an abstract divine agent who is involved in history. Rather, the only way to approach the issue of divine action is to ask, "Who is Jesus Christ for us today?"[4] Over and against Hegel, Barth and Cone insist that God's action in Jesus Christ provides the only trustworthy point of theological reference for discerning divine providence. For both, it is clear that a major reason for this insistence is because of the potential for a doctrine of providence that does not find its center and endpoint in the human being Jesus of Nazareth to idolatrously designate a different human subject for that position.

In addition to their treatment of Christology, each author offers a different account of the relationship between divine providence and humanity. While Hegel once again differs more noticeably from Barth and Cone by relativizing the significance of the human being Jesus of Nazareth, the latter two have differing opinions about how Jesus' humanity relates to humanity in general. For Hegel, the paradigmatic human subject of divine providence is not Jesus Christ, but European man. Hegel resources the doctrine of providence in order to position European humanity as the final site of divine revelation, reconciliation, and eschatological consummation within history. The figure of European man *replaces* Jesus Christ as the human subject in relationship to which God's action in history receives its meaning and purpose.

Barth and Cone are insistent that no other human subject can replace Jesus Christ at the center of the doctrine of providence as the primary locus of God's action in history. Both agree that humanity can only *participate* in divine providence through Jesus himself, yet they configure the relationship between Christ's humanity and general humanity differently, such that they come to different conclusions about the specific human subject that participates most fully. Barth emphasizes humanity's participation in Christ's *rule* over the cosmos, which involves an intellectual *seeing* and *knowing* of providence. Cone emphasizes humanity's participation in Christ's liberating *work* in the world, which involves practical *action* in response to providence.

While most of Barth's energy is dedicated toward critiquing humanity's idolatrous pretension to make itself the divine Subject of the doctrine of providence—to "play the part of world-ruler"—he also affirms that humanity has a positive role in his understanding of the doctrine. Through the Spirit, human creatures, precisely as creatures, have a "genuine and actual share in the universal lordship of God."[5] However, not just any human subject can participate in Christ's lordship. Only the Christian, "the living member of the Christian community," can participate in the "divine world-governance."[6] This participation predominately takes the form of a seeing and knowing of God's providence, even as Barth also affirms the place for action in response to providence as what he calls the creature's "obedience" in cooperating in the work of providence.[7] For Barth, Jesus' reign is transcendent: Christ rules over creation from his throne. Christian participation in providence is, therefore, first and foremost about the Holy Spirit enabling the Christian to see and know this transcendent rule, and secondarily about obedient action in response to this rule as it works itself out in history. Because of Barth's emphasis on sight and knowledge, it is the Christian, the member of Christ's body, who emerges as the quintessential human subject who is able to participate in providence, with that participation understood with an emphasis on its intellectual dimensions.

Cone follows Barth in asserting that Jesus Christ is the one true human subject of divine providence and that it is only by participating in Christ through the Spirit that any other human subject has a share in divine providence. However, for Cone, human participation in divine providence involves, first and foremost, participating in Christ's work through action, as opposed to Barth's emphasis on participating in Christ's rule through knowledge and vision. Action takes precedence over knowledge: participation in providence means working where Christ is at work, more than it means knowing, seeing, and affirming Christ's rule over the cosmos. This alternative construal of participation leads Cone to a slightly different conclusion about the quintessential human subject who participates in divine providence. The human subject who participates in providence is not first and foremost the member of the Christian community, but the one who is at work where Christ is at work. In Cone's context, it is Black humanity engaged in the struggle for liberation who participate most fully in Christ's active presence.

Hegel replaces Jesus Christ with European man as the quintessential human subject of divine providence. Over and against Hegel, both Cone and Barth identify Jesus Christ as the one and only true human subject of the doctrine of divine providence. For both of them, it is only through participation in Christ that any other human being has an active role in divine providence. Because Barth focuses on Christ's *transcendent reign* over the cosmos, he emphasizes the concept of participation—which is first and foremost about sight and knowledge of providence—and identifies the member of the Christian community as the quintessential human subject of that participation. Because Cone focuses on Christ's *immanent work* in history, he emphasizes the concept of presence—in relationship to which human participation primarily takes the form of action—and identifies the person engaged in the struggle for Black liberation as the quintessential subject of that participation.

Finally, pneumatology is an important and ambiguous aspect of all three accounts of divine providence. While playing a critical role in all of their formulations of the doctrine, the Spirit does not receive attention from all of them equally. Indeed, the Spirit tends to either improperly dominate, floating free of Jesus Christ, or be problematically neglected, overshadowed by Christ. For Hegel, spirit is the divine Subject of the doctrine of providence. Spirit does not refer to the third person of the Trinity, but to the dynamic and absolute essence of the divine itself as it becomes incarnate in history. For Hegel, spirit floats free of a determinative connection to Jesus Christ. It simply names the progressive unfolding of the life of the divine in history.

Barth and Cone both hold the Spirit in determinative relationship to Jesus Christ. The subject of their pneumatologies is not abstract "spirit," but the Holy Spirit, the Spirit of Jesus Christ. For Barth, the Holy Spirit makes possible human participation in divine providence. Through the Spirit, Christians are elevated to the throne upon which Christ rules over history: "We are set at God's side and lifted up to Him and therefore to the place where decisions are made in the affairs of His government. . . . We then find ourselves at the very seat of government, at the very heart of the mystery and purpose of all occurrence."[8] The Spirit's role is, therefore, absolutely crucial to Barth's account because it enables him to affirm fully a Christocentric conception of divine providence while still affirming humanity's positive connection to Christ's providential rule over the cosmos. Without the Spirit, humanity's relationship to divine providence could only stand in a competitive relationship with Barth's Christological exclusivism. Either Christ's rule would leave general humanity wholly cut off from divine providence, or humanity would have to seek another path to divine providence other than the one that runs through Jesus Christ. It has to be noted, however, that despite the Spirit's important conceptual role in Barth's understanding of providence, the Spirit does not receive prolonged attention in *Church Dogmatics* III/3. The Spirit tends, rather, to hover just off stage, assumed but not addressed.

Like Barth, Cone prescribes a small yet crucial role for the Holy Spirit in his understanding of divine providence. Once again, the Spirit is tasked with closing the gap between Jesus Christ and general humanity, such that humanity can have a meaningful role in the doctrine of providence without relating to God's action independently of the revelation of the true identity of that God in Israel and Jesus. However, where Barth predominately identifies the work of the Spirit in terms of an epistemological elevation of humanity to the ascended Jesus Christ who rules the cosmos from on high, Cone emphasizes the Spirit's gap-closing work as enabling the presence of Jesus Christ in history. The Spirit still makes possible human participation in divine providence, but that participation is first and foremost a participation in Christ's present *action* in history, as opposed to *knowledge* of Christ's rule over history. Both Barth and Cone rely on the categories of presence and participation to explain the Spirit's work in relationship to a Christocentric account of divine providence, but each emphasizes one to a greater extent than the other. For Barth, humanity *participates* in divine providence as the Spirit makes humanity epistemologically *present* at the throne of Jesus Christ. For Cone, humanity *participates* in divine providence as the Spirit makes Jesus Christ actively *present* in human history.

The prior comparative analysis suggests some consistent themes that run through the accounts of Hegel, Barth, and Cone. In what follows, I identify three such trajectories and explore their ramifications for a contemporary account of divine providence. I then discuss two problems which the developing line of thought in Hegel, Barth, and Cone does not satisfactorily resolve.

The first normative conclusion warranted by the foregoing analysis concerns the centrality of Christology for the doctrine of providence. In short, Christ is the key to the doctrine of providence.[9] Hegel's Eurocentric vision of God's action in history displays how a doctrine of providence that is not Christologically determined easily functions as an abstract framework of divine world-governance through which to theorize the divinization of European humanity and its aspiration to cast itself as the quasi-divine being who rules over the world. Hegel's providential conception of European man is made possible by an operation of Christological displacement, wherein the male European subject replaces Jesus Christ as the one in relationship to whose flesh all of time, space, and humanity finds meaning and receives its ordered place within the cosmos. The Jewish flesh of Jesus is superseded by the bodies of European men.

Both Barth and Cone engage the doctrine of providence in response to exactly this problem, particularly as it was instantiated in political programs and social practices in Nazism in Germany and white supremacy in the United States. When its content is not specifically defined in relationship to the incarnation of the Jewish human being Jesus of Nazareth, the doctrine of providence becomes vulnerable to ideological colonization. Reflection on providence, therefore, must proceed in light of the fact that there is only ever one divine Subject of the doctrine: the particular God revealed in the covenant with Israel and the incarnation of Jesus Christ. Providence is not primarily about abstract concepts like omnipotence, sovereignty, or causality, but about how the God who brought Israel out of slavery in Egypt, became a Jewish human being, and was crucified and resurrected continues to be in an active relationship to creation. Contemporary reflection on the doctrine of providence begins by affirming that God never acts otherwise than God has acted in Israel and Jesus. Theological accounts of providence must fix their vision on the concrete particularity of Jesus Christ.

If, given the Christological thesis previously expounded, humanity ought not to relate to the doctrine of providence as its divine Subject, then what is the proper place of humanity in relationship to the doctrine? Instead of serving as a means of flight from creatureliness toward divinity, the doctrine of providence ought instead to affirm the goodness of finite, limited creaturely existence, by giving an account of how God in Jesus Christ has hallowed creatureliness itself.

Because providence addresses the relationship between God and creation, it is always at risk of becoming a ladder by which the creature seeks to become like God. Improperly construed, the doctrine of providence seems to offer the creature the possibility of escape from the conditions of creaturely existence. Hegel exemplifies this temptation: "Christians are initiated into the *mysteries* of God. Because the essential being of God is revealed in the Christian religion, the *key* to world history is also given to us."[10] Through divine providence, Hegel believes, the creature can obtain a literal "God's eye view" of history. Barth's analysis of these matters differs drastically from Hegel. He argues that the creature who participates in divine providence through Christ "has no *master-key* to all the *mysteries* of the great process of existence. . . . On the contrary, he will be the one man who knows that there is no value in any of the master-keys which man has thought to discover and possess."[11] Similarly, Cone asserts that "Jesus did not give us a blueprint for identifying God and his work or for relevant human involvement in the world."[12] Human creatures have no "guaranteed ethical guide" when it comes to discerning and responding to God's activity in the world. Thus it is always as a "risk" and a "burden" that finite and fallen human creatures attempt to make judgments about where Christ is present in history and how to participate in that presence.[13]

For Cone and Barth, providence does not name a line of flight from creaturely existence and its attendant characteristics of finitude and limitation. Rather, providence addresses precisely how the creature can embrace creatureliness and navigate finite and limited existence faithfully. The doctrine of providence does not provide humanity with a master key, but rather it represents the point at which humanity learns to relinquish the desire for master keys itself. A constructive account of providence must, therefore, address and embrace the conditions of creaturely existence which properly mark human beings in relationship to providence.

The first two constructive conclusions lead to a third. If a constructive doctrine of providence must identify the God revealed in Jesus Christ as the only true Subject of the doctrine, and if it must embrace humanity in all its finitude and creatureliness, then it must also have a robust account of the Spirit as the one who enables a connection between those finite human creatures and the God revealed in Jesus. The previous comparative analysis of Hegel, Barth, and Cone suggests a trajectory of development away from an understanding of the Spirit as a divine abstraction toward a vision of the particular Spirit of Jesus Christ as God who enables human participation in divine providence.

A Christocentric understanding of divine providence requires an account of the Holy Spirit as the one who enables human participation through Christ. For Barth, this participation looks like the Spirit elevating Christians to Christ's throne. For Cone, this participation looks like the Spirit making Christ present in the struggle for Black liberation. For both, the Spirit mediates between Jesus Christ and humanity. The Spirit's presence in creation between ascension and eschaton is a necessary precondition for any attempt to speak of a relationship between human judgment and action and divine providence.

Analyzing the positive developments in the theological trajectory that runs from Hegel through Barth to Cone suggests that Christology, creatureliness, and pneumatology represent three critical themes for a contemporary theology of providence. Yet such an account ought also to be shaped in response to key issues that *fail* to be meaningfully addressed within this trajectory. In this latter regard, two issues in particular require further attention: first, the persistent masculinity of the language used, the theological paradigms invoked, and the creaturely subjects associated with divine providence by all three authors, and second, the reductively competitive relationship between the Holy Spirit and Jesus Christ which manifests in different ways in each account.

The problematic masculinity that underlies all three accounts of divine providence explored in this study manifests itself in at least three ways: in the gender-exclusive language used by the authors, in the theological paradigms deployed to conceptualize divine providence, and in the types of human subjects that each author identifies as participating in divine providence in their respective historical moments.

The first manifestation of masculinity in these accounts of divine providence is the most obvious: all three of the authors employ gender-exclusive language throughout their accounts.[14] These linguistic conventions participate in a long history of excluding women from public and academic discourse by centering male experience and presuming an exclusively male audience. The implicit premise of all three accounts is that they are written by men, for men. Through these subtle linguistic practices, all three authors tacitly render the human subject who stands in relationship to divine providence as normatively male.

The problematic androcentrism that underlies all three accounts of divine providence extends beyond the rather familiar—if no less excusable—issue of gendered language. On a second level, the accounts of divine providence variously wrestle with a tendency to project masculine conceptions of human agency back into their characterizations of God's providential agency in history. While all three authors avoid a stereotypically patriarchal understanding of divine providence, in which God's rule over the cosmos is more or less conceived as a father's rule over his household writ large, the extent to which each author is able to separate his account from the patriarchal model varies.[15]

While Hegel's significant renovation of Christian theological language means that he entirely avoids the problems associated with language of God's fatherhood in traditional Trinitarian accounts, his own account of spirit coming to self-consciousness in history has its own problematic connection to hierarchical gender relationships. Specifically, Hegel believes that the development of spirit's self-consciousness occurs most fully in the masculine domain of the State, and only through transcending the earlier, limited realizations of consciousness in the family. For Hegel, the full emergence of spirit's self-consciousness in distinction from nature proceeds along a gendered trajectory in which "female consciousness" must be suppressed and transcended by the universal.[16] Women lack the self-differentiation that is pre-requisite for spirit's reconciliation with itself, leaving them "outside history and the dialectical movement of the spirit."[17]

Karl Barth attempts to be critical of an account of God based upon patriarchal projection. While he retains the language of "fatherly" to describe God's providential lordship, he deploys it in a strictly relational sense. "Fatherly," as Barth uses it, is not an abstract characteristic describing an "omniscient, omnipotent, and omnioperative being," or even a more benevolent divine patriarch who is "kind," "friendly," or "loving."[18] Rather, it names the relationship between the first person of the Trinity and Jesus Christ. There is no place for an abstract "father" in Barth's understanding of God, only the very specific "Father of Jesus Christ," in which "father" identifies the first person of the Trinity in relationship to Jesus.[19]

Barth makes a concerted effort to avoid projecting masculine characteristics onto God in his understanding of divine providence—the divine subject of the doctrine of providence is Jesus Christ, not some abstract divine patriarch who sits upon a throne high above the cosmos. However, even at this point, questions arise. Barth continues to conceptualize Jesus Christ's relationship to creation in terms of Christ's sovereign reign over it. This is particularly evident when Barth discusses human participation in divine providence in terms of the Spirit elevating humanity to Christ's throne. While there are good Scriptural warrants for this language, it nevertheless raises questions about Barth's consistency with his own method: has Barth wholly avoided a configuration of the doctrine of providence in which the divine patriarch is removed from his throne and Jesus Christ is simply put there in his place? Has Barth sufficiently shaped the meaning of terms like reign, rule, throne, and sovereignty in response to the revelation of Jesus Christ or does he occasionally slip into allowing these terms to shape his understanding of the providential lordship of Jesus Christ? Combined with Barth's continued use of the language of "fatherhood" and "fatherly" as central concepts in his doctrine of providence, these questions certainly raise concerns about the extent to which Barth avoided projecting patriarchal concepts back onto God in his formulation of the doctrine of providence.

Cone's more radical inscription of providence within Christology—in which God's action in history is simply a part of the incarnation rather than an independent doctrine called "providence"—avoids some of the questions about patriarchal imagery raised by Barth's account. Like Barth, Cone identifies Jesus Christ as the central agent of divine providence. However, for Cone, it is not Christ's sovereign reign over creation from a transcendent throne, but Christ's liberating presence to creation through the Spirit that most basically characterizes the nature and shape of divine providence. Cone holds onto Barth's Christocentrism, but jettisons even further any residual imagery associated with a sovereign divine patriarch who rules the universe.

Nevertheless, Cone's account is not without potential problems of its own when it comes to the issue of projecting masculinist conceptions of human agency back onto God's providential agency. As Delores Williams has pointed out, the language of liberation through struggle "assumes an androcentric black history." Indeed, Williams argues, "Masculine indication of person and masculine models of victimization dominate the language and thought of black liberation theology."[20] As Williams makes clear, the struggle for liberation has too often been understood as a struggle undertaken by men and conceptualized in masculine terms.[21] When Cone describes Christ's providential agency in history in terms of liberation and struggle, he is himself running the risk of projecting androcentric categories back onto God's providential agency. Like Hegel and Barth, Cone's doctrine of providence avoids a stereotypically patriarchal vision of God as *paterfamilias* of the universe. Nevertheless, his characterization of divine providence has its own masculinist complications, as he shapes his account of Christ's liberative agency around categories drawn from Black male experiences of racial oppression.

Finally, in addition to gender-exclusive language and masculine theological concepts, the accounts of divine providence developed by Hegel, Barth, and Cone wrestle with a persistent masculinity which characterizes their practical judgments about how God was active in history in their particular historical moments. For Hegel, it was European *man* in whom the divine life became most fully incarnate in history. Likewise, even as Karl Barth identified the human subject who participates in divine providence through the Spirit as the member of the Christian community, he advocated for a hierarchical understanding of gender relations within that community in his work as the chair of a committee on "The Life and Work of Women in the Church" at the World Council of Churches in 1948. Furthermore, the Christian is always a "he" in *Church Dogmatics* III/3. Similarly, James Cone identifies urban rebellions and an early, patriarchal vision of the Black Power movement as the specific sites of Christ's activity in history, locating God's providential activity in events and movements dominated by Black men and characterized in terms of the reclamation of Black masculinity.[22] For all three authors, the institutions, movements, and events in which they see the contemporary manifestations of divine providence are almost exclusively male-dominated.

In sum, while Barth and Cone engage in a sustained critique of the problem on display in Hegel, in which the doctrine of providence is ideologically colonized by a racial imagination exalting the European subject as the subject of the incarnation of the divine in history, neither sufficiently attends to the gendered dimensions of that problem. For Hegel, Barth, and Cone alike, there is little recognition of the heavily masculine characterization of divine providence on display in their gender-exclusive language, their gendered theological conceptions of the divine subject of the doctrine of providence, and their judgments about which human subjects participate most fully in divine providence. The persistent masculinity of the doctrine of providence across all three of the accounts is an unresolved problem in the trajectory charted in this study.

A second key problem that the trajectory of thought running through Hegel, Barth, and Cone fails to resolve concerns the specific role of the Holy Spirit in the doctrine of providence. In all three accounts, there is a tendency to rely on a reductive pneumatology that places the Spirit and Jesus Christ in a competitive relationship in which the Spirit floats free of any determinate relationship to Christ or loses distinctive character and agency by being overshadowed by Christ. Unlike the first problem, in which all three accounts shared the same basic shortcoming, this second problem has two manifestations that are opposites of each other. For Hegel, spirit floats free of the revelation of God in Jesus Christ. For Barth and Cone, the Spirit is held in close relationship to

Jesus Christ, but threatens to lose any distinctive characteristics and become simply reducible to Christ.

The problem with Hegel's decision to sever the connection between spirit and Jesus Christ in his account of providence is that it opens up precisely the sort of abstraction at the heart of the doctrine that makes it vulnerable to ideological colonization. If the agent of divine providence in history is not the particular Spirit of Jesus Christ, then it could just as easily be some other spirit, such as the spirit of Western European humanity. Thus, it is vital to hold the Holy Spirit and Jesus Christ closely together in relationship to divine providence. This is precisely what Barth and Cone propose to do. Yet if there is an attendant weakness to their formulations, it is that, in holding the Spirit and Christ closely together, the Spirit's work can seem reducible to the work of the Son. For both Cone and Barth, it is worth asking Eugene Rogers' question: "Is there nothing the Spirit can do that the Son can't do better?"[23]

Barth identifies the Holy Spirit as the One who enables creaturely participation in divine providence in the form of obedient action. Yet in his treatment of this topic he hedges toward resolving the Spirit's role into Christ's role. He affirms that it is the power of the Spirit that enables the creature to act: "It is only the Holy Spirit who can command him, giving orders and prohibitions which he must and can obey. It is only the Holy Spirit who can really guide him."[24] Yet, he goes on to qualify that claim: "It is only the Holy Spirit: but that is to say, it is only the pure and unbroken Word of God accompanying him where God Himself is hidden."[25] For Barth, "Following the guidance of the Spirit means obedience to the Word of God." The benefit of this position is that it prevents precisely the error on display in Hegel's account, in which a spirit other than the Spirit of Christ leads "the Christian into enterprises which have really nothing to do with obedience and in which he will fulfill anything but the purposes of the Kingdom of God."[26] However, Barth's treatment of the role of the Spirit in the doctrine of providence raises questions as to whether there is any particularity to the Spirit's work other than serving as a conduit to Christ.[27]

A similar tension resides within Cone's account. In one sense, the Holy Spirit has an absolutely crucial role: the Spirit makes Christ present in history between the ascension and the eschaton. Christ's liberating presence in history would not be possible without the Spirit. However, beyond serving as a conduit for Christ's presence, it is not clear what the Spirit actually contributes. When it comes to making judgments about how God is acting in history, the Spirit—having ushered Christ onto the stage—recedes into the background. This is exemplified by the fact that human participation in Christ's presence is not predicated upon a discerning of the Spirit, but rather upon answering the question "Who is Jesus Christ for us today?" It is unclear whether the Spirit contributes anything distinctive to this work. While the advantages of holding the Spirit and Christ closely together are clear, the danger is that the Spirit can simply be assimilated to Christ. It remains to be seen whether this is the necessary price of avoiding a dangerously abstract and independent pneumatology or if it is possible to affirm a determinative connection between the Spirit and Christ that leaves room for the Spirit's distinctiveness as a divine agent.

Given the tendency in all three authors to either free the Spirit from relationship to Christ or assimilate the Spirit to Christ, a constructive theology of providence that wishes to expand upon Barth and Cone's insights must find a way to hold the Spirit and Christ together without simply emptying out the former of any particularity. Fortunately, important contributions have been made in contemporary pneumatology in regard to this matter. The accounts of Barth and Cone can be pushed further through the inclusion of the best insights of contemporary theologians about the Spirit's non-reducible particularity as a divine agent. In what follows, I identify the Spirit's non-reducible particularity in terms of the Spirit's relationship to bodies, community, and time.

In summary, this analysis of Hegel, Barth, and Cone points to a constructive theology of providence that is (1) centered on the incarnation of Jesus Christ as the revelation and paradigmatic instance of God's activity in history, (2) affirms human creatureliness as a gift to be embraced and not a limiting condition to be overcome, and (3) accords the Holy Spirit a central role in uniting Jesus Christ with human creatures. It also suggests that such an account must avoid (1) projecting masculine conceptions of human agency onto God's providential agency and (2) collapsing the work of the Holy Spirit into the work of Jesus Christ. In what follows I develop a constructive account of providence that builds upon these positive themes while addressing the unresolved problems by drawing on important correctives from womanist theology and contemporary pneumatology.

A LIBERATING PROVIDENCE: THE SPIRIT, CHRIST'S PRESENCE, AND CREATURELY PARTICIPATION

A theology of providence in a racialized world will always necessarily exist in a precarious position, delicately poised between irrelevance and idolatry. On the one hand, it must make possible meaningful judgments about the positive relationship between divine providence and the human subject. On the other hand, it faces the reality that modern humanity inhabits a world in which such judgments have been systematically distorted by a racial imagination that has articulated itself precisely in terms of that relationship. Given these realities, to engage in reflection on providence is to place oneself on unstable, perilous ground. However, to think from the site of precarity and instability is to think from the site of creatureliness—the only site at which human reflection on divine providence can hope to be faithful.

From the perspective developed in this study, providence names a twofold work of the Holy Spirit. Objectively speaking, the Spirit makes Christ present to creation in between Christ's ascension and *parousia*. Subjectively speaking, the Spirit relates to bodies, communities, and time to enable human creatures whose existence is marked by precarity and instability to participate in Christ's contemporary presence through discernment, judgment, and action.

Providence as Christ's Presence

God never acts differently in history than God acted in God's covenant relationship with Israel and the incarnation of Jesus Christ. Nevertheless, God's action is not limited to its paradigmatic manifestations in Israel and Jesus, but continues in the present. A constructive account of providence attempts to describe this "nevertheless," which connects God's general providential activities with God's particular actions in relationship to Israel and Jesus. Specifying providence as the work of the Spirit in making Christ present to creation enables an account of God's ongoing action in history that remains faithful to its paradigmatic instantiations in Israel and Jesus, while also doing justice to the universality of God's providential agency in creation.[28] Importantly, articulating providence as Christ's presence to creation through the Spirit enables a characterization of God's relationship to creation as *universal*, without thereby rendering it *abstract*.

Any account of the Spirit's ongoing work in history which makes God's activity in the covenant with Israel and the incarnation of Jesus the normative pattern for the Spirit's wider activities must reconcile these discrete and particular divine initiatives with God's universal and general activities of preserving creation at all times and all places. In short, God's actions in the covenant with Israel and the incarnation of Jesus Christ are individual and particular, while God's providential agency ought at least in part to be universal and continuous. As Kathryn Tanner has argued, theological language ought to "avoid in talk about God's creative agency all suggestions of limitation in scope or manner." Rather, God's agency is "immediate and universally extensive."[29] Providence as Christ's presence holds together a necessary commitment to the particular character of God's providential agency as revealed in Israel and Jesus with the no less necessary commitment to that agency's universal manner and scope.

Through the Spirit, Christ is present to the whole of creation universally, immediately, and simultaneously. Creation *does not* preserve and sustain itself in the normal run of things, apart from perhaps a few particular moments of divine intervention, such as when God makes a covenant with the people of Israel or becomes incarnate in Jesus of Nazareth. As Barth argues, if God does not uphold and sustain every individual aspect of creation at every moment, it will return to nothingness.[30] God's providential agency is not punctiliar. God is present to all of creation at all times in the Son through the Spirit.

However, at this point a problem arises. If God is equally present everywhere and in everything at all times, then it becomes impossible for Christians to make distinctions and judgments about what God is doing in history. A crudely universal model of God's providential agency would only seem to be able to answer the central question of this study—"what is God doing in history?"—by saying "everything." Yet such an answer is clearly insufficient when compared to the Scriptural accounts in which God is almost continuously identified as acting in discrete and particular ways in creation. Indeed, in light of the interests of this study, it is vital to be able to say that God was not active in the African slave trade in the same way that God was active in the Black Power movement. The ability to make such distinctions rests upon a Christological specification of God's providential agency. As both Barth and Cone argue, providence cannot be equated with an abstract omnicausality, even if such an omnicausality helpfully names God's agency as universal and immediate.

Understanding providence specifically in terms of Christ's presence through the Spirit holds together the necessarily universal and immediate scope of divine providence with the concrete particularity of God's paradigmatic activities in the covenant with Israel and the incarnation of Jesus Christ, providing an alternative to both abstractly universal and narrowly punctiliar accounts of the doctrine. On the one hand, in the Son through the Spirit God relates to the entirety of creation in a universal and immediate manner. On the other hand, Christ's presence in creation is not abstract or uniform, but particular and variegated—even as it remains universal and immediate in scope and manner. Indeed, on this Christological and pneumatological account of divine presence, it becomes possible to speak of varying intensities of Christ's presence in creation. Just as radio waves transmitted from a station both permeate the entire coverage area and are weaker or stronger at different points within the coverage area depending on the distance between that point and the source, so also Christ's presence through the Spirit is coextensive with the entirety of creation, even as that presence is weaker or stronger based upon creation's relative participation in its source. Christ's presence through the Spirit is not uniform, predictable, and, therefore, controllable. It is rather a universal presence marked by variegated intensities of creation's participation.

On this model, judgments such as James Cone's—that the urban rebellions represent a special manifestation of divine action in history—need not compete with affirmations of God's universal and immediate activity throughout creation. Christ's presence through the Spirit permeates creation, but the intensity of that presence manifests in creation in a greater or lesser degree depending on the extent to which creation participates in its true identity in Jesus. By extension, sin and evil are those things that cause creation to fail to reflect the presence of Christ through the Spirit.[31] On this account, human creatures relate to Christ's presence through the Spirit as the Spirit enables them to attune themselves to that presence.

Providence and Creaturely Participation

Objectively—independent of creaturely recognition or response—Christ is universally and immediately present to creation through the Spirit. Yet subjectively, creation responds to and reflects Christ's presence to greater and lesser degrees. With regard to human creatures, this responsive relation to Christ's presence takes the form of *participation*. Through the Holy Spirit, human beings are able to participate subjectively in Christ's presence. Furthermore, the process by which human creatures come, through the Spirit, to participate in Christ's providential presence in this way is one of *attunement*, a reorienting of the self through the Spirit toward Jesus Christ.[32] The Spirit provides both the objective means by which Jesus Christ is present to creation and the subjective means by which finite and limited human creatures are able to participate in that presence. Just as radio frequencies require the subjective attunement of a radio receiver to manifest as audible noise, Christ's providential presence in history is universal, immediate, and objective, yet humanity can still be more or less subjectively attuned to that presence through the Spirit, such that they come to participate actively in it.

Within this framework it is possible to make discrete judgments about particular ways in which humanity is able to participate in divine providence, while still affirming the universality and immediacy of God's providential agency in relationship to creation. Given this model, it is possible to understand Cone's identification of Christ's presence in the urban rebellions not as a claim that this is the *only* place where Christ is present to creation, but that at this one particular site we see humanity attuned to and resonating with the frequency of the Spirit such that they are actively participating in Christ's presence in history.

This framework also makes it possible to imagine human participation in providence as functioning on a dynamic model rather than a binary model. It allows us to see Christ's presence in human creatures even as conditions of finitude, sin, and evil prevent it from being fully embodied in them. It renders intelligible Karl Barth's assertion that even the "demonic" state participates in God's work, just to the extent that anything that exists does so because it is related to God.[33] This understanding of human participation frees humanity from the quixotic search for ideological purity and opens the door to the creaturely work of discerning when and where the Spirit might be enabling glimpses of Christ's presence to emerge from human activities even in spite of the inescapable conditions of finitude and sin.

Fundamentally, this understanding of providence reconfigures the relationship between divine action and human agency non-competitively, while still making it possible for human beings to engage in the work of discernment, judgment, and action in the attempt to attune themselves more fully to Christ's presence in history. The Holy Spirit is the condition of possibility for this: objectively mediating Christ's presence to creation, and subjectively enabling human creatures to attune themselves to that presence and in so doing come to actively participate in it. In all of this, Christ remains the sole criterion for discerning God's providence in history. In all of this, human beings are able to participate in God's providence without chaffing against their creaturely finitude and limitation. In all of this, the Spirit occupies a central role in God's providential involvement in creation.

The Work of the Spirit: Bodies, Community, and Time

The Spirit has a particular character as a divine agent that is not simply reducible to that of Jesus Christ. The specific, non-reducible character of the Spirit's activity in creation becomes visible in the Spirit's particular relationship to bodies, communities, and time: the Spirit gives life to material bodies, the Spirit creates surprising communities of intimacy, and the Spirit anticipates the end of time. In these three activities, the Spirit is more than just a hollowed-out conduit for Jesus Christ's presence. Moreover, in these three activities the Spirit undermines traditionally masculinist paradigms of divine action. The specific character of the Spirit's relationship to bodies, communities, and time provides the material content for a pneumatological account of divine providence as Christological presence and anthropological participation.

In *After the Spirit: A Constructive Pneumatology from Resources outside the Modern West*, Eugene Rogers offers a corrective to a tendency in modern theology to collapse the Holy Spirit's role in the triune God's economic activity in creation into that of Jesus Christ. Over and against this tendency, Rogers attempts to rehabilitate the Spirit's role in God's interactions with creation by arguing that the Spirit's integrity and particularity as a divine agent is most fully displayed through interactions with material, embodied humanity—first, in relationship to Christ's body, but, therefore, necessarily also in relationship to the bodies of other human beings.

In the incarnation, Rogers argues, the Spirit characteristically befriends material bodies, resting first on Mary's body in the annunciation, and then on Christ in the baptism of his body, the transfiguration of his body, and the resurrection of his body.[34] After the ascension, the Spirit continues to befriend flesh, resting on the material bodies of human beings and incorporating both human bodies and cosmic bodies into Christ's body.[35] The non-reducible particularity of the Spirit's activity in creation lies in the way the Spirit characteristically relates to material bodies: sanctifying, transfiguring, and giving them life.

If divine providence is the twofold work of this same Spirit in making Christ present to creation and enabling human participation in that presence, then that work must also display the Spirit's characteristic befriending of flesh. Therefore, to answer questions about what God is doing in history, it is necessary to pay attention to what is happening to the material bodies of the human beings on whom the Spirit rests. The Spirit's providential work expresses itself as the Spirit brings life to those bodies who have been overlooked and oppressed by distorted providential visions of imperial and colonial politics, revolutionary ideologies and movements, and even the church.

Such an understanding of the Spirit's work shares much with and is indebted to the work of womanist theologians who have long been developing accounts of God's life-giving presence to ordinary, overlooked, and oppressed human bodies, bodies which in the contexts of the Americas have frequently belonged to women of color. In *Sisters in the Wilderness: The Challenge of Womanist God-Talk*, Delores Williams explores these issues through the consideration of "God's historic relation to black female life."[36] Where Black liberation theology too often saw Christ at work in Black men's heroic reclamation of their masculinity, Williams argues that God is present and active in the lives of "ordinary black women doing what they always do: holding the family and church together; working for the white folks or teaching school; enduring whatever they must so their children can reach for the stars; keeping hope alive in the family and community when money is scarce and white folks get mean and ugly."[37] In her reading of the story of Hagar in the wilderness, Williams draws out God's characteristic concern for ordinary, overlooked, and oppressed material bodies. Hagar, a slave woman with no control over her body, encounters God's presence in the wilderness and experiences that presence in terms of God's care for Hagar's basic material needs: "The Genesis 21 narrative reveals that when their resources for survival (water and bread) had run out, Ishmael was near death and Hagar was a short distance away crying."[38] But God cares for Hagar and Ishmael's material bodies, providing a well from which she and Ishmael could drink. For Williams, the characteristic activity of God in relationship to Black women is to provide for the material survival and quality of life for those struggling to make a way out of no way in the face of incredible adversity.

In a similar vein, in *Enfleshing Freedom: Body, Race, and Being*, M. Shawn Copeland reframes Christian thought about divine action around material bodies. Copeland characterizes Black women's struggle to reclaim their bodies from slavery as a "liturgy of Spirit descending and renewing once despised, used, abused flesh."[39] Copeland sees Jesus Christ at work in the present literally re-membering the bodies of "poor, dark, and despised bodies" that are being "consumed by totalizing dynamics of domination" on a global scale.[40] As "freedom enfleshed," Jesus Christ is at work in the world enfleshing freedom in material bodies through the Holy Spirit. Because of "the body broken and resurrected for us," Christian theology "can never cease speaking of bodies."[41] For Copeland, this attention to bodies necessarily coincides with a criticism of the patriarchal structure of traditional Christian theology and early liberation theology, both of which obscured the importance of the bodies of poor women of color as sites where God is at work in the world enfleshing freedom. To take Jesus' body seriously, Copeland argues, one must change "the anthropological subject of Christian theological reflection" to focus on the bodies of "exploited, despised, poor women of color."[42] If Jesus, as freedom literally enfleshed, reveals the character and content of God's action in history, then accounts of such action must pay attention to the way that God continues to act to enflesh freedom in material bodies through the Spirit.

Providence names the Holy Spirit's work in making Christ present to creation and enabling human participation in that presence. Because this work is the work of the Spirit in particular, it must reflect the Spirit's characteristic relationship to material bodies. Therefore, Christ's presence to creation—and human participation in that presence—manifests when ordinary, exploited, and despised human bodies find healing, survival, support, self-esteem, and quality of life. The Spirit gives life to material bodies.

The Spirit not only gives life to material bodies but also unites those bodies with other bodies in surprising acts of joining, creating unexpected expressions of intimate communion among those who would otherwise be strangers or enemies. The paradigmatic expression of the way that the Spirit enables human participation in Christ's presence by creating surprising forms of intimacy and communion is of course the dramatic reconfiguration of the social life of Israel to include the Gentiles in the books of Acts. The Spirit, as Willie Jennings has suggested, brings new possibilities for intimacy: "On the day of Pentecost the Spirit descended on the disciples and drove them into the languages of the world to enact the joining desired by the Father of Jesus for all people. This is the coming of the one new reality of kinship. . . . In Jesus, Israel's election does a stunning work by opening the possibilities of boundary-shattering love between strangers and enemies."[43] In Acts, the Spirit works to introduce "a new reality of belonging that drew together different peoples into a way of life that intercepted ancient bonds and redrew them around the body of Jesus."[44] The Spirit's presence in Acts creates new and surprising forms of intimacy, drawing together those who ought not otherwise be together—and all this, not as an interruption of or departure from the fulfillment of God's covenant fellowship with Israel in Jesus, but rather as a radical and surprising extension of that covenant fellowship.

Because the Spirit who introduced a "new reality of belonging" to both Jew and Gentile in Acts is the same Spirit who today makes Christ present to creation and enables human participation in that presence, the Spirit's contemporary activity will continue to be marked by the creation of unexpected, boundary-breaking communities. Such communities will not be marked by a bland multiculturalism, but rather a genuine freedom amid difference that runs—often dangerously—against the grain of the dominant social order.[45] The Spirit's joining is not a safe diversity initiative on God's part, but rather a dangerous and uncontrollable coming together of those whom the world says should be kept apart.

This second characteristic of the Spirit's non-reducible particularity as the agent of divine providence once again features centrally in the work of Delores Williams and M. Shawn Copeland. In Williams' interpretation of the story of Hagar, God's providential presence to Hagar and Ishmael in the wilderness manifests not only in the provision of survival and quality of life for their material bodies but also in the creation and preservation of an unexpected community. When God responds to Hagar's cries in Genesis 21, God provides both water and a promise: "Come, lift up the boy and hold him fast with your hand, for I will make a great nation of him."[46] Williams sees this same God at work today in the lives of African-American women engaged in the similar struggle of "building a peoplehood and a community" while working through issues of "survival, surrogacy, motherhood, rape, homelessness, and economic and sexual oppression."[47] The Spirit calls into being surprising and unexpected relationships and communities.

The specific marks of Spirit-birthed communities in the present must match the marks of the Spirit-birthed community in Acts. M. Shawn Copeland identifies the gift of the Holy Spirit in Acts as the "new basis" for a particular type of community: "The *ekklesia*, the church that emerged in the first century, was polyglot, culturally diverse, multiracial, flexible, economically and socially complex, experimental in its service and liturgy, daring in love of neighbor, and unafraid of the martyr's crown. This community lived out the compelling and dangerous memory of the crucified Jesus of Nazareth, whom they confessed as Lord and God."[48] Because it is this same Spirit who remains "the source and principle of the life of the church" in the present, the Spirit's contemporary work can be discerned by the similar fruit which it continues to bear. The Spirit's work disrupts cultural imperialisms and racism because "through the work of the Spirit, peoples of diverse races, ethnicities, and cultures hear and respond to Christ's message and experience this gift as being-in-love with God. The power of the Holy Spirit knits together people of diverse races, ethnicities, and cultures, dissolving every barrier, while regarding difference with dignity. The work of the Holy Spirit brings about unity in diversity and sustains diversity in unity."[49] This is the non-reducible particularity of the Spirit's agency as the one who makes Jesus Christ present to creation and enables human participation in that presence. To see Jesus Christ present through the Holy Spirit, Christians must look for the Spirit's characteristic fruit: the surprising emergence of communities marked by border-crossing, boundary-defying intimacy between those whom the dominant logics of sin and death would keep apart. The Spirit joins.

The final aspect of the Holy Spirit's non-reducible particularity as the agent of divine providence is the Spirit's characteristic *temporality*. The Spirit anticipates the end of time in the midst of the present time. This creates a paradoxical temporality for the Spirit's works: the "already/not yet" of the kingdom of God. On the one hand, the outpouring of the Spirit signals the arrival of the messianic age. On the other hand, the presence of the Spirit is only a down payment on the age to come—not its full realization.[50] The Spirit *anticipates* the end, but does not fully realize it.

Because the Spirit's twofold providential activity takes place in this time between the times—a time helpfully described by Charles Mathewes as "during the world"—Christ's *full* presence in creation, as well as humanity's *full* participation in Christ's presence, awaits the *parousia*.[51] From the perspective of the present, the Spirit's work is necessarily paradoxical, incomplete, obscure, ambiguous, and surprising. This is the final qualification for the specific content of a pneumatological doctrine of providence understood in terms of Christological presence and human participation—it is always both an "already" and a "not yet." Christ is present to creation through the Spirit, but that presence is never straightforward, unambiguous, or controllable.

This final point stands as a qualification of all that has preceded it. Yes, the Spirit makes Christ present to creation. Yes, the Spirit enables human participation in that presence. Yes, the Spirit gives life to material bodies. Yes, the Spirit creates surprising communities. But the Spirit does all this only and ever in a paradoxical relationship to the history of creation that can never be assumed, systematized, or controlled. This is what Karl Barth describes as the "nevertheless" of belief in providence: "What man sees is simply the multiplicity and confusion of the lines of creaturely occurrence. . . . There can be no question of a transparency proper to this occurrence as such, or of an inherent ability of man to see through it. What man sees is simply creation in all the regularity and contingency of its own movement and development."[52]

Thus, Barth argues, the Christian who truly participates in divine providence "will always be the most surprised, the most affected, the most apprehensive and the most joyful in the face of events. He will not be like an ant which has foreseen everything in advance, but like a child in a forest, or on Christmas Eve; one who is always rightly astonished by events . . . [life in the world] will be an adventure for which he for his part has ultimately and basically no qualifications of his own."[53]

Because it is the eschatological Spirit who mediates human participation in Christ's presence to creation, those who attempt to respond to the Spirit's work through discernment, judgment, and action must do so prayerfully and humbly, knowing that their best judgments about how and where the Spirit is at work must be continually open to revision. The Spirit blows freely, working in surprising, uncontrollable, and unpredictable ways.[54]

Delores Williams captures this paradoxical character of the Spirit's providential activity in her suggestion that divine action manifests in making a way out of no way. In Hagar's first sojourn in the wilderness, the angel of the Lord appears and makes a promise that rivals God's promise to Abraham in Genesis 15: "I will so greatly multiply your offspring that they cannot be counted for multitude."[55] Yet this promise for survival and quality of life coincides with a return to slavery and submission to Sarai's abuse. God's presence with Hagar and Ishmael does not lead to a dramatic, unambiguous event of total liberation, but rather enables their survival and quality of life. Hagar does not experience God's action in history as a liberation "by any means necessary" but rather as survival through the provision of "necessary means."[56] Williams sees the Spirit working in the lives of Black women to bring and sustain "whatever is positive in their lives."[57] The Spirit is present to them, enabling them to make a way out of no way, empowering them in their struggle "to resist and rise above the forces seeking to destroy their lives and spirits."[58]

As an anticipation—but not realization—of the end of all things, the Spirit makes Christ present to human beings in the midst of precarity, oppression, and adversity. The Spirit's providential activity is rarely unambiguous. Therefore, as Allen Verhey suggests, "Our talk of God's providence then will often have an 'in spite of' attached to it. 'In spite of' the evil of the Chaldeans, God is at work to fulfill his purpose."[59] God's activity in between Christ's ascension and *parousia* can only be seen clearly from its eschatological end. Yet through the Spirit this end has erupted into our present, and, in the Spirit, human beings are empowered to respond to this eruption through discernment, judgment, and action. Yet this responsive action must always proceed in light of the paradoxical, ambiguous, and even ironic character of the Spirit's relationship to history "during the world." The Spirit anticipates the end.

CONCLUSION

In summary, this pneumatological account of providence is responsive to both the insights and the deficiencies of the trajectory of thought developed in the writings of Hegel, Barth, and Cone. First, understanding providence in terms of Christ's *presence* through the Spirit enables a Christological specification of divine action which prevents dangerous abstractions from taking hold of the doctrine and rendering it vulnerable to ideological colonization by providential visions of European humanity, Western civilization, and white racial supremacy: the particularity of the covenant with Israel and the incarnation of the Word of God as a Jewish human being provides the normative pattern for God's wider activity in history. Moreover, identifying providence as Christ's presence through the Spirit helpfully clarifies the relationship between God's general and special providence, reconciling providence's universal scope with God's discrete and particular action in history.

Second, affirming human *participation* in Christ's presence through attunement to that presence through the Spirit enables an account of the positive relationship between divine providence and human creatures that embraces creaturely existence instead of chaffing against it. The Spirit is not only the objective means by which Christ is present to creation but also the subjective means by which humanity participates in that presence. This dynamic model of human participation in providence relates divine action and human agency non-competitively, enabling humans to exercise creaturely faculties of discernment and judgment regarding where the Spirit might be at work and how they might be called to participate.

Finally, this pneumatological account of providence reflects the Spirit's non-reducible particularity as a divine agent, suggesting that the formal framework of divine providence as the Spirit's twofold work of presence and participation finds its true inner content in the way the Spirit relates to bodies, community, and time. Discernment of the Spirit's twofold work in making Christ present to creation and enabling human participation in that presence must proceed in light of the Spirit's characteristic activities: the Spirit gives life to ordinary, overlooked, and oppressed material bodies; the Spirit engages in surprising acts of joining, creating intimacy and community between those who should be strangers and enemies; the Spirit anticipates—but does not inaugurate—the end. This formulation of the Spirit's particularity as a divine actor both prevents the Spirit from being reduced to an empty cipher for Jesus Christ and resonates deeply with womanist accounts of divine action that seek to deconstruct androcentric projections of human agency onto divine agency.

NOTES

1. *LPWH*, 85; *CD* III/3, 22; *BTBP*, 37.
2. McCarney, *Hegel on History*, 48. "A shift of perspective on the traditional Christian doctrine of incarnation may be said to have taken place, one that subverts it utterly. Instead of being a doctrine of God taking on human form, it becomes the revelation of humanity as the highest form of expression of the divine, thus turning the central drama of Christian theism against its origins."
3. *CD* III/3, 37.
4. *GO*, 99.
5. *CD* III/3, 160, 285.
6. Ibid., 239.
7. Ibid., 254. Barth does not want to be misinterpreted as advocating exclusively for an intellectual creaturely participation in providence: "What we have particularly to emphasize in this connexion is that the Christian attitude to the divine work does not consist merely in looking at it, but in co-operating with it." Nevertheless, on the balance of Barth's analysis, the intellectual dimension of participation receives the lion's share of the treatment and is consistently foregrounded over the practical.
8. Ibid., 287–288.
9. Kathryn Tanner, *Christ the Key* (Cambridge: Cambridge University Press, 2010).
10. *LPWH*, 145. Emphasis added.
11. *CD* III/3, 242. Emphasis added.
12. *BTBP*, 49.
13. *BTL*, 7, 7.
14. James Cone revised the gender-exclusive language in later editions of *A Black Theology of Liberation* and *God of the Oppressed*. However, he chose to retain his original, gender-exclusive language in *Black Theology & Black Power* so that it could serve "as a reminder of how sexist I once was and also that I might be encouraged never to forget it." See *BTBP*, x.
15. For a feminist critique of the patriarchal model of providence, see Kalbryn A. McLean, "Calvin and the Personal Politics of Providence," in *Feminist and Womanist Essays in Reformed Dogmatics*, ed. Amy Plantinga Pauw and Serene Jones (Louisville: Westminster John Knox Press, 2006), 107–124.
16. Lloyd, *Man of Reason*, 82.
17. Laura Werner, "The Gender of Spirit: Hegel's Moves and Strategies," in *Hegel's Philosophy and Feminist Thought: Beyond Antigone?*, ed. Kimberly Hutchings and Tuija Pulkkinen (New York: Palgrave Macmillan, 2010), 206.
18. *CD* III/3, 31, 28.
19. Ibid., 29.
20. Delores Williams, *Sisters in the Wilderness: The Challenge of Womanist God-Talk* (Maryknoll, NY: Orbis Books, 1993), 158.
21. For a programmatic formulation of this argument, see Jacquelyn Grant, "Black Theology and the Black Woman," in *Black Theology: A Documentary History*,

1966-1979, ed. James Cone and Gayraud Wilmore (Maryknoll, NY: Orbis Books, 1979), 418–433.

22. Matthews, "'No One Ever Asks, What a Man's Place in the Revolution Is,'" 278.

23. Eugene F. Rogers Jr., *After the Spirit: A Constructive Pneumatology from Resources outside the Modern West* (Grand Rapids: Wm. B. Eerdmans Publishing Co., 2005), 19.

24. *CD* III/3, 258.

25. Ibid., 258.

26. Ibid., 264, 263–264.

27. Rogers, *After the Spirit*, 20. This ambiguity in Barth's account of the role of the Spirit in the doctrine of providence reflects a wider issue in Barth's theology that has been the topic of much conversation within contemporary theology. Eugene Rogers has argued that Barth "provokes some consensus that his doctrine of the Spirit subsides into his christology." As examples of this consensus position, Rogers cites Robert W. Jenson, "You Wonder Where the Spirit Went," *Pro Ecclesia* 2 (1993): 296–304; Rowan Williams, "Word and Spirit," in *On Christian Theology* (Oxford: Blackwell, 2000), 107–127; Rowan Williams, "Barth on the Triune God," in *Karl Barth: Studies of His Theological Method*, ed. Stephen Sykes (Oxford: Clarendon, 1979), 147–193; Eugene F. Rogers, Jr., "Supplementing Barth on Jews and Gender: Identifying God by Anagogy and the Spirit," *Modern Theology* 14 (1998): 43–81; Eugene F. Rogers, Jr., "The Eclipse of the Spirit in Karl Barth," in *Conversing with Barth*, ed. John McDowell and Michael Higton (Aldershot, Hampshire: Ashgate, 2002), 173–190. For a prominent defense of Barth against this charge, see George Hunsinger, "The Mediator of Communion: Karl Barth's Doctrine of the Holy Spirit," in *The Cambridge Companion to Karl Barth*, ed. John Webster (Cambridge: Cambridge University Press, 2000), 177–194.

28. For an account of providence that is conceptually similar to my own, albeit written with very different governing concerns, see Wright, *Providence Made Flesh*.

29. Kathryn Tanner, *God and Creation in Christian Theology: Tyranny or Empowerment?* (Minneapolis: Fortress Press, 2005), 47, 47.

30. *CD* III/3, 73ff. Without God's preservation, Barth suggest, creation returns to chaos for two reasons. First, created being is participatory being and therefore ceases to be when cut off from that in which it participates. Second, that which constitutes nothingness (the devil and demons) has mounted an open offensive against creation and would actively destroy it barring God's ongoing preservation.

31. From this perspective, sin and evil are unintelligible realities, impossible possibilities. As Kathryn Tanner suggests, identifying sin and evil in this way does not trivialize them, but rather stresses their horror as things "with no right to exist, no place within a divinely instituted order." See Tanner, *God and Creation in Christian Theology*, 174 n. 12.

32. For this concept of attunement, I am indebted to Cristina L. H. Traina's *Erotic Attunement: Parenthood and the Ethics of Sensuality between Unequals* (Chicago: University of Chicago Press, 2011). Traina develops an account of attunement as

a virtue-based alternative to traditional approaches to evaluating intimate conduct between unequals. Attunement, she suggests, "combines perception, imagination, and experimentation in an endless, partnered dance" (217). While it lies beyond the bounds of the present study, a similar account could be developed of the dance between the Holy Spirit and human subjects that leads to the possibility of human participation in divine providence.

33. Karl Barth, "Church and State," in *Community, State, and Church: Three Essays*, ed. David Haddorff (Eugene: Wipf and Stock Publishers, 1960), 111.

34. Rogers, *After the Spirit*, 210.

35. Ibid., 209.

36. Williams, *Sisters in the Wilderness*, 3.

37. Ibid., x.

38. Ibid., 31.

39. M. Shawn Copeland, *Enfleshing Freedom: Body, Race, and Being* (Minneapolis: Fortress Press, 2010), 52.

40. Ibid., 53.

41. Ibid., 57.

42. Ibid., 89.

43. Jennings, *The Christian Imagination*, 267.

44. Ibid., 269.

45. Against an easy misunderstanding of this point, it is important to say that the black church—though racially homogeneous—would represent one such community, growing as it did out of the illegal gatherings of slaves in the hush harbor. Conversely, a contemporary "multicultural" congregation in which diverse peoples are heavily disciplined into a homogeneous performance of faith and worship would not bear the characteristic marks of the Spirit's work of joining.

46. Genesis 21:18.

47. Williams, *Sisters in the Wilderness*, 161, 33.

48. M. Shawn Copeland, "Knit Together by the Spirit as Church," in *Prophetic Witness: Catholic Women's Strategies for Reform*, ed. Colleen M. Griffith (New York: The Crossroad Publishing Company, 2009), 17.

49. Ibid., 21, 21.

50. Fee, *God's Empowering Presence*, 806ff..

51. Charles Mathewes, *A Theology of Public Life* (Cambridge: Cambridge University Press, 2007), 15–18.

52. *CD* III/3, 44.

53. Ibid., 242–243.

54. John 3:8.

55. Williams, *Sisters in the Wilderness*, 21–22.

56. Ibid., 177.

57. Ibid., xiii.

58. Ibid., xi.

59. Allen Verhey, "Calvin's Treatise 'Against the Libertines,'" *Calvin Theological Journal* 15 no. 2 (1980): 202.

Conclusion

This study has explored the way in which different theological conceptions of God's relationship to history help to shape different visions of where and how God is at work in a racialized world. It has done this through three case studies, examining the relationships between G. W. F. Hegel's conception of providence as a progressive teleology of divine incarnation and his theological justifications of European colonialism, Karl Barth's understanding of providence as the lordship of the God revealed in the covenant with Israel and the incarnation of Jesus Christ and his theological critique of National Socialism and the emerging Western capitalist order, and James H. Cone's theology of Christ's liberating presence and his theological judgment that movements for Black liberation represented manifestations of God's action in history.

Having reconstructed these connections, the study has outlined a constructive formulation of the doctrine of providence in response to an analysis of both the exemplary and the problematic aspects of the accounts of Hegel, Barth, and Cone. My final task in this study is to suggest how the constructive account of providence articulated in the last chapter might help to shape judgments about where, how, and in whom the Spirit is making Christ present *now*, in the twenty-first century. However, such an endeavor must be heavily qualified in light of at least two possible misunderstandings of the nature of that task. First, it must be emphasized that different theologies of providence only help to shape different judgments about contemporary divine action. They do not determine such judgments. The latter, idealist misunderstanding wrongly construes Christian doctrine as a theoretical blueprint that can produce right judgment and action if only it can be perfectly formulated. On this account, all we need to do is to place the correct doctrine of providence at the heart of our ethical deliberations and right judgments will necessarily ensue. Such an account would be a thin caricature of the complex nature of moral judgment.

Second, it also needs to be said that the proper venue for discerning Christ's presence through the Spirit is not first and foremost in an academic monograph composed by an individual, but rather in diverse communities of faith that have been shaped by certain types of practices, such as prayer, preaching, and protest—or, even more appropriately, groups of such communities gathered with those of different faiths and no faith. To attempt to discern the Spirit as an individual, apart from participation in wider communities and social practices, is an extremely risky enterprise at best, and a fool's errand at worst, as the limitations of structural location, experience, and a host of other factors—limitations that are exposed and addressed through relationships with others—will distort any one individual's perspective.[1]

The following experimental reflections are, therefore, necessarily incomplete. Against the idealist misunderstanding, they are not presented as the only possible judgments that can result from the particular doctrinal formulation that I have articulated in this study, as though doctrine necessarily and mechanistically determines judgment. Against the individualist misunderstanding, they are not intended as authoritative or universal judgments offered by a properly qualified and objective academician. While on the one hand, they are always and already made possible only by my participation in wider communities and practices, they are, on the other hand, certain to reflect my own limitations of structural location and experience in ways that I am sure I am not yet capable of identifying. The following reflections are offered as the necessarily limited and inadequate judgments of one particular person at one particular time and place, in the knowledge that both the insights and the shortcomings of such judgments will prove instructive. My purpose is broadly to demonstrate how the account of providence developed in the previous chapter might contribute to certain types of judgments about how and where God is active in one particular time and place within the ongoing racial drama that is the modern world: Durham, NC in the second decade of the twenty-first century.

A "POST-RACIAL" SOUTHERN CITY: CONTEMPORARY RACIAL POLITICS IN DURHAM, NC

On October 4, 1971, seventy politicians, business leaders, and academics from across the South gathered in Durham, NC for a summit convened by Duke University and the Research Triangle Institute to prepare for the emergence of a new era of economic and political life in the region: the "Post-Racial South."[2] This characterization of the South as "post-racial," a term coined—apparently for the first time—by Duke University president and former North Carolina Governor Terry Sanford, reflected the belief of those gathered that "race relations are soon to be replaced as a major concern by population increase, industrial development and economic fluctuations."[3] Those in attendance—including future president of the United States Jimmy Carter—oversaw the formation of The Southern Growth Policies Board, whose mission would be to manage and facilitate the transition of the Southern economy into this highly anticipated period of mutually entwined racial harmony and economic growth and expansion. Under the banner of the "Post-Racial South," Sanford, Carter, and others aspired to develop a new vision of Southern politics that, as Roopali Mukherjee has suggested, "urged a departure from the ideological structures of white supremacy, and prioritized modernization, development and securing capitalist expansion as essential to race reform."[4] Yet Durham, NC is more than just the birthplace of this conceptuality of the "post-racial," understood as a "centrist paradigm of racial assimilation organized primarily around economic revitalization."[5] It has also served as its proving ground.

While articulated as early as 1971, this "post-racial" vision of racial assimilation through economic development has, since the turn of the twenty-first century, taken hold as the governing economic and political paradigm in the city of Durham. Beginning in 2000, public and private investments totaling more than $1.2 billion have poured into downtown Durham, facilitated in large part by the 501(c)6 organization Downtown Durham, Inc. which was founded in 1993 to oversee the city's revitalization efforts.[6] In 2017, Durham—a city once popularly associated with urban blight and violence—now appears on *Forbes* magazine's list of the top ten "Best Places for Business and Careers" in the United States and can claim the distinction of being the "South's Tastiest Town" according to *Southern Living* magazine.[7] Indeed, there is a strong case to be made that Terry Sanford's "New South" vision of economic growth and development has largely been realized in the city. However, Sanford's prophecy that such growth would result in increasing racial equality and assimilation has not come to pass.

Durham's economic revitalization, far from inaugurating an age of racial equity, has instead created an affordable housing crisis in historically Black, working-class neighborhoods throughout the city that has drawn national media attention.[8] Indeed, these neighborhoods have experienced the much-lauded wave of economic "resurgence" as a tsunami of gentrification, a ferocious riptide that has torn families from their homes and destroyed tight-knit communities that have existed for generations. The return of economic investment and the elevation of Durham's cultural profile have come at a tremendous cost to working-class people of color and their communities. Neighborhoods that for decades were seen by outsiders as undesirable hotbeds of violence, decay, and urban blight have witnessed a meteoric rise in housing prices as they have—almost overnight—found themselves transformed into much sought after locales perched on the doorstep of a resurgent metropolitan center. Durham, once home to one of the first self-sufficient African-American communities in the South after the Civil War—which had its own schools, library, hotels, hospital, and college alongside thriving businesses and banks—is becoming "whiter, richer, and pricier" with each passing day.[9] Observing this phenomenon, it is hard to deny the truth of James Baldwin's famous assessment: "Urban renewal . . . means Negro removal."[10] At least as far as the city of Durham is concerned, Terry Sanford's vision of a "Post-Racial South" has proven itself to be more of a fanciful projection than a prophecy.

Furthermore, while Sanford and his colleagues were far too sanguine about the power of economic growth to accomplish racial equality, they were equally mistaken in their belief that they stood on the brink of a southern political future marked by the rejection of the ideology of white supremacy and an end to racial discrimination. In the second decade of the twenty-first century, Durham has endured a resurgence, not only in economic growth but also in thinly veiled white supremacist politics and racially discriminatory legislation in the North Carolina General Assembly. Following the Supreme Court's January 2010 decision in Citizens United v. Federal Election Commission, which removed limits on corporate campaign contributions, Republicans—propelled by the very contributions made possible by Citizens United—won majorities in both the state Senate and House of Representatives.[11]

Firmly in control of the General Assembly's redistricting process following the 2010 Census, Republicans redrew the state's legislative maps in 2011 to consolidate their power, in no small part by weakening the power of Black voters by packing them into a handful of districts and widely scattering them over the rest.[12] The General Assembly's redistricting labor bore electoral fruits the following year, as Republicans running in the new districts won veto-proof supermajorities in both chambers of the Assembly. Every elected member of the Republican Party in both chambers was white.[13]

Following the 2012 elections, the all-white Republican delegation began implementing a whole body of legislation that either had disproportionately negative effects on people of color or, in some cases, was found to be intentionally racially discriminatory. The NCGA cut federal unemployment benefits for 170,000 North Carolinians. Legislators passed a bill banning the expansion of Medicaid to 500,000 eligible residents. They also repealed the Racial Justice Act, which had given inmates on death row the right to appeal their sentence on the grounds of racial bias in their sentencing.[14]

Most importantly, the General Assembly enacted legislation to suppress the votes of people of color following the Supreme Court decision in Shelby

County v. Holder, which invalidated key provisions of the Voting Rights Act of 1965 that required certain states with a history of discrimination—including North Carolina—to receive preclearance from the federal government before altering their election laws. HB 589 implemented strict photo ID requirements, cut early voting periods, eliminated same day registration during early voting, and invalidated provisional ballots cast out of precinct—all of which disproportionately affected African-American voters. In 2016, the Fourth Circuit Court of Appeals struck down HB 589, finding that the central provisions of the bill "were enacted with racially discriminatory intent" and targeted "African-Americans with almost surgical precision."[15] In the twenty-first century, Durham, NC has not realized the Southern Growth Policies Board "post-racial" dream. Instead, it has found itself in a nightmare marked by privately and publicly sponsored gentrification at the local level and thinly veiled white supremacist politics at the state level. Where could the Spirit be making Christ present in the midst of all this?

WHERE IS THE SPIRIT MAKING CHRIST PRESENT IN DURHAM TODAY?

If the Holy Spirit makes Christ present to creation between His ascension and *parousia*, and if the Holy Spirit enables human participation in this presence during that time, then where, how, and in whom is the Holy Spirit carrying out this twofold work in Durham, NC in the particular period of time between ascension and *parousia* that is the second decade of the twenty-first century? Such a question can only be answered with any great confidence—at least by human creatures—from the perspective of the end of time. Nevertheless, humanity is called even in the present to engage in the work of discerning, judging, and acting in response to what the Spirit is doing to reveal and to enflesh in creation what God has already accomplished in the incarnation of Jesus Christ. This calling is what Cone identifies as "the risk of faith."[16] The riskiness of the endeavor cannot be overlooked or minimized. As Barth suggests, the Christian who participates in divine providence will be "always rightly astonished by events, by the encounters and experiences which overtake him . . . constantly forced to begin afresh, wrestling with the possibilities which open out to him and the impossibilities which oppose him."[17] Yet it is a necessary risk for those who would believe Jesus' promise to the disciples in John 16: "When the Spirit of truth comes, he will guide you into all the truth; for he will not speak on his own, but will speak whatever he hears, and he will declare to you the things that are to come."[18] Following Jesus requires the risky work of discerning the Spirit.

On the account developed in this study, discerning the Spirit partially entails asking how, where, and in whom the Spirit is making Christ present to creation and enabling human participation in that presence by giving life to ordinary, overlooked, and oppressed bodies, creating surprising communities marked by boundary-breaking intimacy, and anticipating the end of all things in Jesus Christ. Because Christ's presence through the Spirit is at once universal in scope and variegated in intensity, discerning this presence does not require that one identifies a pure, uncompromised, undiluted manifestation of Christ's presence in human actions. Perfect attunement awaits the eschaton. Conversely, to be totally unattuned to the source of our existence is to cease to exist. Discerning the Spirit, therefore, requires making contingent judgments about how particular human initiatives at particular times and places reflect a *relative* attunement to the Spirit, such that the Spirit is at work both "through" and "in spite of" those initiatives in all their finitude and propensity for brokenness. In what follows, I offer just a sketch of what such judgments might look like in relationship to human initiatives in Durham, NC to engage in broad-based community organizing and pursue a mass mobilization of North Carolina's citizens around a vision of multiracial, fusion politics. Such a sketch is representative, not exhaustive; meant to inspire further imaginings, not prematurely foreclose them with a final verdict.

Durham Congregations, Associations, and Neighborhoods (C.A.N.): Campaigning for Affordable Housing

On a humid afternoon in July, several hundred residents of Durham gathered just off Fayetteville Street for a political action staged by Durham C.A.N. Durham C.A.N. is a broad-based community organization affiliated with the Industrial Areas Foundation, the oldest and largest network of community organizations in the United States. On that Wednesday in July, C.A.N. had called a press conference at Fayette Place—popularly known as the Fayetteville Street projects—an abandoned public housing project developed by the Durham Housing Authority in 1967. C.A.N. had chosen Fayette Place as a key battleground on which the thirty local institutions that comprised its membership would seek to stem the tide of gentrification that was rolling through downtown neighborhoods. Long neglected, Fayette Place had suddenly become a site of much interest to local real estate developers, businesses, and universities, all of whom saw in Fayette Place a chance to secure a property with a large footprint in close proximity to downtown at a bargain price. Leaders from C.A.N. had been organizing neighborhood residents over the past several months and the press conference served as the venue for those residents to announce their intention to have a say in the future of their neighborhood.

Durham C.A.N. draws its affiliation, as well as its organizing philosophy, from the Industrial Areas Foundation founded by Saul Alinsky in Chicago in 1940. Influenced by traditions of populism, Judaism, the labor movement, and Christianity, broad-based community organizing emerged as a mode of democratic politics that drew power from local, concrete social relationships to address the conditions of life in industrialized urban centers.[19] As Luke Bretherton argues, Alinsky developed an approach to organizing that was "non-statist, decentralized, and pluralist," intended "to stimulate the appearance of those who are de-politicized or excluded from the decision making process, enabling them to appear and act on their own terms rather than be confined to either a private world of consumerism . . . or a disorganized arena of hostile, fearful, and broken relationships."[20] Broad-based community organizing seeks to enable ordinary people to resist the domination of state and market forces by building the power necessary to have a say in what happens to themselves and their communities.

As a broad-based community organization affiliated with the I.A.F., Durham C.A.N. seeks to develop leaders and build relationships between local institutions in order to aid low and moderate-income citizens of Durham in building the power that they require to address the problems that hamper survival and quality of life in their communities. C.A.N. organizes across religious, racial, ethnic, and class lines to develop shared democratic power that takes religious and racial differences seriously, while discerning the possibilities for realizing a common world of meaning and action that remains rooted in the genuine interests of its various members.

Durham C.A.N.'s affordable housing campaign grew out of a citywide listening session in which ordinary people met in sanctuaries, offices, and homes throughout the city to listen to each other's stories and find common interests and shared desires for change. When affordable housing surfaced from these listening sessions as a priority, C.A.N. did not call in a housing expert to tell its leaders how to fix the problem, nor did it simply place a phone call to elected officials asking them to fix the problem. Rather, it engaged the very people whose neighborhoods were being affected by gentrification to lead the work of researching the problem and developing a strategy to address it. More than increasing the supply of affordable housing, the central goal of C.A.N.'s housing campaign is to identify and develop local leaders and build strong relationships between local institutions in order to help ordinary people resist the domination of their lives by state and market forces. If C.A.N. is successful, the residents of the neighborhood—rather than local government officials or the predatory impulses of the city's real estate market—will determine the future of Fayette Place.

The Spirit is making Christ present to creation and enabling human participation in that presence as people in low-income and working-class Black neighborhoods—along with their allies—work to stem the tide of gentrification surging through downtown Durham. The Spirit is giving life to ordinary, overlooked, and oppressed bodies in these neighborhoods, as residents realize their own leadership abilities and stand together to prevent the displacement of their families and their communities and demand to share in the benefits of the city's economic revitalization. The Spirit is creating community among those that the world says should be kept apart, as cross-class and cross-racial solidarities are developed through face-to-face relational meetings, testimonies, storytelling, and collective social action. Where the market would prefer a citizenry that is disorganized and isolated from one another—and, therefore, easily malleable—some residents of Durham are finding renewed power in listening to one another and standing together against injustice. In all this, the Spirit is anticipating the end, without thereby accomplishing it. The leaders and institutions of Durham C.A.N. continue to struggle with unjust modes of relationship across religious, racial, gender, and class lines. C.A.N.'s work is fragile and faltering, attempting to build a common life among the citizens of Durham, even as those attempts continue to be undermined by enduring injustices in the relationships of its members to one another. Nevertheless, the Spirit continues to bring life to bodies targeted for displacement and to build community among those who would otherwise be strangers or enemies.

The North Carolina NAACP's Moral Movement: Pursuing Fusion Politics

On a cold, overcast Saturday morning in February 2014, participants in North Carolina's Moral Movement gathered in front of Shaw University—the birthplace of the Student Nonviolent Coordinating Committee (SNCC)—for a mass march to the North Carolina State Capitol building. The marchers—as many as 80,000 strong—represented the diverse constituencies of the Historic Thousands on Jones Street (HKonJ), a coalition of the North Carolina NAACP and its partners founded by the Rev. Dr. William J. Barber II. The march was the capstone to a campaign of civil disobedience at the North Carolina General Assembly the previous summer, in which almost a thousand people were arrested for instructing their representatives on the immorality of their legislative agenda. This interfaith, multiracial "fusion" coalition sought to amplify the voices of those most affected by the General Assembly's unjust legislation and build political power across partisan, religious, racial, and class lines based upon a commitment to a common moral framework. When the tens of thousands of marchers reached the State Capitol building, Rev. Barber offered an address that drew equally on the Bible and the U.S. Constitution to cast a new vision for democratic politics in the South.[21]

The Moral Movement founded by the NAACP and its partners self-consciously locates its own identity in relationship to both the Civil Rights tradition of Martin Luther King, Jr.'s Southern Christian Leadership Conference (SCLC) and the multiracial "fusion" populism of the post-Reconstruction South. The rhetoric, aesthetics, and tactics of the movement draw upon King's SCLC. Evoking SCLC's mission to "save the soul of America," Barber invokes the moral more often than he does the political, framing the movement's work as a recovery of the United States' deepest values—a "moral defibrillator" to revive the heart of the nation.[22] The religious aesthetics of the movement also hearken back to King, as Christian, Jewish, and Muslim clergy dressed in clerical attire feature prominently in the movement's public actions and press conferences.[23] Finally, the movement invokes the memory of SCLC's Civil Rights campaigns in its organizational strategy, pairing mass mobilization with strategic engagement in calculated acts of nonviolent civil disobedience.[24]

Movement leaders also regularly invoke North Carolina's history of interracial "fusion" politics, an alliance between white populists and Black Republicans that briefly came to power in North Carolina at the end of the nineteenth century, until white supremacist Democrats staged a race riot in Wilmington in 1898.[25] Rev. Barber regularly positions the movement as a reemergence of this tradition of multiracial, democratic coalition building.[26] By building the movement's priorities around the stories of ordinary people who are being negatively affected by the politics of the General Assembly, Barber seeks to unite groups that would otherwise be split by ideological or partisan divisions: "We had said from the beginning that our agenda wasn't Republican or Democrat, liberal or conservative. We weren't advocating for left or right, but for all that is good *and* right. We had studied our history. We knew that fusion politics was central to our state's history."[27] The Moral Movement's reappropriation of Civil Rights activism and fusion populism seeks to mobilize large numbers of ordinary North Carolinians around an appeal to a basic moral vision derived from the Bible and the U.S. Constitution in order to witness to an alternative to the North Carolina General Assembly's unjust and immoral governing agenda.

The Holy Spirit is making Christ present to creation in the second decade of the twenty-first century in North Carolina's Moral Movement. Through the Spirit, Jesus is giving life to ordinary, overlooked, and oppressed bodies. Attention to these bodies forms the foundation of the movement. Neither a partisan agenda nor an ideological framework—whether progressive or conservative—determines the movement's priorities. Rather, the movement has emerged as a response to the cries of ordinary people whose bodily existence has been rendered precarious by the General Assembly's actions. people who cannot afford cancer treatments because they have been denied

Medicaid expansion; people whose children are hungry because they have lost their unemployment benefits; people on death row who have lost their right to contest racial bias in their sentencing. The movement had indicted the General Assembly, not for being conservative or Republican, but for its cynical refusal to see the suffering bodies of those being affected by its policies. Around these bodies, the Spirit is creating a surprising community. In the movement, the Spirit has drawn together a peculiar group of people. Movement leaders have sought to develop a movement that can include conservatives and liberals, young and old people, Christians, Jews, and Muslims, people of different faiths, people of no faith, members of the LGBTQ community, and white, Black, Latinx, Native American, and Asian people.[28] People who might otherwise have very little reason for being in relationship are being transformed by the Spirit's surprising gifts of unexpected friendship and are responding by seeking similar transformations in their friends, neighbors, and even those who would be their enemies.

The Spirit is doing all this as an anticipation of the end and, therefore, only ever fleetingly and falteringly. Christ's presence through the Spirit is not a property or possession of the Moral Movement. It is itself a surprising gift, always appearing when least expected and never allowing itself to be captured or controlled. The Spirit is at work in spite of efforts by the media and outside interest groups to flatten out the complexity and the radically democratic elements of the movement in order to assimilate the movement into the progressive mainstream. Because the Spirit anticipates the end, Christ's presence to creation may be glimpsed in one moment and obscured in the next.

Attempting to discern the Spirit in this way is risky, contingent, and fragile work. Yet it is necessary. Durham C.A.N. and the North Carolina NAACP represent two particular sites of human activity *through* and *in spite of* which the Spirit continues to make Christ present to creation, joining together those who ought not otherwise be together in order to give life to ordinary, overlooked, and oppressed bodies in anticipation of the end of all things in Jesus Christ.

NOTES

1. On this point, see Luke Bretherton's accounts of listening as a political act and the mutual disciplining of church and *demos* in *Christianity and Contemporary Politics* (Oxford: Wiley-Blackwell, 2010), 71–125, 220 and *Resurrecting Democracy: Faith, Citizenship, and the Politics of a Common Life* (Cambridge: Cambridge University Press, 2015), 76–110.

2. James T. Wooten, "Compact Set Up for 'Post-Racial' South," *New York Times*, October 5, 1971.

3. Ibid., 1.

4. Roopali Mukherjee, "Antiracism Limited," *Cultural Studies* 30 no. 1 (2016): 54.

5. Ibid., 54.

6. Melissa Norton, "Downtown Durham Investment" (oral presentation, Durham C.A.N. Affordable Housing Tour, Durham, NC, January 30, 2016). Norton's timely and significant research on development and gentrification in Durham can be accessed online at https://youtu.be/2u66urIaYS4.

7. Jason deBruyn, "Forbes: Raleigh, Durham rank among top 10 cities for business and careers," *Triangle Business Journal*, August 8, 2013, http://www.bizjournals.com/triangle/blog/2013/08/forbes-raleigh-durham-rank-among-top.html; Paula Disbrowe, "The South's Tastiest Town: Durham, NC," *Southern Living*, January 18, 2013, http://www.southernliving.com/travel/tastiest-town-durham-north-carolina.

8. See, for example, White, "The Downside of Durham's Rebirth."

9. Ibid., 2. In a reflection written in 1912 during a visit to Durham, W.E.B. Du Bois lauded a city in which, "A black man may get up in the morning from a mattress made by black men, in a house which a black man built out of lumber which black men cut and planed; he may put on a suit which he bought at a colored haberdashery and socks knit at a colored mill; he may cook victuals from a colored grocery on a stove which black men fashioned; he may earn his living working for colored men, be sick in a colored hospital, and buried from a colored church; and the Negro insurance society will pay his widow enough to keep his children in a colored school." See W. E. B. Du Bois, "The Upbuilding of Black Durham: The Success of the Negroes and Their Value to a Tolerant and Helpful Southern City," in *World's Work* 23 (1912): 338, via the University of North Carolina at Chapel Hill's *Documenting the American South* archive: http://docsouth.unc.edu/nc/dubois/dubois.html.

10. James Baldwin, interview by Dr. Kenneth Clark, *WGBH*, May 24, 1963.

11. Citizens United v. Federal Election Commission, 558 U.S. 310 (2010).

12. Vann R. Newkirk II, "North Carolina's General Assembly Districts Are Unconstitutional Gerrymanders, Too," *The Atlantic*, June 5, 2017, https://www.theatlantic.com/politics/archive/2017/06/north-carolinas-general-assembly-districts-are-unconstitutional-gerrymanders-too/529212/. Federal courts have since ruled that two federal congressional seats, nine state senate seats, and nineteen state house seats drawn up in the 2011 redistricting process are unconstitutional racial gerrymanders.

13. Pat McCrory's victory in the gubernatorial race only further cemented Republican control of the state government.

14. For further analysis of the General Assembly's legislative activity, see William J. Barber II, with Jonathan Wilson-Hartgrove, *The Third Reconstruction: Moral Mondays, Fusion Politics, and the Rise of a New Justice Movement* (Boston, Beacon Press: 2016), 55–98.

15. Michael Wines and Alan Blinder, "Federal Appeals Court Strikes Down North Carolina Voter ID Requirement," *The New York Times*, July 29, 2016. In the decision, the judges found that "before enacting that law, the legislature requested data on the use, by race, of a number of voting practices. Upon receipt of the race data, the General Assembly enacted legislation that restricted voting and registration in five different ways, all of which disproportionately affected African Americans."

16. *BTL*, 7.

17. *CD* III/3, 243.
18. John 16:13.
19. Bretherton, *Resurrecting Democracy*, 21–56. For further background on Alinsky and the origins and background of the Industrial Areas Foundation, see Sanford D. Horwitt, *Let Them Call Me Rebel: Saul Alinsky—His Life and Legacy* (New York: Alfred A. Knopf, 1989); Robert A. Slayton, *Back of the Yards: The Making of a Local Democracy* (Chicago: University of Chicago Press, 1986); Neil Betten and Michael J. Austin, *The Roots of Community Organizing, 1917-1939* (Philadelphia: Temple University Press, 1990).
20. Bretherton, *Resurrecting Democracy*, 38, 45.
21. Barber, *The Third Reconstruction*, 108.
22. David J. Garrow, *Bearing the Cross: Martin Luther King, Jr., and the Southern Christian Leadership Conference* (New York: William Morrow, 1986), 160, 671.
23. For an interpretation of the Civil Rights movement as primarily a religious event, see David L. Chappell *A Stone of Hope: Prophetic Religion and the Death of Jim Crow* (Chapel Hill: The University of North Carolina Press, 2004), 87–104.
24. Adam Fairclough, *To Redeem the Soul of America: The Southern Christian Leadership Conference and Martin Luther King, Jr.* (Athens: The University of Georgia Press, 1987), 85–142; Thomas R. Peake, *Keeping the Dream Alive: A History of the Southern Christian Leadership Conference from King to the Nineteen-Eighties* (New York: Peter Lang, 1987), 65–96.
25. Omar H. Ali, *In the Lion's Mouth: Black Populism in the New South, 1886-1900* (Jackson: University of Mississippi Press, 2010), 135–144; Lawrence Goodwyn, *The Populist Movement: A Short History of the Agrarian Revolt in America* (New York: Oxford University Press, 1978), 199, 285
26. Barber, *The Third Reconstruction*, 7, 52–53, 56–57, 62.
27. Ibid., 52.
28. Ibid., 88.

Bibliography

Adams, Nicholas. *Eclipse of Grace: Divine and Human Action in Hegel.* Oxford: Wiley-Blackwell, 2013.
Ali, Omar H. *In the Lion's Mouth: Black Populism in the New South, 1886-1900.* Jackson: University of Mississippi Press, 2010.
Anderson, Victor. *Beyond Ontological Blackness: An Essay on African American Religious and Cultural Criticism.* New York: Continuum Publishing Co., 1995.
———. "The Mimesis of Salvation and Dissimilitude in the Scandalous Gospel of Jesus." In *Christology and Whiteness: What Would Jesus Do?*, edited by George Yancy, 196–211. New York: Routledge, 2012.
Aquinas, Thomas. *The Summa Theologiae.* Translated by Fathers of the English Dominican Province. New York: Benziger Bro., 1948.
Augustine, *The City of God.* Translated by Babcock. Hyde Park, NY: New City Press, 2012.
———. *The Retractions.* Translated by Sister M. Inez Bogan. Baltimore, MD: The Catholic University of America Press, 1968.
Avineri, Shlomo. *Hegel's Theory of the Modern State.* Cambridge: Cambridge University Press, 1972.
Baelz, Peter R. *Prayer and Providence: A Background Study.* New York: The Seabury Press, 1968.
Baker-Fletcher, Garth. "Black Theology and the Holy Spirit." In *The Cambridge Companion to Black Theology*, edited by Dwight N. Hopkins and Edward P. Antonio, 111–125. Cambridge: Cambridge University Press, 2012.
Baldwin, James. Interview by Dr. Kenneth Clark. *WGBH*, May 24, 1963.
Barber, William J. with Jonathan Wilson-Hartgrove, *The Third Reconstruction: Moral Mondays, Fusion Politics, and the Rise of a New Justice Movement.* Boston, Beacon Press, 2016.
Barth, Karl. *Against the Stream: Shorter Post-war Writings 1946-1952.* New York: Philosophical Library, 1954.

———. *Church Dogmatics*. Edited and translated by G. W. Bromiley and T. F. Torrance. 14 vols. Edinburgh: T&T Clark, 1956–1975.
———. *Community, State, and Church: Three Essays*. Edited by David Haddorff. Eugene: Wipf and Stock Publishers, 1960.
———. "No Christian Marshall Plan," *The Christian Century* 65, no. 49 (1948): 1330–1333.
Beiser, Frederick C. "Hegel and Ranke: A Re-examination." In *A Companion to Hegel*, edited by Houlgate and Baur, 332–350. Oxford: Blackwell Publishing Ltd., 2011.
Berkouwer, G.C. *The Providence of God*. Translated by Lewis B. Smedes. Grand Rapids, MI: Wm. B. Eerdmans Publishing Company, 1952.
Bernasconi, Robert. "Hegel at the Court of the Ashanti." In *Hegel after Derrida*, edited by Barnett, 41–63. London: Routledge, 1998.
———. "'The Ruling Categories of the World': The Trinity in Hegel's Philosophy of History and the Rise and Fall of Peoples." In *A Companion to Hegel*, edited by Houlgate and Baur, 315–331. Oxford: Blackwell Publishing Ltd., 2011.
———. "With What Must the Philosophy of World History Begin? On the Racial Basis of Hegel's Eurocentrism." *Nineteenth-Century Contexts* 22 (2000): 170–201.
Bernhardt, Reinhold. *Was heißt "Handeln Gottes"?: Eine Rekonstruktion der Lehre von der Vorsehung*. Gütersloh: Chr. Kaiser/Gütersloher Verlagshaus, 1999.
Betten, Neil and Michael J. Austin. *The Roots of Community Organizing, 1917-1939*. Philadelphia: Temple University Press, 1990.
Bourdieu, Pierre and Loïc J. D. Wacquant, *An Invitation to Reflexive Sociology*. The University of Chicago Press, 1992.
Bourdieu, Pierre. *The Logic of Practice*. Translated by Richard Nice. Stanford: Stanford University Press, 1990.
Bowdich, Thomas Edward. *Mission from Cape Coast Castle to Ashantee, with a Statistical Account of that Kingdom and Geographical Notices of other Parts of the Interior of Africa*. London: John Murray, 1819.
Braun, Theodore E. D. and John B Radner, eds. *The Lisbon Earthquake of 1755: Representations and Reactions*. Oxford: Voltaire Foundation, 2005.
Bretherton, Luke. *Christianity and Contemporary Politics*. Oxford: Wiley-Blackwell, 2010.
———. *Resurrecting Democracy: Faith, Citizenship, and the Politics of a Common Life*. Cambridge: Cambridge University Press, 2015.
Brito, Emilio. *La Christologie de Hegel: Verbum Crucis*. Translated by B. Pottier. Paris: Beauchesne, 1983.
Brody, David. "Donald Trump, Paula White and the Gospel." *Christian Broadcasting Network*, June 21, 2016. https://www1.cbn.com/thebrodyfile/archive/2016/06/21/donald-trump-paula-white-and-the-gospel.
Buck-Morss, Susan. *Hegel, Haiti, and Universal History*. Pittsburgh: University of Pittsburgh Press, 2009.
Burrow, Jr., Rufus. *James H. Cone and Black Liberation Theology*. London: McFarland & Company, Inc., 1994.

Busch, Eberhard. *Karl Barth: His Life from Letters and Autobiographical Texts*. Translated by John Bowden. Eugene, OR: Wipf & Stock Publishers, 1975.
Butler, Judith. "Sexual Politics, Torture, and Secular Time." *The British Journal of Sociology* 59, no. 1 (2008): 1–23.
Calhoun, John C. "Further Remarks in Debate on His Fifth Resolution." In *The Papers of John C. Calhoun*, edited by Clyde N. Wilson. Columbia, SC: University of South Carolina Press, 1981.
Calvin, John. *Institutes of the Christian Religion*. Edited by John T. McNeill and translated by Ford Lewis Battles. Louisville, KY: Westminster John Knox Press, 2011.
Carmichael, Stokely and Charles V. Hamilton. *Black Power: The Politics of Liberation in America*. New York: Random House, 1967.
Carter, J. Kameron. *Race: A Theological Account*. Cambridge: Cambridge University Press, 2008.
Césaire, Aimé. *Discourse on Colonialism*. Translated by Joan Pinkham. New York: Monthly Review Press, 2000.
Chappel, James. "The Catholic Origins of Totalitarianism Theory in Interwar Europe." *Modern Intellectual History* 8, no. 3 (2011): 561–590.
Chappell, David L. *A Stone of Hope: Prophetic Religion and the Death of Jim Crow*. Chapel Hill: The University of North Carolina Press, 2004.
Chappelle, Albert. *Hegel et la religion*. Paris: Éditions Universitaires, 1967.
Citizens United v. Federal Election Commission. 558 U.S. 310 (2010).
Cleaver, Kathleen. "Women, Power, and Revolution." In *Liberation, Imagination, and the Black Panther Party*, edited by Kathleen Cleaver and George Katsiaficas, 123–127. New York: Routledge, 2001.
Collier-Thomas, Bettye and V. P. Franklin, eds. *Sisters in the Struggle: African American Women in the Civil Rights-Black Power Movement*. New York: New York University Press, 2001.
Cone, James. *A Black Theology of Liberation*. Maryknoll, NY: Orbis Books, 1986.
———. *Black Theology and Black Power*. Maryknoll, NY: Orbis Books, 1997.
———. *The Cross and the Lynching Tree*. Maryknoll, NY: Orbis Books, 2012.
———. *For My People: Black Theology and the Black Church*. Maryknoll, NY: Orbis Books, 1984.
———. *God of the Oppressed*. Maryknoll, NY: Orbis Books, 1975.
———. *My Soul Looks Back*. Maryknoll, NY: Orbis Books, 1985.
———. *Risks of Faith: The Emergence of a Black Theology of Liberation, 1968-1998*. Boston: Beacon Press, 1999.
———. *Speaking the Truth: Ecumenism, Liberation, and Black Theology*. Grand Rapids: Wm. B. Eerdmans Publishing Co., 1986.
———. *The Spirituals and the Blues*. Maryknoll, NY: Orbis Books, 1972.
Copeland, M. Shawn. "The (Black) Jesus of Detroit: Reflections on black power and the (white) American Christ." In *Christology and Whiteness: What Would Jesus Do?*, edited by George Yancy. New York: Routledge, 2012.
———. *Enfleshing Freedom: Body, Race, and Being*. Minneapolis: Fortress Press, 2010.

———. "Knit Together by the Spirit as Church." In *Prophetic Witness: Catholic Women's Strategies for Reform*, edited by Colleen M. Griffith. New York: The Crossroad Publishing Company, 2009.

Cornelius, Deborah S. *Hungary in World War II: Caught in the Cauldron*. New York: Fordham University Press, 2011.

Da Silva, Denise Ferreira. *Toward a Global Idea of Race*. Minneapolis: University of Minnesota Press, 2007.

Daniels, David D. and Ted A. Smith. "History, Practice, and Theological Education." In *For Life Abundant: Practical Theology, Theological Education, and Christian Ministry*, edited by Dorothy C. Bass and Craig Dykstra. Grand Rapids, MI: William B. Eerdmans Publishing Co., 2008.

Dante. *Monarchy*. Edited by Prue Shaw. Cambridge: Cambridge University Press, 1996.

Davis, David Brion. *Antebellum American Culture: An Interpretive Anthology*. Lexington, MA: D. C. Heath and Co., 1979.

———. *Slavery and Human Progress*. Oxford: Oxford University Press, 1984.

De Nys, Martin J. *Hegel and Theology*. London: T&T Clark International, 2009.

DeBruyn, Jason. "Forbes: Raleigh, Durham Rank Among top 10 Cities for Business and Careers." *Triangle Business Journal*, August 8, 2013. http://www.bizjournals.com/triangle/blog/2013/08/forbes-raleigh-durham-rank-among-top.html.

Desmond, William. *Hegel's God: A Counterfeit Double?*. Burlington, VT: Ashgate Publishing Co., 2003.

DiAngelo, Robin. "White Fragility," *International Journal of Critical Pedagogy* 3, no. 3 (2011): 54–70.

Disbrowe, Paula. "The South's Tastiest Town: Durham, NC." *Southern Living*, January 18, 2013. http://www.southernliving.com/travel/tastiest-town-durham-north-carolina.

Dorrien, Gary. *The Barthian Revolt in Modern Theology: Theology without Weapons*. Louisville: Westminster John Knox Press, 2000.

Du Bois, W. E. B. "The Upbuilding of Black Durham: The Success of the Negroes and Their Value to a Tolerant and Helpful Southern City." *World's Work* 23 (1912): 338. http://docsouth.unc.edu/nc/dubois/dubois.html.

Dussel, Enrique. "Eurocentrism and Modernity (Introduction to the Frankfurt Lectures)." *boundary 2* 20, no.3 (1993): 65–76.

———. *The Underside of Modernity: Apel, Ricouer, Rorty, Taylor, and the Philosophy of Liberation*, translated by Mendieta. Atlantic Highlands: Humanities Press, 1996.

Echeverria, Eduardo. *Berkouwer and Catholicism: Disputed Questions*. Leiden: Brill, 2013.

Fackenheim, Emil. *The Religious Dimension in Hegel's Thought*. Bloomington, IN: Indiana University Press, 1967.

Fairclough, Adam. *To Redeem the Soul of America: The Southern Christian Leadership Conference and Martin Luther King, Jr.* Athens: The University of Georgia Press, 1987.

Farley, Benjamin W. *The Providence of God*. Grand Rapids, MI: Baker Book House, 1988.

Fee, Gordon. *God's Empowering Presence: The Holy Spirit in the Letters of Paul.* Grand Rapids: Baker Academic, 2009.

Fergusson, David. *The Providence of God: A Polyphonic Approach.* Cambridge: Cambridge University Press, 2018.

Fine, Sidney. *Violence in the Model City: The Cavanagh Administration, Race Relations, and the Detroit Riots of 1967.* Ann Arbor, MI: The University of Michigan Press, 1989.

Fulkerson, Mary McClintock. *Places of Redemption: Theology for a Worldly Church.* Oxford: Oxford University Press, 2007.

Garrow, David J. *Bearing the Cross: Martin Luther King, Jr., and the Southern Christian Leadership Conference.* New York: William Morrow, 1986.

Gilkey, Langdon. "The Concept of Providence in Contemporary Theology." *Journal of Religion* 43, no. 3 (1963): 171–192.

———. *Reaping the Whirlwind: A Christian Interpretation of History.* New York: The Seabury Press, 1976.

Goodwyn, Lawrence. *The Populist Movement: A Short History of the Agrarian Revolt in America.* New York: Oxford University Press, 1978.

Gorringe, T. J. *God's Theatre: A Theology of Providence.* London: SCM Press Ltd., 1991.

———. *Karl Barth: Against Hegemony.* Oxford: Oxford University Press, 1999.

Grant, Jacquelyn. "Black Theology and the Black Woman." In *Black Theology: A Documentary History, 1966-1979*, edited by James Cone and Gayraud Wilmore, 418–433. Maryknoll, NY: Orbis Books, 1979.

Green, Christopher C. *Doxological Theology: Karl Barth on Divine Providence, Evil, and the Angels.* London: Bloomsbury T&T Clark, 2011.

Greene, Christina. *Our Separate Ways: Women and the Black Freedom Movement in Durham, North Carolina.* Chapel Hill, NC: The University of North Carolina Press, 2005.

Gregory, Brad. *The Unintended Reformation.* Cambridge: The Belknap Press, 2012.

Guyatt, Nicholas. *Providence and the Invention of the United States, 1607-1876.* Cambridge: Cambridge University Press, 2007.

Hammond, James Henry. *Remarks of Mr. Hammond of South Carolina on the Question of Receiving Petitions for the Abolition of Slavery in the District of Columbia.* Washington DC: Duff Green, 1836.

Hart, Julian N. "Creation and Providence." In *Christian Theology: An Introduction to Its Traditions and Tasks*, edited by Peter C. Hodgson and Robert H. King. Minneapolis, MN: Fortress Press, 1994.

Harvey, Jennifer. *Dear White Christians: For Those Still Longing for Racial Reconciliation.* 2nd ed. Grand Rapids: Wm. B. Eermans Publishing Co., 2020.

———. *Raising White Kids: Bringing Up Children in Racially Unjust America.* Nashville: Abingdon Press, 2017.

Hegel, G. W. F. *Elements of The Philosophy of Right.* Translated by Nisbet. Cambridge: Cambridge University Press, 1991

———. *Lectures on the Philosophy of World History: Introduction.* Translated by H.B. Nisbet. Cambridge: Cambridge University Press, 1975.

———. *Lectures on the Philosophy of World History: Volume 1: Manuscripts of the Introduction and the Lectures of 1822-3*. Edited and translated by Robert F. Brown and Peter C. Hodgson with the assistance of William G. Geuss. Oxford: Oxford University Press, 2011.

———. *Vorlesungen über die Philosophie der Weltgeschichte (Berlin 1822/23)*. Edited by Ilting, Brehmer, and Seelmann. Hamburg: Felix Meiner Verlag, 1996.

———. *Vorlesungsmanuskripte II (1816-31)*. Edited by Walter Jaeschke. Hamburg: Felix Meiner 1995.

Helm, Paul. *The Providence of God*. Downers Grove, IL: InterVarsity Press, 1994.

Herman, Max Arthur. *Fighting in the Streets: Ethnic Succession and Urban Unrest in Twentieth-Century America*. New York: Peter Lang, 2005.

———. *Summer of Rage: An Oral History of the 1967 Newark and Detroit Riots*. New York: Peter Lang, 2013.

Hodgson, Peter C. *Hegel and Christian Theology: A Reading of the* Lectures on the Philosophy of Religion. Oxford: Oxford University Press, 2005.

———. "Providence." In *A New Handbook of Christian Theology*, edited by Donald W. Musser and Joseph L. Price, 394–396. Nashville, TN: Abingdon Press, 1992.

———. *Shapes of Freedom: Hegel's Philosophy of World History in Theological Perspective*. Oxford: Oxford University Press, 2012.

Hoffheimer, Michael H. "Hegel, Race, Genocide." *The Southern Journal of Philosophy* 39 (2001): 35–62.

Holcombe, William Henry. "The Alternative." In *Antebellum American Culture*, edited by Davis. Lexington, MA: D. C. Heath and Co., 1979.

Hook, Sidney. *From Hegel to Marx*. New York: Humanities Press, 1950.

Hopkins, Dwight N. "Black Theology on Theological Education." In *Black Faith and Public Talk: Critical Essays on James H. Cone's* Black Theology and Black Power, edited by Dwight N. Hopkins. Maryknoll, NY: Orbis Books, 1999.

Horwitt, Sanford D. *Let Them Call Me Rebel: Saul Alinsky—His Life and Legacy*. New York: Alfred A. Knopf, 1989.

Hunsinger, George. "The Mediator of Communion: Karl Barth's Doctrine of the Holy Spirit." In *The Cambridge Companion to Karl Barth*, edited by John Webster, 177–194. Cambridge: Cambridge University Press, 2000.

Ill'in, Ivan. *Die Philosophie Hegels als kontemplative Gotteslehre*. Bern: A. Francke, 1946.

Jaeschke, Walter. "World History and the History of the Absolute Spirit." In *History and System: Hegel's Philosophy of History*, edited by Perkins. Albany, NY: State University of New York Press, 1984.

Jantzen, Matt R. "Neither Ally, Nor Accomplice: James Cone and the Theological Ethics of White Conversion." *Journal of the Society of Christian Ethics* 40, no. 2 (2020).

Jameson, Frederic. "Future City." *New Left Review* 21 (May/June 2003): 65–79.

———. *The Political Unconscious: Narrative as a Socially Symbolic Act*. Ithaca: Cornell University Press, 1981.

Jennings, Willie James. *The Christian Imagination: Theology and the Origins of Race*. New Haven: Yale University Press, 2010.

———. "Overcoming Racial Faith." *Divinity* (Spring 2015): 5–9.
Jenson, Robert W. "You Wonder Where the Spirit Went." *Pro Ecclesia* 2 (1993): 296–304.
Johnson, Patricia Altenbernd. "Comment for Walter Jaeschke." In *History and System: Hegel's Philosophy of History*, edited by Perkins. Albany, NY: State University of New York Press, 1984.
Jones, Charles E., ed. *The Black Panther Party [Reconsidered]*. Baltimore: Black Classic Press, 1998.
Jones, Major. *Black Awareness: A Theology of Hope*. Nashville: Abingdon Press, 1971.
———. *Waiting 'Til the Midnight Hour: A Narrative History of Black Power in America*. New York: Henry Holt and Co., 2006.
Kant, Immanuel. "Idea for a Universal History with a Cosmopolitan Intent." In *Perpetual Peace and Other Essays: On Politics, History, and Morals*, translated by Humphrey, 29–40. Cambridge: Hackett Publishing Co., 1983.
———. "To Perpetual Peace: A Philosophical Sketch." In *Perpetual Peace and Other Essays: On Politics, History, and Morals*, translated by Humphrey, 107–144. Cambridge: Hackett Publishing Co., 1983.
Kenez, Peter. *Hungary from the Nazis to the Soviets: The Establishment of the Communist Regime in Hungary, 1944-1948*. Cambridge University Press, 2006.
Kennedy, Darren M. *Providence and Personalism: Karl Barth in Conversation with Austin Farrer, John Macmurry, and Vincent Brümmer*. Oxford: Peter Lang, 2011.
Kim, Sung-Sup. *Deus providebit: Calvin, Schleiermacher, and Barth on the Providence of God*. Minneapolis, MN: Fortress Press, 2014.
Kipling, Rudyard. "The White Man's Burden." In *100 Poems Old and New*, edited by Thomas Pinney, 111–113. Cambridge: Cambridge University Press, 1997.
Krötke, Wolf. Review of *Was heisst 'Handeln Gottes'?*. *Theologische Literaturzeitung* 125 (2000): 1190–1193.
Langford, Michael J. *Providence*. London: SCM Press Ltd., 1981.
Lilla, Mark. *The Stillborn God: Religion, Politics, and the Modern West*. New York: Vintage Books, 2008.
Lloyd, Genevieve. *The Man of Reason: "Male" and "Female" in Western Philosophy*. Minneapolis: University of Minnesota Press, 1984.
Lloyd, Vincent. "Paradox and Tradition in Black Theology." *Black Theology* 9, no. 3 (2011): 265–286.
Luther, Martin. "On Secular Authority." In *Luther and Calvin on Secular Authority*, edited by Harro Höpfl. Cambridge: Cambridge University Press, 1991.
MacIntyre, Alasdair. *Whose Justice? Which Rationality?*. Notre Dame: University of Notre Dame Press, 1989.
Magee, Glenn Alexander. *Hegel and the Hermetic Tradition*. Ithaca, NY: Cornell University Press, 2001.
Markoe, Lauren. "Did God choose Trump? What it means to believe in divine intervention." *Religion News Service*, January 17, 2017. http://religionnews.com/2017/01/17/did-god-choose-trump-what-belief-in-divine-intervention- really-means/.

Marsilius of Padua. *The Defender of Peace*. Edited and translated by Annabel Brett. Cambridge: Cambridge University Press, 2005.

Mathewes, Charles. *A Theology of Public Life*. Cambridge: Cambridge University Press, 2007.

Matthews, Tracye. "'No One Ever Asks, What a Man's Place in the Revolution Is': Gender and the Politics of the Black Panther Party 1966-1971." In *The Black Panther Party [Reconsidered]*, edited by Charles E. Jones, 267–304. Baltimore: Black Classic Press, 1998.

McCarney, Joseph. *Hegel on History*. London: Routledge, 2000.

———. "Hegel's Racism?: A Response to Bernasconi." *Radical Philosophy* 119 (2003): 32–35.

McCormack, Bruce. "The Actuality of God: Karl Barth in Conversation with Open Theism." *Engaging the Doctrine of God: Contemporary Protestant Perspectives*, edited by Bruce L. McCormack, 185–244. Grand Rapids: Baker, 2008.

McGee, Timothy. "Against (White) Redemption: James Cone and the Christological Disruption of Racial Discourse and White Solidarity." *Political Theology* (2017): 1–18.

———. "God's Life In and As Opening: James Cone, Divine Self-Determination, and the Trinitarian Politics of Sovereignty." *Modern Theology* 32, no. 1 (2016): 100–117.

McLaughlin, Malcolm. *The Long, Hot Summer of 1967: Urban Rebellion in America*. New York: Palgrave Macmillan, 2014.

McLean, Kalbryn A. "Calvin and the Personal Politics of Providence." In *Feminist and Womanist Essays in Reformed Dogmatics*, edited by Amy Plantinga Pauw and Serene Jones, 107–124. Louisville: Westminster John Knox Press, 2006.

McNeill, John T. *The History and Character of Calvinism*. London: Oxford University Press, 1967.

Merleau-Ponty, Maurice. *Sense and Non-Sense*. Translated by Dreyfus and Dreyfus. Chicago: Northwestern University Press, 1964.

Mignolo, Walter D. *The Darker Side of Western Modernity: Global Futures, Decolonial Options*. Durham, NC: Duke University Press, 2011.

Milbank, John. *Theology and Social Theory: Beyond Secular Reason*. Oxford: Blackwell Publishing, 1990.

Mitchell, Beverly Eileen. "Karl Barth and James Cone: The Question of Liberative Faith and Ideology." PhD diss., Boston College, 1999. ProQuest (9930882).

Moses, A. Dirk. *German Intellectuals and the Nazi Past*. Cambridge: Cambridge University Press, 2007.

Mukherjee, Roopali. "Antiracism Limited." *Cultural Studies* 30 no. 1 (2016): 47–77.

Mumford, Kevin. *Newark: A History of Race, Rights, and Riots in America*. New York: New York University Press, 2007.

Murphy, Francesca Aran and Philip G. Ziegler, eds. *The Providence of God: Deus Habet Consilium*. London: T&T Clark, 2009.

Neder, Adam. *Participation in Christ: An Entry into Karl Barth's* Church Dogmatics. Louisville: Westminster John Knox Press, 2009.

Neiman, Susan. *Evil in Modern Thought: An Alternative History*. Princeton: Princeton University Press, 2002.
Newkirk, Vann R. "North Carolina's General Assembly Districts Are Unconstitutional Gerrymanders, Too." *The Atlantic*, June 5, 2017. https://www.theatlantic.com/politics/archive/2017/06/north-carolinas-general-assembly-districts-are-unconstitutional-gerrymanders-too/529212/.
Niebuhr, H. Richard. *The Kingdom of God in America*. Middletown, CT: Wesleyan University Press, 1988.
Nimmo, Paul T. *Being in Action: The Theological Shape of Barth's Ethical Vision*. London: T&T Clark, 2007.
Noll, Mark. *The Civil War as a Theological Crisis*. Chapel Hill, NC: University of North Carolina Press, 2006.
Norton, Melissa. "Downtown Durham Investment." Oral presentation at Durham C.A.N. Affordable Housing Tour, Durham, NC, January 30, 2016.
O'Brien, George Dennis. *Hegel on Reason and History: A Contemporary Interpretation*. Chicago: The University of Chicago Press, 1975.
O'Regan, Cyril. *The Anatomy of Misremembering: von Balthasar's Response to Philosophical Modernity: Volume 1: Hegel*. New York: The Crossroad Publishing Company, 2014.
———. *The Heterodox Hegel*. Albany, NY: State University of New York Press, 1994.
Outler, Albert C. *Who Trusts in God: Musings on the Meaning of Providence*. New York: Oxford University Press, 1968.
Painter, Nell Irvin. *The History of White People*. New York: W.W. Norton, 2010.
Pannenberg, Wolfhart. *Jesus, God and Man*. Translated by Lewis L. Wilkins and Duane A. Priebe. Philadelphia: Westminster Press, 1968.
Patten, Alan. *Hegel's Idea of Freedom*. Oxford: Oxford University Press, 1999.
Peake, Thomas R. *Keeping the Dream Alive: A History of the Southern Christian Leadership Conference from King to the Nineteen-Eighties*. New York: Peter Lang, 1987.
Pinn, Anthony B. "Looking Like Me? Jesus images, Christology, and the limitations of theological blackness." In *Christology and Whiteness: What Would Jesus Do?*, edited by George Yancy, 169–179. New York: Routledge, 2012.
Plamenatz, John. "History as the Realization of Freedom." In *Hegel's Political Philosophy: Problems and Perspectives*, edited by Pelczynski. Cambridge: Cambridge University Press, 1971.
Rabinach, Anson. *In the Shadow of Catastrophe: German Intellectuals between Apocalypse and Enlightenment*. Berkeley: University of California Press, 1997.
Reinders, Hans S. *Disability, Providence, and Ethics: Bridging Gaps, Transforming Lives*. Waco, TX: Baylor University Press, 2014.
Roberts, J. Deotis. *Liberation and Reconciliation: A Black Theology*. Philadelphia: Westminster Press, 1971.
Rogers Jr., Eugene F. *After the Spirit: A Constructive Pneumatology from Resources outside the Modern West*. Grand Rapids: Wm. B. Eerdmans Publishing Co., 2005.

———. "The Eclipse of the Spirit in Karl Barth." In *Conversing with Barth*, edited by John McDowell and Michael Higton, 173–190. Aldershot, Hampshire: Ashgate, 2002.

———. "Supplementing Barth on Jews and Gender: Identifying God by Anagogy and the Spirit." *Modern Theology* 14 (1998): 43–81.

Rousseau, Jean-Jacques. *The Social Contract*. In *The Social Contract and Other Later Political Writings*, edited by Victor Gourevitch. Cambridge: Cambridge University Press, 1997.

Sanders, John. *The God Who Risks: A Theology of Providence*. Downers Grove, IL: InterVarsity Press, 1998.

Sandoval, Chela. *Methodology of the Oppressed*. Minneapolis: University of Minnesota Press, 2000.

Schlitt, Dale M. *Hegel's Trinitarian Claim: A Critical Reflection*. Leiden: E. J. Brill, 1984.

Schröder, Caroline. "'I See Something You Don't See': Karl Barth's Doctrine of Providence." In *For the Sake of the World: Karl Barth and the Future of Ecclesial Theology*, edited by George Hunsinger. Grand Rapids: Eerdmans, 2004.

Seipel, Brooke. "Michele Bachmann on Trump Victory: 'God Did This.'" *The Hill*, November 9, 2016. https://thehill.com/blogs/ballot-box/presidential-races/305227-michele-bachmann-on-trump-victory-god-did-this.

Shanks, Andrew. *Hegel Versus 'Inter-Faith Dialogue': A General Theory of True Xenophilia*. Cambridge: Cambridge University Press, 2015.

———. *Hegel's Political Theology*. Cambridge: Cambridge University Press, 1991.

Singleton III, Harry H. *Black Theology and Ideology: Deideological Dimensions in the Theology of James H. Cone*. Collegeville, MN: The Liturgical Press, 2002.

Slayton, Robert A. *Back of the Yards: The Making of a Local Democracy*. Chicago: University of Chicago Press, 1986.

Smith, Ted A. *The New Measures: A Theological History of Democratic Practice*. Cambridge: Cambridge University Press, 2007.

Splett, Jörg. *Die Trinitätslehre G.W.F. Hegels*. Freiburg: K. Alber, 1965.

Springer, Kimberly. "Black Feminists Respond to Black Power Masculinism." In *The Black Power Movement*, edited by Peniel E. Joseph, 105–118. New York: Routledge, 2006.

Sugrue, Thomas J. *The Origins of the Urban Crisis: Race and Inequality in Postwar Detroit*. Princeton: Princeton University Press, 1996.

Tanner, Kathryn. *Christ the Key*. Cambridge: Cambridge University Press, 2010.

———. "Creation and Providence." In *The Cambridge Companion to Karl Barth*, edited by John Webster. Cambridge: Cambridge University Press, 2000.

———. *God and Creation in Christian Theology: Tyranny or Empowerment?*. Minneapolis: Fortress Press, 2005.

Taylor, Charles. *Hegel*. Cambridge: Cambridge University Press, 1975.

———. *A Secular Age*. Cambridge, MA: Harvard University Press, 2007.

———. *Sources of the Self: The Making of the Modern Identity*. Cambridge, MA: Harvard University Press, 1989.

Traina, Cristina L. H. *Erotic Attunement: Parenthood and the Ethics of Sensuality between Unequals*. Chicago: University of Chicago Press, 2011.

Tupper, E. Frank. "The Providence of God in Christological Perspective." *Review & Expositor* 82 (1985): 579–595.

———. *A Scandalous Providence: The Jesus Story of the Compassion of God*. Macon, GA: Mercer University Press, 1995.

Verhey, Allen. "Calvin's Treatise 'Against the Libertines.'" *Calvin Theological Journal* 15, no. 2 (1980): 190–219.

Walker, Cardinal Aswad. "Princes Shall Come Out of Egypt: A Theological Comparison of Marcus Garvey and Reverend Albert B. Cleage Jr." *Journal of Black Studies* 39, no. 2 (2008): 194–251.

Wendte, Martin. *Gottmenschliche Einheit bei Hegel: eine logische und theologische Untersuchung*. New York: Walter de Gruyter, 2007.

Werner, Laura. "The Gender of Spirit: Hegel's Moves and Strategies." In *Hegel's Philosophy and Feminist Thought: Beyond Antigone?*, edited by Kimberly Hutchings and Tuija Pulkkinen. New York: Palgrave Macmillan, 2010.

West, Cornel. "Black Theology and Human Identity." In *Black Faith and Public Talk: Critical Essays on James H. Cone's Black Theology and Black Power*, edited by Dwight N. Hopkins. Maryknoll, NY: Orbis Books, 1999.

White, Gillian B. "The Downside of Durham's Rebirth." *The Atlantic*, March 31, 2016. https://www.theatlantic.com/business/archive/2016/03/the-downside-of-durhams-rebirth/476277/.

Wilkins, Burleigh Taylor. *Hegel's Philosophy of History*. Ithaca, NY: Cornell University Press, 1974.

Williams, Delores. *Sisters in the Wilderness: The Challenge of Womanist God-Talk*. Maryknoll, NY: Orbis Books, 1993.

Williams, Rhonda Y. "Black Women, Urban Politics, and Engendering Black Power." In *The Black Power Movement*, edited by Peniel E. Joseph, 79–104. New York: Routledge, 2006.

Williams, Rowan. "Barth on the Triune God." In *Karl Barth: Studies of His Theological Method*, edited by Stephen Sykes, 147–193. Oxford: Clarendon, 1979.

———. *Wrestling with Angels: Conversations in Modern Theology*. Edited by Mike Higton. Grand Rapids, MI: William B. Eerdmans Publishing Co., 2007.

Wilmore, Gayraud. *Black Religion and Black Radicalism*. Garden City, NY: Doubleday, 1972.

———. "Black Theology at the Turn of the Century: Some Unmet Needs and Challenges." In *Black Faith and Public Talk: Critical Essays on James H. Cone's Black Theology and Black Power*, edited by Dwight N. Hopkins. Maryknoll, NY: Orbis Books, 1999.

Wines, Michael and Alan Blinder. "Federal Appeals Court Strikes Down North Carolina Voter ID Requirement." *The New York Times*, July 29, 2016.

Winters, Joseph R. *Hope Draped in Black: Race, Melancholy, and the Agony of Progress*. Durham: Duke University Press, 2016.

Wood, Charles M. "Providence." In *The Oxford Handbook of Systematic Theology*, edited by Kathryn Tanner, John Webster, and Iain Torrance. Oxford: Oxford University Press, 2007.

———. *The Question of Providence*. Louisville, KY: Westminster John Knox Press, 2008.

Wooten, James T. "Compact Set Up for 'Post-Racial' South." *New York Times*, October 5, 1971.

Wright, Terry J. *Providence Made Flesh: Divine Presence as a Framework for a Theology of Providence*. Milton Keynes: Paternoster Press, 2009.

X, Malcolm and Alex Haley. *The Autobiography of Malcolm X*. New York: Grove Press, 1965.

Yerkes, James. *The Christology of Hegel*. Albany, NY: State University of New York Press, 1983.

Zachman, Randall C. "Response to: 'I See Something You Don't See.'" In *For the Sake of the World: Karl Barth and the Future of Ecclesial Theology*, edited by George Hunsinger. Grand Rapids: Eerdmans, 2004.

Zantop, Susanne. *Colonial Fantasies: Conquest, Family, and Nation in Precolonial Germany, 1770-1870*. Durham, NC: Duke University Press, 1997.

Ziegler, Philip. "The Uses of Providence in Public Theology." In *The Providence of God: Deus Habet Consilium*, edited by Murphy and Ziegler. London, T&T Clark, 2009.

Index

Alinsky, Saul, 173
Anaxagoras, 43–44
Aquinas, Thomas, 86
Ashanti, 37–38
Augustine, 20–21; context of, 28; on providence, 27, 30, 40, 60n13

Bachmann, Michele, 1
Baldwin, James, 170
Barber, William J., 174–75
Barth, Karl, 4–6, 26, 101n15, 109, 111, 137, 139; Christological account of providence and, 7, 70–72, 74–75, 77, 79–80, 83–85, 88–93, 97, 99, 102n54, 110, 132n29, 140, 142–43; *Church Dogmatics* III/3 and, 5, 7, 26, 69–72, 75–76, 79–80, 84–85, 99, 138, 140, 144, 150; on Communism, 77–78, 101n29; critiques Hegel, 7, 70–71, 99, 138, 140; critiques Western cultural and religious supremacy, 72–76, 79–83, 85, 90–91, 95, 99, 141; defines providence, 85–88; distinguishes Communism and Nazism, 69, 75–76, 78, 81–82; Hungarian tour of, 68, 72, 75, 77; nihilism and, 73–74; on participation in providence, 89, 92, 97–98, 105n21, 139, 142–46, 149, 160–61, 164n30, 171; pneumatology of, 90, 98, 144, 150–51, 160–62; political theology of, 70–72, 76–77, 79, 132n29; on postwar Europe and East-West conflict and, 69–73, 75, 80–83, 96, 141; problematic masculinity of, 147–50; rejects abstract conception of divine lordship and history, 70–71, 74, 85, 87–88, 90–95, 99, 147, 154, 167; on salvation history and world history, 76–77, 80–84, 86, 88–90, 92, 96; theological critique of Nazism, 26–28, 69–71, 73–75, 79–80, 83, 95–97, 145, 167; World Council of Churches and, 69, 72, 78. *See also* Cone, James; Hegel, G. W. F.
Bavinck, Herman, 14
Berkouwer, G. C., 6, 24; decline of the doctrine of providence and, 12–16, 22–23; neglects colonialism and racism, 17, 22, 25. *See also* Gilkey, Langdon
Bernasconi, Robert, 42
Blackness. *See* Cone, James
Black Power, 5, 7, 154; James Cone's theology of providence and, 26, 109–16, 126, 141, 150. *See also* Cone, James

Black Theology and Black Power (1969). *See* Cone, James
A Black Theology of Liberation (1970). *See* Cone, James
Blanding, Tonya, 108
Bonaventure, 86
Bourdieu, Pierre, 4
Bowdich, Thomas Edward, 37–38
Breckinridge, Robert J., 21
Bretherton, Luke, 173
Brunner, Emil, 69, 72, 77–78. *See also* Barth, Karl

Calhoun, John C., 16–17
Calvin, John, 28; context of, 27, 33n44; Hegel departs from, 40; providential doctrine of, 40, 60n13, 88, 103n85
capitalism, 2, 26, 71, 141, 167, 169
Carter, Jimmy, 169
Carter, J. Kameron, 113, 115, 135n116
Cavanaugh, Jerome P., 108
Césaire, Aimé, 24–25
"The Christian Message in Europe Today" (1946). *See* Barth, Karl
Christology: G. W. F. Hegel diminishes, 6–7, 40, 45, 47–48, 57–58, 70–71, 110, 144–52; James Cone's account of, 110–28, 131n29, 132n31, 134n109, 140, 143–52, 155, 157, 167; Karl Barth reformulates, 7, 70–72, 74–77, 79–99, 110, 131n29, 140–52; pneumatological interpretation of, 7–8, 123–24, 126, 132n31, 138–39, 141, 144–62, 167, 171–76. *See also* participation; pneumatology
"The Church between Easy and West" (1949). *See* Barth, Karl
Church Dogmatics (1932-67). *See* Barth, Karl
Citizens United v. Federal Election Commission (2010), 170
The City of God (c. 420). *See* Augustine
civil rights, 107–9, 114–15, 171, 174–75
Civil War, the, 2, 9n1, 21, 170
Cleage, Albert, 124

Clinton, Hillary, 1
Cold War, 5, 7, 69, 141
Communism: detested by Westerners, 7, 70, 72, 80, 83, 91, 141; in Hungary, 68–69, 77; Karl Barth and, 69–70, 72, 75–78, 82–83, 141. *See also* Barth, Karl; National Socialism
community organizing, 8, 107, 171–76
Cone, James, 4, 6, 8, 131n29, 139, 147, 162, 171; analyzes eschatology, 111–12, 123; androcentrism and, 138, 149–50, 163n14; on the Blackness of Christ, 115, 118, 120, 124–27; Christology of, 110–17, 120–24, 126–27, 134n109, 142–43, 149–52; connects Black Power and providence, 109–11, 114–18, 124; the contemporaneity of Christ and, 110–11, 115, 117, 119–23, 126–28, 137, 140, 155; criticizes white Christianity, 121–22; critiques abstract theology, 112, 115–17, 121, 127, 154; defines Black Power, 130n24; develops hermeneutical framework, 124–26; early theological work of, 108–10; emphasizes revelation, 108, 112–13, 117–21; engages Karl Barth, 5, 111, 130n20, 138; God's liberating providence and, 7, 26, 99–100, 110–13, 118, 121, 124, 127, 137, 141–44, 167; notoriety of *Black Theology and Black Power* (1969), 109; on participation, 139, 142–45; pneumatology of, 114, 117–18, 120, 122, 126, 132n31, 144–45, 149–52; stresses Jesus' Jewishness, 115, 117, 122, 124–27; white criticisms of, 120. *See also* Barth, Karl; Black Power; race
Copeland, M. Shawn, 8, 129n9, 139, 158–59
creatureliness: Christological providence and, 62n30, 86–95, 98–99, 138–39, 146–47, 151–55, 162; defined

by G. W. F. Hegel, 57; in James
Cone's doctrine of providence,
120, 125; in Karl Barth's doctrine
of providence, 86–99, 143, 151,
156, 163n7; participation and, 7–8,
89–93, 98–99, 120, 155–56, 162.
See also Christology; participation;
pneumatology

Dante, 27, 30
Durham, NC, 2, 8, 168–76
Durham C.A.N., 172–74, 176
Dussel, Enrique, 24

Enlightenment, the, 53, 58, 65n101
eschatology, 7, 48, 57, 67, 122–23,
172; Civil War America and, 21–22;
distinguished from providence, 20; in
history, 49–50, 112, 138, 147, 151,
161; Western supremacy and, 41, 51,
55–59, 70–71, 99, 140, 142; within
Black Christianity, 111–12. *See also*
Cone, James; Hegel, G. W. F.

Fergusson, David, 12
Ferreira da Silva, Denise, 58–59
Fulkerson, Mary McClintock, 12
fusion politics, 8, 172, 174–75

Gans, Eduard, 51, 61n20
gentrification, 2, 169–74
gerrymandering, 170
Gilkey, Langdon, 6, 28; on the fall
of providential doctrine, 11–12,
14–15, 23–24, 31n1; ignores
colonialism and racism, 13, 16–17,
22–25; influence of, 12, 14. *See also*
Berkouwer, G. C.
God of the Oppressed (1975). *See* Cone,
James
Graham, Franklin, 1
Gregory, Brad, 28
Guyatt, Nicholas, 20–21

Hammond, James Henry, 17

Hegel, G. W. F., 4, 6–7, 93, 147,
152, 162; concept of spirit, 47–48,
51–52, 54–56, 67, 71, 144; critiques
traditional Christianity, 40, 45, 57,
140, 146, 151; defends his historical
theory, 43–45; eschatology of,
49–50, 55, 57; on gender, 61n17,
70, 138–39, 148–49; geography and
space, and, 52, 54–55, 72; influence
of, 10n17, 31; James Cone differs
from, 111–13, 131n28, 142–44; Karl
Barth critiques, 70, 111, 138, 142–
44; nineteenth century Germany and,
5, 26, 39, 137; philosophical history
and, 38–40, 42, 46, 48, 50–52, 57; on
providence in history, 39–42, 45–48,
50–51, 54–58, 70–72, 99, 109, 140,
146, 151; racializes humanity, 58–59,
70, 110, 137, 140; sacralizes Western
civilization, 41, 49, 51–59, 67, 70,
95, 99, 109, 137, 140–45, 150; use
of incarnation, 45–48, 56–58, 71, 99,
109, 141, 167. *See also* Barth, Karl;
Cone, James; race
history. *See* Barth, Karl; Cone, James;
Hegel, G. W. F.
Hitler, Adolph, 68, 73, 75, 96; Karl
Barth critiques, 78, 88. *See also*
Barth, Karl; National Socialism
Hobbes, Thomas, 29–30
Hodgson, Peter, 47, 52
Hoffmeister, Johannes, 51, 61n20
Holcombe, William Henry, 19
Holocaust, the, 13, 70, 73
Hopkins, Dwight N., 109
Hughes, Richard, 107

incarnation. *See* Christology
Industrial Areas Foundation, 172–73

James, Frederick, 37–38
Jennings, Willie James, 3, 17, 158

Kant, Immanuel, 5, 62n28
King, Jr., Martin Luther, 108–9, 175

Kirschbaum, Charlotte von, 69, 73
Koechlin, Alphons, 77
Kuyper, Abraham, 14

Lasson, George, 51, 61n20
Lectures on the Philosophy of World History (1837). *See* Hegel, G. W. F.
Lilla, Mark, 29–30, 34n50
Lloyd, Vincent, 126
Lombard, Peter, 86

MacIntyre, Alasdair, 28, 34n48
Malcolm X, 114–15
Mathewes, Charles, 160
McCarney, Joseph, 57–58, 65n101
McGee, Timothy, 125
Milbank, John, 28
modernity: Christian theology during, 3, 12–13, 58; European colonialism and, 6, 12, 16, 24–25; providence and race in, 2–4, 6, 8, 17–19, 22, 26–27, 30–31, 109, 137, 152, 168; theological critiques of, 26, 85, 140; violence during, 12–13, 16; Western supremacy and, 5, 24–25, 40, 58, 85, 141. *See also* Barth, Karl; Cone, James; Hegel, G. W. F.; race
Moltmann, Jürgen, 123
Moral Movement, 174–76
Mukherjee, Roopali, 169

National Association for the Advancement of Colored People (NAACP), 174–76
nationalism, 1–2, 5, 7, 26, 73, 141, 145, 162, 167. *See also* Barth, Karl; Hegel, G. W. F.; National Socialism
National Socialism, 73–74, 77; compared to Communism, 78, 82–83; Karl Barth and, 70–72, 80, 88, 91, 94–99; spurs Barth's Christological providential doctrine, 5, 7, 75, 80, 84–85, 88, 91, 167. *See also* Barth, Karl; Hitler, Adolf

Nazism. *See* National Socialism
Niebuhr, H. Richard, 5
Niebuhr, Reinhold, 69, 101n15
North Carolina General Assembly, 169–76

O'Regan, Cyril, 46, 50

Painter, Nell Irvin, 4
Palmer, Benjamin, 21
participation: Christ's enablement of, 97–98, 142–47, 154–62, 171–72; gendered language of, 147, 149–50; Holy Spirit and, 120, 126, 138, 144–45, 151, 154–62, 171–72; political activity of the church and, 77–78, 95, 143; in providence, 7–8, 50, 57, 92–93, 138–39, 142, 156–62; race and, 41, 53–54, 116, 126–27, 147. *See also* Barth, Karl; Cone, James; Hegel, G. W. F.
Patten, Alan, 49
Plamenatz, John, 49
pneumatology: Christological presence and, 7–8, 90, 98, 110–18, 120, 123, 127–28, 138–41, 144, 147, 150–59, 162, 167–68, 171–76; freedom and, 158–61, 171–76; Hegel's "spirit" and, 39, 41–58, 67, 71, 144, 151; James Cone employs, 7, 108, 110–18, 120, 122, 126–28, 132n31, 141–42, 145, 152; Karl Barth applies, 90, 98, 143–44, 150, 152; providence and, 8, 138–39, 141, 144, 147, 149, 152–54, 156, 160; reductive forms of, 138, 150, 152, 162. *See also* Christology; participation
populism, 173, 175
The Providence of God (1952). *See* Berkouwer, G. C.

race: Christ and, 115, 117–28; liberative providence and, 8, 22, 30, 110, 117–28, 149–50, 159–62; pro-slavery theories of, 16–17, 19; providential doctrine and, 2–3, 13–14, 18–19, 22, 25–31, 54–55, 58, 100, 109–10, 141, 152; shapes modern Protestantism, 4–6, 13, 18, 137–38; theologies of colonialism and, 18–22, 25–26, 54–55, 58, 100; whiteness and, 4, 8, 10n15, 19–22, 31; within contemporary Durham, NC, 168–76. *See also* Cone, James; Hegel, G. W. F.; modernity

Ranke, Leopold von, 43

Reformation, the, 2, 11, 53

Rogers, Eugene, 151, 156–57, 164n27

Romney, George, 108

Sandoval, Chela, 23

Sanford, Terry, 169–70

Schweitzer, Albert, 119

Shelby County v. Holder (2013), 170–71

Smith, John Hope, 37

Socrates, 43–44

Southern Christian Leadership Conference (SCLC), 175

space. *See* Hegel, G. W. F.

Stalin, Joseph, 68

Student Nonviolent Coordinating Committee (SNCC), 174

Tanner, Kathryn, 153

Taylor, Charles, 28, 34n48

Tildy, Zoltán, 68–69

Trump, Donald, 1

Verhey, Allen, 161

Voltaire, 27

Voting Rights Act (1965), 171

White, Paula, 1–2

Williams, Delores S., 8, 139, 149, 157, 159, 161

Wilmore, Gayraud, 116, 121

Winters, Joseph R., 59

World Council of Churches. *See* Barth, Karl

World War I, 12–13, 67, 76

World War II, 12–14, 26; European Christianity and, 76; Karl Barth's doctrine of providence and, 67–70, 72–73. *See also* Barth, Karl

Zantop, Susanne, 39

Ziegler, Philip, 18

About the Author

Matt R. Jantzen (ThD, Duke University) is Visiting Assistant Professor of Ministry Studies and Director of the Emmaus Scholars Program at Hope College.

www.ingramcontent.com/pod-product-compliance
Lightning Source LLC
Chambersburg PA
CBHW050905300426
44111CB00010B/1394